Paris 2010

WHAT'S NEW | WHAT'S ON | WHAT'S BEST

www.timeout.com/paris

Contents

Don't Miss: 2010

Itineraries

Paris by Area

Essentials

Published by Time Out Guides Ltd
Universal House
251 Tottenham Court Road
London W1T 7AB
Tel: + 44 (0)20 7813 3000
Fax: + 44 (0)20 7813 6001
Email: guides@timeout.com
www.timeout.com

Managing Director Peter Fiennes
Editorial Director Ruth Jarvis
Business Manager Dan Allen
Editorial Manager Holly Pick
Assistant Management Accountant Ija Krasnikova

Time Out Guides is a wholly owned subsidiary of Time Out Group Ltd.

Chairman Tony Elliott
Chief Executive Officer David King
Group General Manager/Director Nichola Coulthard
Time Out Communications Ltd MD David Pepper
Time Out International Ltd MD Cathy Runciman
Time Out Magazine Ltd Publisher/Managing Director Mark Elliott
Production Director Mark Lamond
Group IT Director Simon Chappell
Marketing & Circulation Director Catherine Demajo

This edition first published in Great Britain in 2009 by Ebury Publishing
A Random House Group Company
Company information can be found on www.randomhouse.co.uk
Random House UK Limited Reg. No. 954009
10 9 8 7 6 5 4 3 2 1

Distributed in the US by Publishers Group West
Distributed in Canada by Publishers Group Canada

For further distribution details, see www.timeout.com

ISBN: 978-1-84670-132-0

A CIP catalogue record for this book is available from the British Library.

Printed and bound in Germany by Appl.

The Random House Group Limited supports The Forest Stewardship Council (FSC), the leading international forest certification organisation. All our titles that are printed on Greenpeace approved FSC certified paper carry the FSC logo. Our paper procurement policy can be found at www.rbooks.co.uk/environment.

Time Out carbon-offsets all its flights with Trees for Cities (www.treesforcities.org).

Paris Shortlist

The **Time Out Paris Shortlist 2010** is one of a new series of annual guides that draws on Time Out's background as a magazine publisher to keep you current with what's going on in town. As well as Paris's key sights and the best of its eating, drinking and leisure options, it picks out the most exciting venues to have opened in the last year and gives a full calendar of events from September 2009 to December 2010. It also includes features on the important news, trends and openings, all compiled by locally based editors and writers. Whether you're visiting for the first time in your life or the first time this year, you'll find the *Time Out Paris Shortlist* contains all you need to know, in a portable and easy-to-use format.

The guide divides central Paris into ten areas, each containing listings for Sights & Museums, Eating & Drinking, Shopping, Nightlife and Arts & Leisure, and maps pinpointing their locations. At the front of the book are chapters rounding up these scenes city-wide, and giving a shortlist of our overall picks. We include itineraries for days out, plus essentials such as transport information and hotels.

Our listings give phone numbers as dialled within France. From abroad, use your country's exit code followed by 33 (the country code for France) and the number given, dropping the initial '0'.

We have noted price categories by using one to four euro signs (€-€€€€), representing budget, moderate, expensive and luxury. Major credit cards are accepted unless otherwise stated. We also indicate when a venue is NEW, and give **Event highlights**.

All our listings are double-checked, but places do sometimes close or change their hours or prices, so it's a good idea to call a venue before visiting. While every effort has been made to ensure accuracy, the publishers cannot accept responsibility for any errors that this guide may contain.

Venues are marked on the maps using symbols numbered according to their order within the chapter and colour-coded as follows:

1 Sights & Museums
1 Eating & Drinking
1 Shopping
1 Nightlife
1 Arts & Leisure

Map key

Major sight or landmark	
Hospital or college	
Railway station	
Park	
River	
Autoroute	
Main road	
Main road tunnel	
Pedestrian road	
Arrondissement boundary	
Airport	
Church	
Métro station	M
RER station	RER
Area name	LES HALLES

Time Out **Paris** Shortlist 2010

EDITORIAL
Editor Dominic Earle
Proofreader Mandy Martinez

DESIGN
Art Director Scott Moore
Art Editor Pinelope Kourmouzoglou
Senior Designer Henry Elphick
Graphic Designers Kei Ishimaru, Nicola Wilson
Advertising Designer Jodi Sher

Picture Editor Jael Marschner
Deputy Picture Editor Lynn Chambers
Picture Researcher Gemma Walters
Picture Desk Assistant Marzena Zoladz
Picture Librarian Christina Theisen

ADVERTISING
Commercial Director Mark Phillips
International Advertising Manager Kasimir Berger
Head of French Advertising Sales Charlie Sokol

MARKETING
Marketing Manager Yvonne Poon
Sales & Marketing Director, North America & Latin America Lisa Levinson
Senior Publishing Brand Manager Luthfa Begum
Art Director Anthony Huggins

PRODUCTION
Production Manager Brendan McKeown
Production Controller Damian Bennett
Production Co-ordinator Kelly Fenlon

CONTRIBUTORS
This guide was researched and written by Anna Brooke, Simon Cropper, Alison Culliford, Jonathan Derbyshire, Natasha Edwards, Rosa Jackson, Julien Sauvalle, Rich Woodruff and the writers of *Time Out Paris*.

PHOTOGRAPHY
All photography by Olivia Rutherford, except: pages 8, 50, 55, 122, 127 Jean-Christophe Godet; pages 9, 47, 49, 106, 132, 133, 119 (right) Heloise Bergman; pages 22, 36, 41, 42, 43, 44, 45, 85, 112, 161 Oliver Knight; pages 34, 35 CSI/Arnaud Legrain; page 38 Pascale Simard; page 48 Musée du Louvre; pages 52, 138 Elan Fleisher; page 96 Pierre-Emmanuel Rastoin; pages 121, 148 Karl Blackwell; page 124 Musée Rodin/J Manoukian; page 150 Musée National du Sport.

The following images were provided by the featured establishments/artists: pages 21, 93, 158.

Cover image: Jupiter Images.

MAPS
JS Graphics (john@jsgraphics.co.uk).

About **Time Out**

Founded in 1968, Time Out has expanded from humble London beginnings into the leading resource for those wanting to know what's happening in the world's greatest cities. As well as our influential what's-on weeklies in London, New York and Chicago, we publish more than a dozen other listings magazines in cities as varied as Beijing and Mumbai. The magazines established Time Out's trademark style: sharp writing, informed reviewing and bang up-to-date inside knowledge of every scene.

Time Out made the natural leap into travel guides in the 1980s with the City Guide series, which now extends to over 50 destinations around the world. Written and researched by expert local writers and generously illustrated with original photography, the full-size guides cover a larger area than our Shortlist guides and include many more venue reviews, along with additional background features and a full set of maps.

Throughout this rapid growth, the company has remained proudly independent, still owned by Tony Elliott four decades after he started Time Out London as a single fold-out sheet of A5 paper. This independence extends to the editorial content of all our publications, this Shortlist included. No establishment has been featured because it has advertised, and no payment has influenced any of our reviews. And, for our critics, there's definitely no such thing as a free lunch: all restaurants and bars are visited and reviewed anonymously, and Time Out always picks up the bill.
For more about the company, see www.timeout.com.

Don't Miss 2010

Musée du Louvre

WHAT'S BEST

Sights & Museums

Paris could well be on the threshold of the most monumental changes since the middle of the 19th century – that is, if the global economic downturn doesn't scotch the plans. In 2008, President Sarkozy convened a panel of top international architects, including Richard Rogers and Norman Foster, to examine ways in which the city and its suburbs can be retooled for the future. It's an open secret that Sarkozy wants a 'greater Paris' more in line with the London model than the French capital's current set-up, and bringing that aim to fruition will entail vast building projects that would make the *grands projets* of his predecessors – such as the Louvre pyramid (p74), the Opéra Bastille (p115) and the Musée du Quai Branly (p126) – look like a child's Lego set.

The main focus of the building projects now sprouting like mushrooms after a shower – more skyscrapers at La Défense, a skyscraper just inside the city ring road (*horreur!*) and the remaking of a great swathe of the east of the city – is economic, not cultural; but Sarkozy's fixation with status is offset by the more fun-loving, arts-oriented agenda of the city's mayor, Bertrand Delanoë, now into his second term of office. On his watch, Paris has produced some superb new additions to its line-up of museums and attractions

– things like the Cité de l'Architecture et du Patrimoine (p57), the 104 multimedia arts centre built in premises previously occupied by the city's undertakers (p159), and the Cité de la Mode et du Design (p152), part of the renewal of a strip of run-down warehouses by the Seine.

Across the rest of the city, the list of sights worth your time is almost endless – from iconic treasures like the Eiffel Tower (p122) to lesser-known gems on the periphery like the Musée Fragonard (p159). All this, and much more that we haven't yet mentioned, in a city that's a manageable size and boasts one of the best transport networks anywhere in the world.

The lie of the land

Parisians identify parts of their city by two systems: there are the named districts, whose frontiers

SHORTLIST

Best new
- Cité de la Mode et du Design (p152)

Best revamped
- Musée Fragonard (p159)
- Musée de la Chasse et de la Nature (p105)

Best secret
- Les Egouts de Paris (p122)
- Musée Gustave Moreau (p89)
- La Promenade Plantée (p107)

Best art
- Centre Pompidou (p100)
- Musée du Louvre (p74)
- Musée d'Orsay (p134)
- Musée National Picasso (p106)
- Palais de Tokyo (p61)

Best dead
- Cimetière du Montparnasse (p154)
- Cimetière du Père-Lachaise (p101)

Best outdoors
- Jardin du Luxembourg (p132)
- Palais-Royal (p75)
- Parc des Buttes-Chaumont (p96)

Best views
- Arc de Triomphe (p56)
- Eiffel Tower (p122)
- Institut du Monde Arabe (p142)
- Cathédrale Notre-Dame (p118)
- Sacré-Coeur (p90)
- Tour Montparnasse (p156)

Best tours
- Bateaux-Mouches (p56)
- Canauxrama (p95)
- Vedettes du Pont-Neuf (p116)

Exclusive: A bar on board

La terrasse: summer restaurant

Get a sample of the best monuments

aren't always clear – the Marais, the Latin Quarter, Montparnasse and so on – and the 20 numbered arrondissements that spiral out, clockwise and in ascending order, from the Louvre. Together they comprise an urban jigsaw that the novelist Julien Green once compared to a model of the human brain. Each piece has a particular connotation or function: the fifth is academic; the sixth is arty and chic; the 16th is wealthy and dull; while the 18th, 19th and 20th arrondissements are riotously multicultural. Residents are frequently assessed, on first meeting at least, by their postcode, and as a consequence often develop a fierce sense of local pride. Indeed, many of them will tell you that Paris isn't so much a city as a jumble of villages, each pungently and defiantly distinctive.

We've divided this book into areas, though not necessarily into shapes that residents would recognise; we've imagined the city as a series of visitor-friendly concentrations of shops, sights, restaurants and bars. The Champs-Elysées & Western Paris section has the famous avenue as its spine, lined with high-end shops and showrooms. It also contains fashion's most glamorous thoroughfare, avenue Montaigne, which is almost matched in lustre and allure by rue du Faubourg-Saint-Honoré.

Montmartre & Pigalle has, at its northern end, picturesque Montmartre with its vertiginous flights of steps, narrow winding streets and the massive bulk of Sacré-Coeur (p90). To the south lies Pigalle, famous for the Moulin Rouge and its strip clubs and scuzzy bars (though it's a good deal more salubrious today than it once was).

Opéra to Les Halles used to be the centre of royal power in Paris, and you can get a sense of this by taking a stroll around the Palais-Royal (p75). Today, however, it's

Cité de la Mode et du Design p9

the city's commercial and cultural powerhouse: it's home to the massive Les Halles shopping complex, the jewellers and fashion houses of place Vendôme, and to the Louvre, Palais Garnier (p86) and Musée de l'Orangerie (p74).

North-eastern Paris is the area visitors from the UK are likely to see first: Eurostar trains terminate at the Gare du Nord (p95) in the tenth arrondissement. The area is on the up, with its main artery, the charming Canal St-Martin, lined with chic boutiques and cafés. Further north and east of here is the magnificently odd Parc des Buttes-Chaumont (p96), a warren of cliffs and grottoes carved out of a former quarry. Marais, Bastille & Eastern Paris is barfly territory, especially along rue Oberkampf, rue Jean-Pierre Timbaud and rue St-Maur. The ever-trendy Marais is chock-full of independent galleries and quirky shops, and is also the centre of gay life in Paris.

The Islands – the Ile de la Cité, the oldest part of the city and home to Notre-Dame cathedral (p118), and the more elegant Ile St-Louis, with its shops and restaurants – are highly distinctive and essential ports of call.

Undeniably, the main attraction of the affluent (and sometimes stuffily institutional) 7th & Western Paris area is the Eiffel Tower, the universal emblem of the French capital. Its elegant ironwork is most alluring at night, when it is lit up by tens of thousands of shimmering lightbulbs. This is also the best time to climb it, because the queues are at their shortest.

For many years, St-Germain-des-Prés was the intellectual heartland of the city, home to Sartre and de Beauvoir. But these days it's more about fashion than philosophy, and the expensive cafés are no place for starving writers. The city's most beautiful park, the Jardin du Luxembourg (p132), won't cost you a sou, however; and the Musée d'Orsay (p134), although not free, is still excellent value. Due east, the Latin Quarter is home to several of Paris's most august academic institutions, including the Sorbonne. And to the south, Montparnasse, although no longer the artistic stronghold it was in the 1920s, still boasts a number of excellent cafés and restaurants, and the resting place of some of France's most illustrious dead, the Cimetière du Montparnasse (p154).

Getting around

In 2007, the mayor launched Vélib, a municipal bike scheme that put 20,000 bicycles at the disposal of residents and visitors. But if you don't feel confident about your chances in Paris traffic, invest in a Mobilis pass and travel around the city sans cash. The Paris métro is one of the oldest public transport networks in the world, and buses are clean, frequent and cheap. Some of the bus routes are worth riding just for the sightseeing opportunities they offer: no.24 takes you through St-Germain-des-Prés and the Latin Quarter; no.69 runs all the way from Gambetta in the east, via the Louvre, to the Champ de Mars in the west; and no.73 connects the Champs-Elysées to the futuristic concrete jungle of La Défense.

But when all is said and done, you can't beat walking. Paris is compact enough to be navigated on foot, and this is the best way to hear the heartbeat of the city. This way you'll discover that far from being a 'museum city' suffocating under the weight of its 'heritage', Paris is a thriving capital that looks to the future without ever forgetting its past.

Café Charbon p19

WHAT'S BEST

Eating & Drinking

It takes more than *la crise*, as the global economic crisis is known in France, to put Parisians off their restaurant food. The most popular bistros are booked up weeks or even months in advance, while fashionable new spots have no trouble winning a clientele. Perhaps, in a country that has long valued pleasure at the table, good food is the last thing people are willing to sacrifice. The good news for visitors is that chefs are starting to pay more attention to value, particularly when it comes to wines. It's not unusual to pay €3 for a glass of wine or €10 for a half-litre carafe even in a relatively pricey bistro, which helps keep the overall cost of a meal down. In times of crisis, lobster, caviar and truffles give way to sardines, sweetbreads and oxtail, which is no bad thing considering that these humble ingredients seem to inspire chefs even more. Paris is not ready to throw in the luxury towel, however: one of the most popular new restaurants, Pizza Chic (13 rue de Mézières, 6th, 01.45.48.30.38), boasts of serving the priciest pizzas in town (€16 for a Nutella pizza).

Another result of tough economic times is that restaurants are more flexible. Instead of imposing a three-course meal, most bistros now offer a quicker lunch menu that might consist of two courses or even a bento box-style tray which includes the starter, main course and dessert, as at Alain Ducasse bistro Spoon (14 rue de Marignan, 8th, 01.40.76.34.37). This makes sense when you consider that the

French now spend an average of 30 minutes on lunch, and that soup, salad, sushi and sandwich spots are proving ever more popular.

Bistro boom

Thankfully, the bistro boom continues in Paris. This is where locals go to be greeted with a handshake and a smile, where wine comes in carafes and the dishes make you feel warm inside. Many, like L'Ambassade d'Auvergne (p107), deliberately serve only time-honoured (often regional) dishes, but others are swaying from traditional cuisine, putting a modern spin on French classics. Le Pré Verre (p146), La Cerisaie (p156), L'Ami Jean (p126), Itinéraires (p146), Le Gaigne (p109) and La Gazzetta (29 rue de Cotte, 12th, 01.43.47.47.05) all push the boundaries of bistro cooking. Though a full bistro meal rarely comes in at less than €30 without drinks, it's often better value than a mediocre café or brasserie.

Brasseries still have their appeal, even if most now belong to chains such as the Flo group, the Frères Blanc or the Costes. The spectacle of sitting amid art nouveau extravagance, as waiters in black and white rush between tables serving platters of oysters and choucroute, comes at a price, but is cheaper at lunchtime or late at night. Bofinger (p108) and La Coupole (p156), both part of the Flo chain, pull in a multigenerational crowd of locals and tourists. The Costes brothers set the standard for the modern brasserie experience in Paris with stylish restaurants like Le Georges (6th floor, Centre Pompidou, 19 rue Beaubourg, 4th, 01.44.78.47.99); they have also taken over a few vintage bistros such as Chez Julien (1 rue du Pont Louis-Philippe, 4th, 01.42.78.31.64).

SHORTLIST

Best new
- L'Epigramme (p136)
- Le Gaigne (p109)
- Itinéraires (p146)

Best value
- A la Bière (p96)
- Le Baron Rouge (p108)
- Chez Toinette (p90)
- L'Encrier (p109)

Most glamorous
- Alain Ducasse au Plaza Athénée (p61)
- Les Ambassadeurs (p63)
- L'Arpège (p127)
- Café de la Paix (p76)
- Le Jules Verne (p127)
- Lapérouse (p146)

Bars with character
- Andy Wahloo (p108)
- Café Charbon (p109)
- De la Ville Café (p76)
- La Fourmi (p91)
- La Palette (p136)

Cocktail classics
- Le Brébant (p90)
- Le Crocodile (p145)
- Le Fumoir (p77)
- Lizard Lounge (p110)
- Palais de Tokyo (p61)

Best for nighthawks
- Le Brébant (p90)
- Le Fanfaron (p109)
- Harry's New York Bar (p77)
- Le Tambour (p79)
- Le Sancerre (p92)

Regional stars
- L'Ambassade d'Auvergne (p107)
- L'Ami Jean (p126)
- Le Ch'ti Catalan (p90)
- Granterroirs (p63)
- Un Jour à Peyrassol (p77)

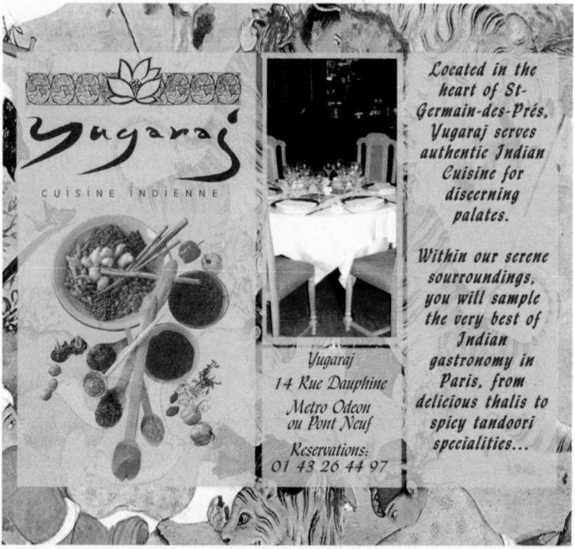
Yugaraj
CUISINE INDIENNE
Yugaraj
14 Rue Dauphine
Metro Odeon
ou Pont Neuf
Reservations:
01 43 26 44 97
Located in the heart of St-Germain-des-Prés, Yugaraj serves authentic Indian Cuisine for discerning palates.
Within our serene sourroundings, you will sample the very best of Indian gastronomy in Paris, from delicious thalis to spicy tandoori specialities...

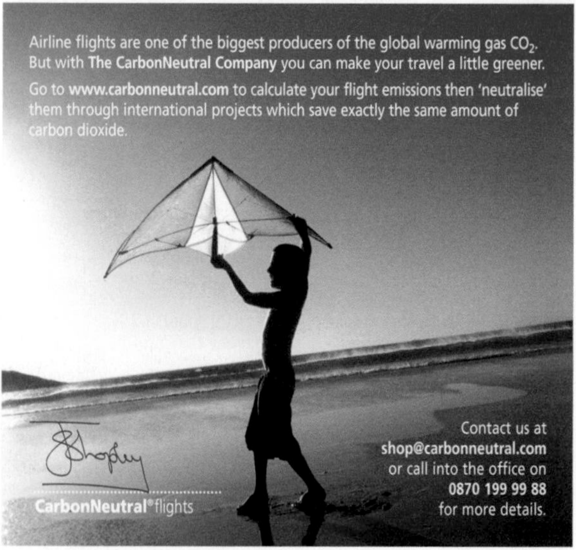
Airline flights are one of the biggest producers of the global warming gas CO_2.
But with **The CarbonNeutral Company** you can make your travel a little greener.
Go to **www.carbonneutral.com** to calculate your flight emissions then 'neutralise' them through international projects which save exactly the same amount of carbon dioxide.
Contact us at **shop@carbonneutral.com** or call into the office on **0870 199 99 88** for more details.
CarbonNeutral® flights

Top tables

To crank it up a notch, you could opt for a spot of all-out luxury in one of the city's haute cuisine restaurants. Nothing can beat the feeling of being treated like royalty. What's more, these high-class establishments are swapping their revered classicism for something more fun. Les Ambassadeurs (p63) in the Crillon is a perfect example. Inside the lavish marble and gilt dining room, chef Jean-François Piège serves a Michelin-starred menu featuring an Explosion de Pizza – a little doughy ball of pizza, on a spoon, that literally explodes inside your mouth. Service remains impeccably five-star, but the dress code is more flexible than in days gone by. Other sumptuous dining experiences are to be had at Le Meurice (p78), Le Cinq (31 av George V, 8th, 01.49.52.70.00), Alain Ducasse au Plaza Athenée (p61), and the Ducasse-run Jules Verne (p127) in the Eiffel Tower.

Restaurants where you can easily spend €200 or more a head often have lunch menus for €75-€80 – still a lot of money, but for this you are treated to a full-blown experience from *amuse-bouches* to *mignardises*. Ordering the lunch menu often means having a more limited choice of dishes, but they are likely to draw on the freshest ingredients from the market. A notch down from haute cuisine, restaurants such as Le Restaurant (p136) and Pétrelle (p91) offer sumptuous dining experiences for less than €100 per person.

Café culture

A growing trend is the Anglo-style snack shop. Cojean (17 bd Haussmann, 9th, 01.47.70.22.65), La Ferme (55 rue St-Roch, 1st, 01.40.20.12.12), Bioboa (3 rue Danielle-Casanova, 1st, 01.42.61.17.67) and Bob's Juice Bar (15 rue Lucien Sampaix, 10th, 06 82 63 72 74) all serve healthy sandwiches, soups, salads and juices to eat in or take out. The Anglo theme continues at boho-chic Rose Bakery (p91) and Rose Bakery II (30 rue Debelleyme, 3rd, 01.49.96.54.01), where organic soups, quiches and inventive salads have shown Parisians that the British know a thing or two about nosh. Bread & Roses (p135) is a mostly organic bakery run by a French couple that is passionate about British food, especially cakes.

The ubiquitous Parisian café, where wine is cheaper than water, is still present, although the iconic, scruffy neighbourhood haunt with its peeling paintwork is fortunately becoming a thing of the past. Many cafés have upgraded their interiors and prices accordingly, but you can still find affordable snacks such as omelettes and croques monsieur. Just a handful of addresses nostalgically cling to their shabby-chic image – generally in the artsy

Bread & Roses

Located in the heart of the LatinQuarter, the Bouillon Racine combines art nouveau charm and exceptionally tasty food.

Open daily noon-11pm
Live jazz 1st & 3rd Tuesdays of the month
3 rue Racine, 6th. Mº Odéon.
Tel: 01.44.32.15.60
Email.bouillon.racine@wanadoo.fr
www.bouillonracine.com

north-east. A perfect example is Chez Jeanette (47 rue du Faubourg-St-Denis, 10th, 01.47.70.30.89), which despite the new owner's decision to preserve the 1970s decor, grease 'n' all, has never been busier. If grime gets you down, you still can't beat a chic café experience in the famous (if jaw-droppingly expensive) Left Bank institutions Les Deux Magots (p135) and Café de Flore (p135), or at Café de la Paix (p76), whose millefeuilles are unrivalled.

If you're after something stronger, the 10th and 11th, especially around rue Oberkampf, continue to be the most happening areas for bars. Café Charbon (p109), which acts as both a restaurant and pre-club cocktail bar, and L'Alimentation Generale (p107), whose excellent concerts give stage space to up-and-coming musicians, are the places to be seen. Other trendy locals gravitate to grungy all-nighters like Le Sancerre (p92) or La Fourmi (p91).

For those with money to burn, the city's other party central is the area around Champs-Elysées. Abandoned by all but a 'wannabe' crowd a few years ago, the area has regained favour with the smart set and now boasts some very posh addresses indeed. If you're curious, have a tipple in Le Dada (p63) and count the designer handbags.

In the know

If your heart is set on somewhere specific, it's always a good idea to book ahead. Some of the most popular restaurants, such as Le Comptoir (p135) and Spring (p92), can be booked up months in advance. Once you're at the table, it's yours until you decide to leave (it is considered the height of rudeness for the waiter to bring you the bill before you've asked), except at popular bistros with multiple sittings, where you'll be expected to leave before the next guests arrive. Also remember that tips are usually included in the bill and that you are not expected to leave anything, although one or two euros per person for great service will always be appreciated.

As a general rule, the closer the tourist site and the better the view, the worse the food – although there are exceptions, such as bistro Au Bon Accueil (14 rue de Monttessuy, 7th, 01.47.05.46.11), which serves sophisticated fare with a view of the Eiffel Tower from its small pavement terrace.

If you are looking for a snack, bear in mind that the hundreds of Chinese '*traiteurs*' in Paris are almost uniformly mediocre, reheating dishes in a microwave while you wait. You are much better off finding a bakery or packing a picnic and saving your cash for a special dinner. There are a number of decent crêperies around Montparnasse, where the Bretons originally settled, or you could try gourmet crêperie Breizh Café (109 rue Vieille-du-Temple, 3rd, 01.42.72.13.77) in the Marais.

Apart from fast-food outlets, non-French food is increasingly popular. The streets around Belleville (20th) and the southern end of the 13th are crammed with decent Chinese, Vietnamese and Laotian restaurants; the 2nd, around rue Ste-Anne, is flourishing with Japanese eateries, including the excellent Kai (p77). Rue des Rosiers in the Marais is a centre for Jewish cooking, and Italian, Indian, Moroccan and Lebanese cuisine can be found across the city.

Finally, try to avoid anywhere with a menu labelled 'menu touristique' or 'we speak English'. As tempting as it may be, these are sure-fire signs of mediocre cooking.

Sonia Rykiel p25

WHAT'S BEST

Shopping

Who would have guessed that France was in recession with all the new store openings over the past few months? British fashion designers, in particular, have continued their invasion. Stella McCartney has opened her longed-for showcase in the Palais-Royal; Jimmy Choo has opened a large store on rue St-Honoré, and All Saints has opened its first Paris boutique on rue Etienne-Marcel.

With all this feverish activity happening on the Right Bank, it's a wonder there are any shopfronts left for fashion brands to take over. 'NoMa' (north of the Marais), the area of the 3rd around rue Charlot and rue Poitou, is a prime example. Anyone who has not visited in a few months will find a host of new boutiques here, making it a focus for youth brands. The other, more upmarket, focus for fashion is the Palais-Royal, whose cloisters must be one of the most beautiful places to shop in any city.

The concept shop trend is now a central feature of the shopping scene, crossing the boundaries between clothes, music and product design. Colette (p80) celebrated its tenth anniversary with a facelift by Japanese designer Masamichi Katayama, better known as Wonderwall. The massive LE66 (p66), which opened on the Champs-Elysées last year showcasing original fashion, has been joined by Bubble Wood (4 rue Elzévir, 3rd, 01.44.78.03.86) in the Marais, with a quirky selection

Diptyque

of clothes, cosmetics, music and interior design, as well as Stéphane Plassier's personal selection of fashion, furniture and amusing gifts at Set Galerie (7 rue d'Uzès, 2nd, 01.40.16.56.49). On the high-tech front, Sony has opened its first European concept store, Sony Style, on avenue George V (p67).

It has also been the year of Yamamoto, *père et fille*. Yohji has achieved a long-held dream of opening a flagship store on rue Cambon (p83) – a three-floor temple to his aesthetic. Only a month later his rebel daughter Limi, who showed her collection in Paris in 2007 to great acclaim, opened her boutique and showroom Limi Feu on rue de Turbigo (p82). Not to be outdone, Issey Miyake has set up at 11 rue Royale.

Boutique chic

The stretch of rue St-Honoré and rue du Fbg-St-Honoré from the Hôtel Costes to the Hôtel Bristol is wall-to-wall fashion boutiques. With the exception of trash temple Just Cavalli (50 rue du Fbg St-Honoré, 8th, 01.42.66.25.68, www.robertocavalli.com), it's all taste and intimacy, with Givenchy (p66), Lanvin (p82) and Jimmy Choo (376 rue St-Honoré, 8th, 01.58.62.50.40) the three major highlights.

Rue Boissy d'Anglas has a branch of L'Eclaireur with its Fornassetti café (8 rue Boissy d'Anglas, 8th, 01.53.43.03.70, www.leclaireur.com) and Paris's other famous fashion picker Maria Luisa (7 rue Rouget de Lisle, 1st, 01.47.03.96.15) is just a step away.

Avenue Montaigne's headliners include Fendi at no.22, the Roberto Cavalli flagship at no.50 and, next door at no.52, Ralph Lauren's new three-floor womenswear store in the former home of couturier Madeleine Vionnet. Agnès B has joined the more casual crowd infiltrating the Golden Triangle (38 av George V, 01.40.73.81.10), and iconic jeweller Jean Dinh Van has opened on the Champs-Elysées (123 av des Champs-Elysées, 8th, 01.47.23.59.08), away from the main jewellery centre on Place Vendôme. The small streets criss-crossing the Golden Triangle also have a few surprises, such as Lola.J (15 rue Clément Marot, 8th, 01.47.23.87.40), a new boutique that brings together luxury clothes with attitude for men and women, including Ni-Search Swarovski-studded jeans and Diego Dolcini shoes.

Palais-Royal & around

If you're visiting Colette, don't miss a detour to the Marché St-Honoré. This former food market, rebuilt in glass by Ricardo Bofill, combines bistros and boutiques, with Marc by Marc Jacobs (p82) the big attraction.

Easily reached on foot from here, the Palais-Royal just gets better and better. On the eastern side, galerie du Valois has Stella McCartney (p83), cult Swedish brand Acne Jeans at no.124, the covetable and racy gloves of Maison Fabre at no.128, and Paris star Robert Normand (p83). Opposite, with the idyllic gardens in between, is galerie de Montpensier containing jewellery shop Casoar at no.29, Marc Jacobs (p82), and vintage wear from Didier Ludot (p80), as well as Martin Margiela in the road behind (23 & 25bis rue de Montpensier, 1st, 01.40.15.07.55). Also in the area is Kitsuné (52 rue de Richelieu, 1st, 01.42.60.34.28), the record label now selling its own brand clothing, including Scottish cashmere and Japanese jeans.

Further east, the Etienne-Marcel area is the centre for club and streetwear with All Saints (49 rue Etienne-Marcel, 1st, 01.44.88.21.30), Kiliwatch (p81) and Royal Cheese (24 rue Tiquetonne, 2nd, 01.40.28.06.56).

Marais mode

The northern part of the Marais, now dubbed NoMa, has sealed its identity as the essential district for hot and hip fashion. Here, you'll find multi-label boutique Shine (p114), and young French label Swildens (22 rue de Poitou, 3rd, 01.42.71.19.12) which boasts Carla Sarkozy as a client. Dolls (56 rue de Saintonge, 3rd, 01.44.54.08.21) stocks cutting-edge labels and brand-name jeans, and April 77 (49 rue de Saintonge, 3rd, www.april77.fr) offers skinny jeans and faux leather jackets in a beatnik setting. Among the newcomers are Tigersushi Furs (27 rue de Saintonge, 3rd, www.tigersushi.com), a record label that, like

SHORTLIST

Best new
- Limi Feu (p82)
- Stella McCartney (p83)
- Yohji Yamamoto (p83)

Best concept stores
- Base One (p92)
- Colette (p80)
- LE66 (p66)
- Sony Style (p67)

Best handpicked fashion
- L'Eclaireur (p113)
- Shine (p114)

Best for accessories
- Marc by Marc Jacobs (p82)
- Sonia Rykiel (p140)

Best for eveningwear
- Lanvin (p82)
- Lefranc.ferrant (p139)
- Yves Saint Laurent (p140)

Best souvenirs
- Diptyque (p147)
- La Galerie du Carrousel du Louvre (p80)

Best food and wine
- Christian Constant (p138)
- Fromagerie Quatrehomme (p128)
- Jean-Paul Hévin (p139)
- Julien, Caviste (p113)
- Du Pain et des Idées (p113)
- Pierre Hermé (p140)

Literary life
- I Love My Blender (p113)
- Red Wheelbarrow (p114)
- Shakespeare & Company (p148)

The classics
- Le Bon Marché (p138)
- Galeries Lafayette (p80)
- Printemps (p83)

Kitsuné, is producing its own cashmere and polos, Corpus Christie's 'pocket store' for Thierry Gougenot's rock gothic jewellery (64 rue Vieille-du-Temple, 3rd), and concept shop Bubble Wood. Stylish menswear is also strong here with Frenchtrotters Homme (114 rue Vieille-du-Temple, 3rd, 01.44.61.00.14. www.frenchtrotters.fr), Jacenko's impeccable selection of preppy jackets, pullovers and accessories (38 rue de Poitou, 3rd, 01.42.71.80.38), Christophe Lemaire's lounge lizard separates (28 rue de Poitou, 3rd (01.44.78.00.09), and Laurel Store (70 rue Vieille-du-Temple, 3rd, 01.42.74.17.42) for the currently in-vogue Fred Perry look. For vintage check out Marie Louise de Monterey (1 rue Charles François Dupuis, 3rd, 01.48.04.83.88) and Studio W (6 rue du Pont-aux-Choux, 3rd, 01.44.78.05.02).

Going Gauche

The long-established shopping area of St-Germain tends to be more conservative, but is increasingly offering a mirror image of the Right Bank with brands insisting on a presence on both sides of the Seine. These include Paul & Joe (p139) and Vanessa Bruno (p140). Shoe heaven is found along rue de Grenelle with all the top brands. Newcomers include bobo bags in colourful fabrics and denim from the former prêt-à-porter designer Jérome Dreyfuss (1 rue Jacob, 6th, 01.43.54.70.93), Hélène Lamey's French-made nightwear and childrenswear at Bluet (18 rue du Pré-aux-Clercs, 7th, 01.45.44.00.26), and attractive multi-brand shop Kyrie Eleison (15 carrefour de l'Odéon, 6th, 01.46.34.26.91) with lush creations by Orla Kiely, Eros-Erotokritos, Velvet and La Fée Parisienne.

On the luxury scene two big names have revamped their boutiques: at Yves Saint Laurent (p140) opium-coloured walls and lacquered ceilings provide a sumptuous showcase for Stephane Pilati's creations, while at Sonia Rykiel's enlarged St-Germain flagship (p140) black mosaics, smoked glass and multiple mirrors evoke a '70s nightclub. And if you're in the market for something special and rather avant-garde, visit Lefranc.ferrant (p139), a talented Paris duo who approach couture with a surreal eye.

Foodie heaven

The new layout of Fauchon (28 & 30 pl de la Madeleine, 8th, 01.70.39.38.00), with different areas (pâtisserie, bakery, fruit and vegetables, etc) and chefs on hand at each to offer advice and recipes, provides an excuse to indulge at this luxury food store. Food markets, both permanent and temporary, are found in all arrondissements – two of the most popular are the historic Marché d'Aligre in the 12th, and the relatively new Marché des Enfants Rouges in the 3rd, which focuses on organic produce. For a full list, see www.paris.fr. Foodie streets include rue de Buci (6th), rue des Martyrs (9th) and rue Mouffetard (5th).

Practicalities

VAT at 19.6% is included in the price of most items. Opening hours are generally 10am to 7pm Monday to Saturday, with some shops closing for lunch and on Monday mornings. Department stores stay open late on Thursdays. Many Marais shops and those on the Champs-Elysées are open on Sundays.

Batofar

WHAT'S BEST

Nightlife

Beneath an apparently uneventful surface, there are loads of great venues in Paris and the locals know how to let their hair down – after a cocktail or three. True to cliché, the city has some of the most stylish clubs in the world, but gaze beyond the sparkle and you'll find shabby-chic bars with celebrity DJs, boats rocking from dusk 'til dawn and club-restaurants offering late-night meals and a boogie. Music wise, electro pop and rock reign, but jazz, blues and *chanson* still reel in the punters.

Nightclubs

New additions adding verve to Paris's increasingly cool clubbing scene are Le World Place (32-34 rue Marbeuf, 8th, 01.56.88.36.36), a brand new lobster restaurant/ lounge bar/nightclub just off the Champs Elysées, and the recently opened Showcase (p69), in a former warehouse underneath the Pont Alexandre II. In a similar vein, Djoon (22 bd Vincent-Auriol, 13th, 01.45.70.83.49) provides a superclub experience as a restaurant, bar and club mixing an industrial setting with baroque frescoes and an electro, garage and house sound.

For big-room clubbing, Queen (p69) is a gay-friendly club known for its wild disco nights, while Rex (p84) offers mainstream and experimental electro on one of the best sound systems in Europe.

For standard house try Folies Pigalle (p94) or Red Light (p157), but don't ignore the city's smaller venues, which frequently feature leading DJs. It is not unusual to find Berlin's DJ M.A.N.D.Y at Elysée Montmartre (p94), Jarvis Cocker at the Nouveau Casino (p115) or Birdy Nam Nam at the Social Club (142 rue Montmartre, 2nd, www.parissocialclub.com). These intimate gigs are also where you'll discover most of Paris's 'after' parties too, with almost as many early Sunday morning events as there are Saturday nighters. Worth checking out are the floating Batofar (p152) and, in summer, the Bateau Concorde Atlantique (Porte de Solférino, 25 quai Anatole-France, 7th, 01.47.05.71.03).

Straightforward hip hop nights are held at the Opus Café (167 quai de Valmy, 10th, 01.40.34.70.00); the Ram di Boat reggae night happens most Tuesdays at Batofar; for drum 'n' bass, don't miss the monthly Para Siempre at Glaz'Art (7 avenue Porte de la Villette, 19th, 01.40.36.55.65). Trance and hardcore tend to stay outside Paris, with outdoor events organised by local collectives and sound systems, although Red Light salutes French techno with regular tecktonik nights with DJ Dess. Dance music of every stripe gets an outing at the Paris Techno Parade (p34), which takes place in September and draws thousands.

If you like your clubbing cosy, plenty of bars around Bastille, Oberkampf and the Grands Boulevards are willing to oblige. The new Panic Room (101 rue Amelot, 11th, 01.58.30.93.43) is one of the hippest around with a stream of French electro nights. Traditionalists can choose their poison too; a host of school disco-type nights where the DJ is no superstar take place at the twice-monthly Bal at Elysée Montmartre, and salsa and world music get a good hammering at Le Divan du Monde (p94).

SHORTLIST

Best new/revamped
- Les Trois Baudets (p94)
- Le World Place (p26)

Best bands
- Le Bataclan (p114)
- La Cigale (p94)
- Le Point Ephémère (p99)

Best sound systems
- Djoon (p26)
- Rex (p84)

All night long
- Nouveau Casino (p115)
- Red Light (p157)

Sunday sessions
- Wagg (p140)

Perfect for posing
- Le Baron (p67)
- Le ParisParis (p84)

Best for star DJs
- Rex (p84)
- Social Club (p27)

Best for party snacks
- Café Charbon (p109)
- Le Showcase (p69)

Best gay club
- Queen (p69)

Best for jazz
- Caveau de la Huchette (p148)
- New Morning (p98)
- Le Petit Journal Montparnasse (p157)
- Le Sunset/Le Sunside (p84)

Killer cocktails
- Djoon (p26)

Life is a cabaret
- Le Lido (p67)
- Moulin Rouge (p94)

Bateau Concorde Atlantique p27

Because Paris clubs don't really get going until 2am, people usually hit a DJ bar beforehand and diehards finish their evening at an 'after' on Sunday morning. Free passes can be found on various flyers; flyer information is available at www.flyersweb.com. Other good sites are www.radiofg.com, www.novaplanet.com and www.lemonsound.com. Also look out for big, one-off events in venues such as Rex and Point Ephémère (p99) where cool labels, DJs and crews like Dirty Sound System, Bob Sinclair and David Guetta run their own show.

The last métro leaves at around 12.45am (1.45am on Friday and Saturday), and the first gets rolling at 5.45am; in between you'll have to use a night bus, Vélib or taxi.

Rock, roots & jazz

If you'd set your heart on a late-night gig, think again. Trendsetters may flock to Paris to meet, plan and jam, but many punters complain that the powers-that-be – the people who dreamed up the *lutte contre le bruit*, or noise clampdown – are spoiling the party. So if you want live music, you'll have to arrive before 10.30pm (sometimes earlier).

If you're in need of Francophonia delivered by husky-voiced ladies, you'll be glad to know that *chanson* continues to thrive in places such as La Bellevilloise (19 rue Boyer, 20th, 01.53.27.35.77), founded in 1877 as a socialist cooperative and now a multi-purpose exhibition and concert venue, and new arrival Les Trois Baudets (p94).

Rock is on the rise, especially in Bastille where the three-level Méchanique Ondulatoire (p115) and Le Motel (p115) hold regular live gigs; and in Menilmontant's La Maroquinerie (23 Rue Boyer, 20th, 01.40.33.35.05), which doubles as an excellent restaurant.

On the down side, jazz has been suffering of late and three famous joints – the Slow Club, Bilboquet and 7 Lézards – have thrown in the towel. All is not lost, though: the New Morning (p98), Sunset (p84), Caveau de la Huchette (p148) and Duc des Lombards (p84) still offer consistently high standards and a stream of big names.

Paris also has a lively world music scene – often Arabic and African – at places like Le Bataclan (p114). US and UK indie acts drop by on tour to places like Olympia (p84) and La Cigale (p94).

Listings can be found in the weekly *Les Inrockuptibles*, whose database at www.lesinrocks.com has all that's hot in town. Monthly *Lylo* is distributed free at Fnac (p65) and in some bars. Virgin Megastore (p67) and Fnac have their own ticket offices. Get to a gig at the time given on the ticket; they usually start on time.

Cabaret

The promise of busty babes slinking across stage in frilly knickers has turned glamour cabarets into some of the hottest spots around. The Moulin Rouge (p94) popularised the skirt-raising concept in the 19th century, and since then venues such as Le Lido (p67) have institutionalised garter-pinging forever.

These days, a cabaret is an all-evening, smart-dress affair, with a pre-show meal and champers. The Moulin Rouge is the most traditional revue and the only place with cancan. Toulouse-Lautrec posters, glittery lamp-posts and fake trees lend tacky charm, while 60 Doriss dancers cover the stage with faultless synchronisation. Sadly, elbow room is nil, with tables packed in like sardines. But if you can bear intimacy with international businessmen, it's the cheapest of the food-serving cabarets and won't disappoint.

For space go to Le Lido. With 1,000 seats, this classy venue is the largest, priciest cabaret of the lot: the art nouveau hall's high-tech touches optimise visibility and star chef Paul Bocuse has revolutionised the menu. The slightly tame show, with 60 Bluebell Girls, has boob-shaking, wacky costumes and numerous oddities.

For a cheaper, more risqué performance, try the Crazy Horse (12 ave George V, 8th, 01.47.23.32.32) whose neo-Dadaist 'l'art du nu' (the art of nudity) concept was invented by Alain Bernadin in 1951. The new show, Forever Crazy, is an ode to feminine beauty with 11 clone-like dancers, clothed only in psychedelic light (and some judiciously placed black sticky tape), who put on tantalising numbers with names like *Teasing* and *Legmania*.

Le Grand Rex

WHAT'S BEST

Arts & Leisure

A number of cultural developments and innovations, and several new sites, have given a significant lift to Paris's cultural scene. In 2008, the Maison des Métallos (p115), a former trade union centre, reopened as a cutting-edge showcase for up-and-coming artists; and an old funeral parlour was transformed into 104 (p159), a centre for contemporary art. The Théâtre de la Gaîté Lyrique, meanwhile, is set to reopen as a hub for digital arts and contemporary music in 2010.

Construction has also begun on the Cité Européenne du Cinéma in the northern suburb of St-Denis. Due for completion in 2010, the complex will house nine studios and promises to give the national film industry a massive boost. Even so, the French film industry remains in extremely good health. In 2008, the home-grown comedy *Bienvenue Chez les Ch'tis* became the country's second biggest grossing film of all time, and actress Marion Cotillard took home an Oscar for her interpretation of Edith Piaf in *La Vie en Rose*.

What's especially good about the arts here is the accessibility: there are any number of festivals and discount promotions throughout the year, many organised by the city council, that bring what Brits often consider to be 'elitist' art forms within the reach and appreciation of the general public.

Film

Cinema-going is a serious pastime in Paris. More tickets per head are bought here than anywhere else in

Europe, and in any given week there's a choice of some 350 movies – not including the numerous festivals (p34), many of which offer free or discounted entry. The city houses nearly 90 cinemas and around 400 screens, almost a quarter of which show nothing but arthouse. Even the multiplexes regularly screen documentaries and films from Eastern Europe, Asia and South America. This vibrant scene is constantly evolving, with new multi-screen complexes under construction and classic picture houses constantly under renovation.

Visiting one of the city's many picture palaces is an experience in itself – from the glorious faux-oriental Pagode (p128) and kitsch excesses of the Grand Rex (p86) to the innovative Forum des Images (p86), which reopened at the end of 2008 after a major facelift.

New releases hit the screens on Wednesdays – when certain cinemas offer reduced rates.

Opera & classical

It's all change at the Opéra National de Paris (p86). After years under controversial modernist director Gérard Mortier, the Paris opera company enters a new era under Nicolas Joel, who comes to the capital after 18 years at Toulouse Opera. With a reputation for traditional values, Joel is likely to favour a more classical repertoire, while talented new music director Philippe Jordan will offer some youthful energy. The Opéra Comique (p86), meanwhile, continues to capitalise on new financial security following its promotion to National Theatre status by offering a crowd-pleasing season of revivals and classics.

Plans are underway to construct a new 2,400-seat symphonic concert hall in the Parc de la Villette for

SHORTLIST

Wonderful settings
- Le Grand Rex (p86)
- Palais Garnier (p86)
- Théâtre des Champs-Elysées (p69)

Most innovative
- International opera at the Festival d'Automne (p34)

Most romantic
- Candlelit recitals for the Festival Chopin (p38)
- Lovers' seats at MK2 Bilbliothèque (p152)

Best bargains
- Film tickets at €3.50 during Printemps du Cinéma (p36)
- Free concerts at Paris Jazz Festival (p38)
- Free museum entry during Printemps des Musées (p37)

Best alfresco
- Cinéma en Plein Air (p39)
- Festival Classique au Vert (p34)
- Fête de la Musique (p39)

Best film venues
- Le Grand Rex (p86)
- La Pagode (p128)

Best opera venues
- Opéra Comique (p86)
- Palais Garnier (p86)

Original creations
- 104 (p159)
- Maison des Métallos (p115)
- Quinzaine des Réalisateurs at Forum des Images (p38)

Culture after dark
- Midnight closing at Palais de Tokyo (p61)
- Nuit Blanche (p35)
- La Nuit des Musées (p37)

2012; in the meantime, the city's current largest classical venue, the Salle Pleyel (p69), remains home to the Orchestre de Paris. Elsewhere, director Jean-Luc Choplin provides a populist touch at Châtelet (p86).

Contemporary composition remains a strong suit, thanks to the work of IRCAM, the Ensemble Intercontemporain and the active involvement of Pierre Boulez. Another Parisian forte is Early Music, led by William Christie's Les Arts Florissants, which has become an international benchmark for the Baroque repertoire.

Many venues offer cut-rate tickets to students (under 26) an hour before curtain-up – but be suspicious of smooth-talking touts around the Opéra. On the Fête de la Musique (21 June) all events are free, and year-round freebies crop up at the Maison de Radio France and the Conservatoire de Paris.

Dance

Although the sumptuous ballet productions at the Palais Garnier and international companies at Châtelet will always delight audiences, it's in the sphere of contemporary dance that Paris currently shines brightest. The prestigious Centre National de la Danse (1 rue Victor-Hugo, 93507 Pantin, 01.41.83.27.27), just outside the city centre, has given France an impressive HQ for its 600-plus regional dance companies. Every season sees some kind of contemporary dance festival in or near Paris; Paris Quartier d'Eté (p39) is one of the biggest.

Theatre

French-speaking theatre buffs can choose from some 450 productions every week: from offbeat shows in small, independent venues to high-brow classics in grandiose auditoriums like the Comédie Française (2 rue Richelieu, 1st, 08.25.10.16.80), whose staples include Molière and Racine.

Fortunately for Anglophones, the Paris theatre scene is becoming ever more international. The restored and re-baptised Odéon Théatre de l'Europe (pl de l'Odéon, 6th, 01.44.85.44.00) offers plays in a number of languages, including at least one per season in English. Anglophone performances are occasionally programmed at the Théatre des Bouffes du Nord (37bis bd de la Chapelle, 10th, 01.46.07.34.50), which remains under the direction of maverick Brit-born director Peter Brook until 2011, while the cutting-edge MC93 Bobigny (1 bd Lénine, 93000 Bobigny, 01.41.60.72.72) regularly hosts international companies performing in their mother tongue. Meanwhile, the Improfessionals (www.improfessionals.com) stage regular improv performances in English, and the Monday at 7 troupe brings British plays to life at the Sudden Théatre (14bis rue Ste-Isaure, 18th, 01.42.62.35.00). Shakespeare in English is performed every summer at the Bois de Boulogne's Théâtre de Verdure du Jardin Shakespeare (01.40.19.95.33) by London's Tower Theatre Company (www.towertheatre.org.uk).

What's on

For listings, see weekly magazines *L'Officiel des Spectacles* or *Pariscope*. When it comes to films, take note of the two letters printed near the title: VO (*version originale*) means a screening in the original language with French subtitles; VF (*version française*) means that it's dubbed into French. Cinema seats can be reserved at www.allocine.fr.

WHAT'S ON

Calendar

Nuit Blanche

This is the pick of events that had been announced as we went to press. On public holidays, or *jours feriés*, banks, many museums, most businesses and a number of restaurants close. New Year's Day, May Day, Bastille Day and Christmas Day are the most piously observed holidays. Dates highlighted in **bold** indicate public holidays.

September 2009

Early Sept
Festival Classique au Vert
Parc Floral de Paris
www.classiqueauvert2009.com
A series of free classical recitals held in a park setting.

Early Sept **Jazz à la Villette**
Parc de la Villette
www.jazzalavillette.com
One of the best local jazz festivals.

4 Sept-11 Oct **Festival Paris Ile-de-France**
Various venues
www.festival-ile-de-france.com
The capital's own film festival.

Mid Sept **Techno Parade**
www.technopol.net
This parade (finishing up at Bastille) marks the start of the electronic music festival Rendez-vous Electroniques.

Mid Sept-end Dec
Festival d'Automne
Various venues
www.festival-automne.com
Major annual festival of challenging theatre, dance and modern opera.

19-20 **Journées du Patrimoine**
Various venues
www.journeesdupatrimoine.culture.fr
Embassies, ministries and scientific establishments open their doors.

October 2009

Ongoing Festival d'Automne (see Sept); Festival Paris Ile-de-France (see Sept)

Early Oct **Nuit Blanche**
Various venues
www.nuitblanche.paris.fr
For one night, galleries, museums, swimming pools, bars and clubs stay open till very late.

3, 4 Oct **Prix de l'Arc de Triomphe**
Hippodrome de Longchamp
www.prixarcdetriomphe.com
France's richest flat race attracts the elite of horse racing.

Mid Oct **Fête des Vendanges de Montmartre**
Various venues
www.fetedesvendangesde montmartre.com
The modest 1,000-bottle harvest of the Clos Montmartre vineyard is the pretext for a weekend of street parties.

22-25 **FIAC**
Paris-Expo
www.fiacparis.com
Respected international art fair.

November 2009

Ongoing Festival d'Automne (see Sept)

Early Nov **Festival Inrockuptibles**
Various venues
www.lesinrocks.com
Rock, pop and trance festival curated by rock magazine *Les Inrockuptibles*.

11 L'Armistice (Armistice Day)
Arc de Triomphe
The President lays wreaths to honour French combatants who died in the World Wars.

19 **Fête du Beaujolais Nouveau**
Various venues
www.beaujolaisgourmand.com
The new vintage is launched to packed cafés and wine bars.

Nov-Dec **Africolor**
Various venues in St-Denis
www.africolor.com
African music festival with a spirited wrap party.

December 2009

Ongoing Africolor (see Nov); Festival d'Automne (see Sept)

Dec-Mar **Paris sur Glace**
Various venues
www.paris.fr
Three free outdoor ice rinks.

24-**25 Noël (Christmas)**

31 **New Year's Eve**
Huge crowds on the Champs-Elysées.

Journées du Patrimoine

Paris sur Glace p35

January 2010

Ongoing Paris sur Glace (see Dec)

1 **Jour de l'An (New Year's Day)**
The Grande Parade de Paris brings floats, bands and dancers.

6 **Fête des Rois (Epiphany)**
Pâtisseries all sell *galettes des rois*, frangipane-filled cakes in which a *fève*, or tiny charm, is hidden.

20 **Mass for Louis XVI**
Chapelle Expiatoire
Royalists and right-wing crackpots mourn the end of the monarchy.

February 2010

Ongoing Paris sur Glace (see Dec)

Early Feb-mid Mar **Six Nations**
Stade de France
www.rbs6nations.com
Paris is invaded by Brits and Celts for big weekends of rugby.

14 **Nouvel An Chinois**
Various venues
Dragon dances and martial arts demos celebrate the Chinese new year.

March 2010

Ongoing Paris sur Glace (see Dec); Six Nations (see Feb)

Early Mar-Apr **Banlieues Bleues**
Various venues in Seine St-Denis
www.banlieuesbleues.org
Five weeks of top-quality French and international jazz, blues, R&B and soul.

Mid Mar **Printemps du Cinéma**
Various venues
www.printempsducinema.com
Film tickets across the city are cut to a bargain €3.50 for three days.

April 2010

Ongoing Banlieues Bleues (see Mar)

Early Apr-end May **Foire du Trône**
Pelouse de Reuilly
www.foiredutrone.com
France's biggest funfair.

2 **Le Chemin de la Croix (Way of the Cross)**
Square Willette
Good Friday pilgrimage as crowds follow the Archbishop of Paris from the bottom of Montmartre to Sacré-Coeur.

4 Pâques (Easter Sunday)

Mid Apr **Marathon de Paris**
Av des Champs-Elysées to av Foch
www.parismarathon.com
37,000 runners take in the sights.

End Apr-mid May **Foire de Paris**
Paris-Expo
www.foiredeparis.fr
Enormous lifestyle salon, full of craft and food stores, plus health exhibits.

End Apr-early May **Grand Marché d'Art Contemporain**
Place de la Bastille
www.organisation-joel-garcia.fr
Contemporary artists display and sell their work at this annual arts fair.

May 2010

Ongoing Foire du Trône (see Apr); Foire de Paris (see Apr); Grand Marché d'Art Contemporain (see Apr)

1 Fête du Travail (May Day)
Key sights close; unions march in eastern Paris via Bastille.

1 Jour de l'Ascension

Early May **Printemps des Musées**
Various venues
www.printempsdesmusees.culture.fr
For one Sunday in May, selected museums open for free.

8 Victoire 1945 (VE Day)

Mid May **La Nuit des Musées**
Various venues
www.nuitdesmusees.culture.fr
For one night, the landmark museums across Paris stay open late and put on special events.

Mid May **Art St-Germain-des-Prés**
Various venues
www.artsaintgermaindespres.com
See box right.

Artful partying

Join in the fun at a Paris *vernissage*.

Timing your trip to Paris with a night of *vernissages* (private views) gives a taste not only of the art on offer but of the personalities who frequent the art scene, a real entrée into Paris life. Providing you look the part – and obvious freeloading is ill-advised – you can turn up at most private views without an invitation.

The journal *L'Officiel Galeries & Musées*, which you can pick up free in most galleries, has a diary of *vernissages*. The second and last Thursdays of the month are the most popular dates, with ten to 15 galleries opening a new exhibition. But the big rendezvous of the year – unmissable if you are serious about this – is **Art St-Germain-des-Prés** (www.artsaintgermaindespres.com) in May. Nicknamed the 'block party', it sees almost 50 galleries get together to showcase their top artists, with red carpets spread outside each gallery.

The galleries are mostly concentrated on rue de Seine, rue des Beaux-Arts, rue Visconti, rue Guénégaud and rue Mazarine, and a whole cross-section of boho locals turn out for a drop of wine and conversation: artists, dealers, ageing musicians, film directors, eccentrics, fur-clad ladies, rich kids and celebrities (Kylie's ex Olivier Martinez likes to bring his friends) – this is most definitely one weekend when *flânerie* will get you everywhere.

Etés de la Danse

Mid May **Festival Jazz à Saint-Germain-des-Prés**
St-Germain-des-Prés, various venues
www.espritjazz.com
A ten-day celebration of jazz and blues.

Mid May-early June **Quinzaine des Réalisateurs**
Forum des Images
www.quinzaine-realisateurs.com
The Cannes Directors' Fortnight programme comes to Paris.

24 Lundi de Pentecôte (Whit Monday)

End May **Le Printemps des Rues**
Various venues
www.leprintempsdesrues.com
Annual street-theatre festival.

End May-mid July
Foire St-Germain
Various venues
www.foiresaintgermain.org
Concerts, theatre and workshops.

End May-early June
French Tennis Open
Stade Roland Garros
www.rolandgarros.com
Glitzy Grand Slam tennis tournament.

June 2010

Ongoing Quinzaine des Réalisateurs (see May); French Tennis Open (see May); Foire St-Germain (see May)

Early June **Tous à Vélo**
Across Paris
www.tousavelo.com
Cycling tours and activities as Paris's two-wheelers take to the streets.

Early June-July **Paris Jazz Festival**
Parc Floral de Paris
www.parcfloraldeparis.com/ www.paris.fr
Free jazz at the lovely Parc Floral.

Early June-early July **Festival de St-Denis**
Various venues in St-Denis
www.festival-saint-denis.com
Four weeks of concerts showcasing top-quality classical music.

June-July **Festival Chopin à Paris**
Orangerie de Bagatelle
www.frederic-chopin.com
Romantic candlelit piano recitals in the Bois de Boulogne.

Late June **Fête de la Musique**
Various venues
www.fetedelamusique.fr
Free gigs (encompassing all musical genres) take place across the city.

Late June **Gay Pride March**
www.inter-lgbt.org
Outrageous floats and costumes parade towards Bastille, followed by an official party and various club events throughout the city.

Late June-early July **La Goutte d'Or en Fête**
Eglise St Bernard
www.gouttedorenfete.org
Raï, rap and reggae.

July 2010

Ongoing Foire St-Germain (see May); Paris Jazz Festival (see June); Festival de St-Denis (see June); Festival Chopin à Paris (see June); La Goutte d'Or en Fête (see June)

Early July **Paris Cinéma**
Various venues
www.pariscinema.org
Premieres, tributes and restored films at the city's excellent summer film-going initiative.

Early July **Solidays**
Hippodrome de Longchamp
www.solidays.com
A three-day music bash for AIDS charities, featuring French, world and new talent.

Early-late July **Etés de la Danse**
Centre Historique des Archives Nationales
www.lesetesdeladanse.com
International classical and contemporary dance festival.

July-Aug **Cinéma en Plein Air**
Parc de la Villette
www.villette.com
A summer fixture on the city calendar: a themed season of free films screened under the stars.

14 Quatorze Juillet (Bastille Day)
Various venues
France's national holiday commemorates 1789. On the 13th, Parisians dance at place de la Bastille. At 10am on the 14th, crowds line the Champs-Elysées as the President reviews a military parade. By night, the Champ de Mars fills for a huge firework display.

Mid July-mid Aug
Paris, Quartier d'Eté
Various venues
www.quartierdete.com
Classical and jazz concerts, plus dance and theatre, in outdoor venues.

Mid July-mid Aug **Paris-Plage**
Pont des Arts to Pont de Sully
www.paris.fr
Palm trees, huts, hammocks and around 2,000 tonnes of fine sand on both banks of the Seine bring a seaside vibe to the city. Not only this, there's a floating pool and a lending library too.

Late July **Tour de France**
Av des Champs-Elysées
www.letour.fr
The ultimate cycle endurance test climaxes on the Champs-Elysées.

August 2010

Ongoing Cinéma en Plein Air (see July); Paris, Quartier d'Eté (see July); Paris-Plage (see July)

15 Fête de l'Assomption (Assumption Day)
Cathédrale Notre-Dame de Paris
Notre-Dame again becomes a place of religious pilgrimage.

Late Aug **Rock en Seine**
Domaine National de St-Cloud
www.rockenseine.com
Two days, two stages, one world-class rock line-up.

September 2010

Early Sept **Jazz à la Villette**
Parc de la Villette

www.jazzalavillette.com
One of the best jazz festivals in the city.

Sept **Festival Classique au Vert**
Parc Floral du Paris
www.paris.fr
Free classical recitals in a park setting.

Mid Sept **Techno Parade**
Various venues
www.technopol.net
This parade (finishing up at Bastille) marks the start of electronic music festival Rendez-vous Electroniques.

Mid Sept **Journées du Patrimoine**
Various venues
www.jp.culture.fr
Embassies, ministries and scientific establishments throw open their doors to the general public. See *Le Parisien* for a full programme.

Mid Sept-late Dec **Festival d'Automne**
Various venues
www.festival-automne.com
Major annual festival for all kinds of challenging theatre, dance and modern opera performances.

October 2010

Ongoing Festival d'Automne (see Sept)

Early Oct **Prix de l'Arc de Triomphe**
Hippodrome de Longchamp
www.prixarcdetriomphe.com
France's richest flat race.

Early Oct **Nuit Blanche**
Various venues
www.paris.fr
For one night, a selection of galleries, museums, swimming pools, bars and clubs stay open until very late.

Mid Oct **Fête des Vendanges à Montmartre**
Various venues
www.fetedesvendangesde montmartre.com
The modest 1,000-bottle harvest is the pretext for a weekend of street parties.

Mid Oct **FIAC**
Various venues
www.fiacparis.com
Respected international art fair.

End Oct **Grand Marché d'Art Contemporain**
Place de la Bastille
www.organisation-joel-garcia.fr
Annual arts fair.

November 2010

Ongoing Festival d'Automne (see Sept)

1 Toussaint (All Saints' Day)

Early Nov **Festival Inrockuptibles**
Various venues
www.lesinrocks.com
Rock, pop and trance festival curated by rock magazine *Les Inrockuptibles*.

11 L'Armistice (Armistice Day)
Arc de Triomphe
The President lays wreaths to honour French dead of both World Wars.

Late Nov **Fête du Beaujolais Nouveau**
Various venues
www.beaujolaisgourmand.com
The new vintage is launched.

December 2010

Ongoing Festival d'Automne (see Sept)

Dec-Mar **Paris sur Glace**
Various venues
www.paris.fr

Mid Dec **Africolor**
Various venues in St-Denis
www.africolor.com
African music festival.

24-**25 Noël (Christmas)**

31 **New Year's Eve**

Itineraries

Rest in Pieces

Paris has some of history's most influential characters buried on its soil; the Père-Lachaise cemetery alone shelters hundreds of influential writers, artists and politicians within its confines. But these are the lucky ones. Other historical figures did not always get to their final resting place in one piece – much like Britney's used gum for today's eBayers, their bones, hair or innards led to great traffic back in the day. This itinerary around central Paris gives you the chance to get up close and personal with some of the city's more macabre relics.

START: Place du Palais-Royal, 1st (M° Palais Royal Musée du Louvre). Turn your back on the Louvre and walk into the **Comédie Française** (2 rue de Richelieu, 1st). Founded in 1640 by Louis XIV with Molière as its lead playwright, 'La Comédie' is still the only state theatre with a permanent troupe of actors. In the foyer, look out for an old armchair inside a glass cage. It is believed to be the one from which Molière delivered his last lines at a performance of *Le Malade Imaginaire* in 1673. He died shortly after the curtain fell. As a tribute to the playwright, the seat is put back on stage every 15 January, the anniversary of his birth.

In the same room, the statue of an old man regards theatre-goers with a sarcastic smile. You may have recognised Voltaire, the French Enlightenment philosopher, immortalised here by sculptor Jean-Antoine Houdon. But it is a lesser known fact that the statue serves as reliquary for the philosopher's brain, sealed inside its pedestal.

After Voltaire's death in 1778, the apothecary who performed the autopsy removed his brain and heart and put them in boiling alcohol to solidify them. Voltaire's brain then passed through many

Comédie Française

hands before finally ending up at the Comédie in 1924.

As for his heart, it remained on display for a long time at the Château de Ferney, where Voltaire died. It was only when the philosopher's body was declared 'property of the state' in 1791 that the heart was given to Napoleon III, who decided to keep it at the Imperial Library, now the **Bibliothèque Nationale – Richelieu**. Walk to the entrance at 58 rue de Richelieu, around the corner from the Comédie, and ask to see the *salon d'honneur*, a stunning oak-veneered room presided over by a statue of Voltaire identical to the one at the Comédie. The heart is enclosed in its wooden pedestal.

The next destination is on the Left Bank, a perfect opportunity to test out Vélib, Paris's hugely popular municipal bike scheme. There is a *borne* opposite the library, at 71 rue de Richelieu.

Head south and turn left into rue des Petits Champs. Cycle across place des Victoires and turn right into rue du Louvre. Follow the traffic all the way down to the river, and turn left on to quai du Louvre, a section of riverbank lined with *bouquinistes*. Carry on to Pont au Change, where you can use the bus lane to cycle across the bridge. Once on the island, keep going south, passing the impressive gates of the Palais de Justice, and turn left on to quai du Marché Neuf. Go straight ahead until you're facing Notre-Dame cathedral. You can drop your bike at the *borne* on the side of the square, on rue d'Arcole.

Head south across Pont au Double. On quai de Montebello, walk around the small park in front of you and take rue de la Bûcherie. If you're feeling peckish after all that cultural dissection, you can indulge yourself with a dish of gently sautéed brains at offal specialist **Ribouldingue** (p146) around the corner.

With rested feet and a full stomach, you're ready for more relic-hunting. Find rue St-Jacques at the end of rue de la Bûcherie and walk down to rue Soufflot. The

Bibliothèque Nationale – Richelieu p43

columns of the **Panthéon** (p145) should be clear to see on your left. As the last home of many French *grands hommes*, the Panthéon could be seen as the ultimate reliquary, even though there's not much to peep at in terms of old bones. The crypt gathers the shrines of over 70 illustrious Frenchmen, including Victor Hugo, Alexandre Dumas and our old friend Voltaire, whose carcass – or what remains of it – can finally rest in peace here.

A somewhat more sensational relic can be found in the **Eglise St-Etienne-du-Mont** (p141), just around the corner from the Panthéon. The church, a masterpiece of Flamboyant Gothic architecture, displays a finger bone belonging to Sainte Geneviève, patron saint of Paris, in a glass reliquary next to her sarcophagus.

Next, retrace your steps towards boulevard St-Michel and brace yourself for a particularly creepy rendezvous. You can pick up a Vélib from the *borne* at 174 rue St-Jacques or cross through the Jardin du Luxembourg for some much-needed greenery.

From boulevard St-Michel, take rue de Médicis, followed by rue de Vaugirard which hugs the north side of the Jardin du Luxembourg. After passing the Sénat, turn right into rue Garancière, then left into rue St-Sulpice. Carry on along rue du Vieux Colombier until you reach rue de Sèvres. Look out for Vaneau métro station and the Vélib *borne* around the corner.

Find the Chapelle des Lazaristes, identifiable by its tall green doors next to no.95 rue de Sèvres, and climb up the stairs to the side of the altar. Here lies the surprisingly fresh-looking corpse of Saint Vincent de Paul, patron saint of the poor. While his skeleton was preserved in its entirety, his face and hands were covered in wax and moulded to resemble the deceased,

Musée de l'Homme

giving the disturbing impression that he passed away only minutes ago. The people of Paris, very attached to Saint Vincent de Paul, clubbed together to pay for the sumptuous silver and gold coffin in which the body lies.

Pick up a Vélib on rue Vaneau and head north. Turn left into rue de Babylone and then right into boulevard des Invalides. Keep cycling towards the Seine, with the golden dome of **Les Invalides** (p124) on your left, the last resting place of Napoleon. The emperor could easily win the title of most scattered cadaver in history. While his heart and innards are in Austria, you will need to travel to New York to get near his penis, bought at auction by a urologist for $3,800.

After such intense reflections, you should arrive on quai d'Orsay, by the Seine. Cross the Pont Alexandre III and turn left on to cours Albert I. At place de l'Alma, where other pilgrims are gathered by the Princess Diana memorial, take avenue du Président Wilson on your right. Carry on until you reach place du Trocadéro. A Vélib *borne* on avenue d'Eylau, third right on the roundabout, will allow you to dispose of your bike.

Buy a ticket to the **Musée de l'Homme** (17 place du Trocadéro, 16th) in the Palais de Chaillot. In the anthropology gallery, you can compare the plaster skull of a Cro-Magnon with that of footballer Lilian Thuram and philosopher René Descartes. The original skull of the latter is in the museum's safe.

The rest of Descartes' body is buried on the Left Bank, which makes the perfect start to another trek. But by the time you leave the museum you will probably have had your share of gravestones for the day. Instead, take a seat in the Café de l'Homme, order a coffee and enjoy one of the best views there is of the city. Chances are you've never felt more alive.

The Lesser Known Louvre

There are several approaches to visiting the Louvre, but certainly no one logical route and years of potential for discovering all its secret treasures. You can be systematic and do a trail through the greatest hits, by department, by wing or by theme, or you can follow the route mapped out here and let yourself be sidetracked and beguiled by Flemish landscapes, Byzantine icons, Ancient Egyptian funerary chapels, and France's earliest portrait.

Part of the fascination of the Louvre is that it is not just a museum, but was a royal and later imperial palace and seat of government (part of it continued to be used by the ministry of finance until the 1980s). The building's history is entwined with that of Paris and France. Behind the 35,000 works of art and 8.5 million annual visitors, and amid the modern lifts, escalators and postcard stalls, you'll also find the giant staircases, sumptuous ceilings and carved panelling of the original palace.

Start on rue du Louvre with its pedimented classical façade and go through the central doorway into the Cour Carrée. Although the main entrance is now via the glass pyramid, this courtyard, with its richly sculpted western façade by Pierre Lescot and Jean Goujon, marked the introduction of Renaissance taste to Paris by François 1er as he established his court in the capital. Head through the arch to the Cour Napoléon, where the two long wings added under Napoléon III are set off by I M Pei's glass pyramid in the centre – main entrance since 1993, exactly 200 years after part of the Louvre first became a museum. Be sure to pick up a plan of the museum at the welcome desk.

Start by the Richelieu wing, going up to the Cours Puget glazed sculpture court, on the lower ground floor. Here four vast green bronze captives by Martin van den Bogaert, which originally stood at the foot of a statue in place des Victoires, represent Spain, Brandenburg, Empire and Holland, territories conquered by France. Next go through to the Cours Marly with its pairs of equestrian sculptures by Guillaume Coustou and Antoine Coysevox, and other statues comissioned by Louis XIV for the park of his favourite château at Marly-le-Roi.

Up the stairs to the side, the French Renaissance sculpture galleries are crammed with caryatids, monuments and fireplaces. Here, you'll find treasures such as the Fontaine de Diane from Anet, a whimsical confection of stag and nude huntress sitting on an urn, plus nymphs, sea beasts and swirling waves by Jean Goujon from the Fontaine des Innocents.

***Portrait de l'Abbé de Saint-Non* by Jean Honoré Fragonard**

Next, take the Escalier Lefuel to the first floor decorative arts department. Sidetrack through the OTT apartments of Napoléon III, a feast of 19th-century bad taste, to admire the sheer excess of the dining room with its carved, sculpted and gilded ceiling, and the *grande salle* where the padded circular sofa evokes palmy days of official functions.

Head to the medieval gallery (rooms 1-4) for Byzantine icons and ivories, the medieval treasure of St-Denis (golden eagle wings around an antique porphyry vase) and lively Limoges enamel reliquaries and caskets, before taking the escalators up to the 2nd floor, whichis home to the departments of French and northern European painting.

Here, your first stop should be the Galerie Médicis (room 18), one of the places where the history of France and the museum coincide in 24 virtuoso canvases by Rubens depicting episodes in the life of Marie de Médici – including Henri IV receiving her portrait, her arrival by boat in Marseille accompanied by thrashing sea monsters, her accession as regent and the marriage of Louis XIII.

There's more Rubens just around the corner (room 21) with his two sensitive portraits of his second wife Hélène Fourment. Continue through Flemish landscapes and Dutch paintings, with Rembrandt in all his registers, from the tenderness of *Bathsheba at her Bath* to the raw meat and thick brushstrokes of *The Flayed Ox* (room 31), Vermeer's *Lacemaker* and Franz Post's Brazilian landscapes (room 38).

ITINERARIES

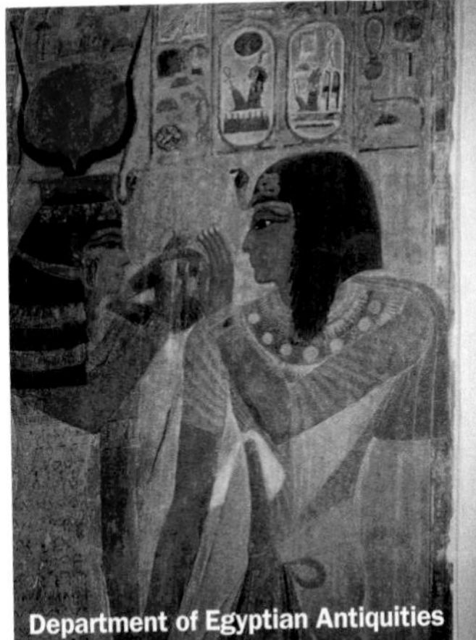
Department of Egyptian Antiquities

Back out on the landing, follow signs for French painting, said to start (room 1) with the 14th-century *Portrait of Jean II the Good*, deemed to be France's earliest independent portrait. There's a much more Gothic verve to Enguerrand Quarton's extraordinary *Pietà*, all angular angst and emotion against a golden background, painted during the Avignon papacy, while Jean Clouet's *François 1er* is a stripey-sleeved incarnation of the dashing Renaissance monarch, a precursor to the wispy figures of the Ecole de Fontainebleau and Antoine Caron's paintings of court festivities.

Against the colour and bravura of 17th-century official Baroque painting for church and state, there is a more ascetic edge in Lubin Baugin's pared back *Still Life with Wafers* (room 27), while Georges de la Tour's paintings (room 28) still inspire awe with their incredible stillness and calm, simplification of forms, moulding by candlelight and shadow in *Mary Magdelene* or the more worldy moral theme of *The Card Cheat*.

Cross the Salle Alexandre (room 32), a vision of grandiose official history painting in Charles Le Brun's massive battle scenes full of thrashing horses and muscled bodies. This is followed by the 18th-century lightness and frivolity of Watteau's *Gilles*, the dreamy portraits and still lifes of Chardon, and paintings by Fragonard, at his best not in sugary moral subjects but in his wonderfully free 'fantasy portraits' (room 48).

You've already done Neo-Classicism and Romanticism at its best so exit by the spiral staircase down to Ancient Egypt on the ground floor, always swarming with children. If space allows, pop into the Mastaba of Akhethetep (room 4), a circa 2400 BC funerary chapel of a royal dignitary from Saqqara with an interior chamber covered in painted reliefs.

End your walk where it all began – the underground remains of the sturdy defensive walls, moats and conical towers of the medieval Louvre – before the glass pyramid brings you back to earth.

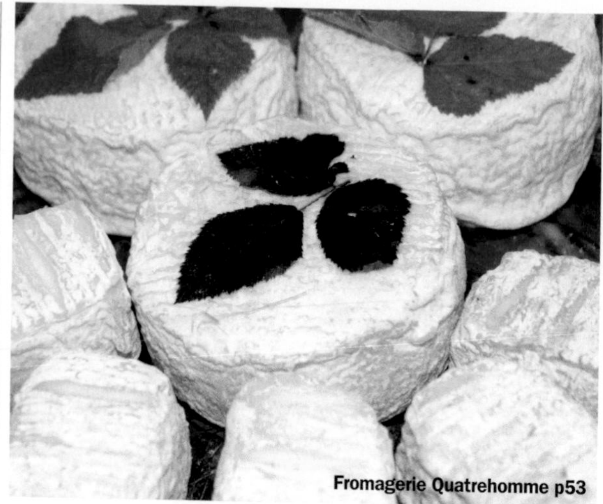
Fromagerie Quatrehomme p53

Left Bank Picnic

St-Germain-des-Prés may be rather more Louis Vuitton than Boris Vian these days, but there are still enough small galleries and bookshops in the neighbourhood to ensure that it retains a whiff of its bohemian past. Aside from art and books, the 6th arrondissement (and its neighbour the 7th) is also a great place to shop for food, since it boasts some of the finest artisanal bakeries and traiteurs in Paris.

And thanks to **Vélib** (www. velib.paris.fr), it's easier than ever to get around the *quartier* in order to stock up. What's more, the standard-issue bike is equipped with a fairly capacious basket that should accommodate everything you'll need for a sumptuous picnic – which we recommend taking in the elegant surroundings of the Jardin du Luxembourg.

Since you'll be deliberating over your purchases each time you stop, this itinerary will probably take you the best part of two hours. And remember, after the first half hour on Vélib, which is free, there's a sliding scale of charges. Don't bother searching for a station each time you need to stop; just use the chain provided to lock your bike.

START: Station Vélib, 1 rue Jacques Callot, 6th (M° Mabillon).

Detach your bike from the *borne* and cycle down rue Mazarine as far as the carrefour de Buci. Turn left into rue de Buci and carry on until the junction with rue de Seine. The stretch of rue de Seine between here and boulevard St-Germain is lined with butchers and greengrocers. Ignore the smell of roasting chickens (you'll be getting cooked meat elsewhere), and just buy salad leaves and fruit. Then head back

Bread & Roses p53

down rue de Seine (it's one way, like many of the narrow streets round here) towards the river. About halfway down, turn left into rue Jacob, a typically well-heeled slice of Left Bank real estate – all furniture shops, galleries, boutiques and elegantly turned-out *femmes d'un certain age*.

Cross rue Bonaparte and take the next left into rue St-Benoît. Pause for a moment to look in the window of the **Librairie Saint Benoît des Prés** (2 rue St-Benoît, 6th, 01.46.33.16.16), which specialises in rare books, original manuscripts, letters and autographs. On our most recent visit, letters written by

Poilâne

George Sand and Charles de Gaulle were on prominent display.

Continue down rue Saint-Benoît as far as place St-Germain-des-Prés, where you'll find three venerable St-Germain institutions: **Café de Flore** (p135), **Les Deux Magots** (p135) and **La Hune** bookshop (p139). The Flore and the Deux Magots throng more with tourists than writers these days, though the former is still a favoured haunt of ageing enfant terrible Bernard-Henri Lévy. If you spot a man with a mane of black hair and a white shirt open to the navel poring over a notebook, it's probably 'BHL'. Next door, La Hune, which opened in 1949, is a kind of holy shrine for that nearly extinct species, the Left Bank Intellectual.

But it's not books we're after, it's bread; so pick your way across boulevard St-Germain and follow rue Gozlin round into the rue de Rennes. This is a broad, thunderously busy main road lined with chain stores. There's not a great deal to distract as you bowl south for half a kilometre or so, until you reach rue du Vieux Colombier on the right. You'll have to do battle with buses and taxis in this narrow cut-through which leads to the altogether more charming rue du Cherche-Midi. On the left-hand side of the street, wedged in among the usual expensive boutiques, jewellers and galleries, stands **Poilâne** (p140), the renowned family bakers. You can expect to have to queue here for the famous Poilâne loaf – but it's worth waiting for: dark, firm and distinctively flavoured. The tarts and the biscuits are wonderful too.

Having loaded the bread into your basket, carry on down rue du Cherche-Midi. Go straight across boulevard Raspail. Take the first right into rue Dupin (there's a coffee merchant's on one corner, a fishmonger on the other). Running down one side of this quiet street is a fine, if forbidding, example of 1930s art deco municipal housing.

You'll eventually reach rue de Sèvres. Lock your bike up against the railings here and cross the road on foot to La Grande Epicérie, the food hall in Paris's oldest department store, **Le Bon Marché** (p138). This is a gastronome's paradise, a super-abundant temple to food. Make your way to the traiteurs in the centre of the hall and choose from a staggering array of cooked meats – succulent hams and pungent garlic sausages in dizzying profusion. While you're here, you can also pick up dressing for the salad and a bottle of wine (and a corkscrew if you need one).

It just remains to buy some cheese, and for this you'll need to get back on your bike and cycle a little further south down rue de Sèvres, deeper into a residential corner of the 7th arrondissement. You'll pass on the right the wonderful art deco entrance to the Vaneau metro station, with its green iron lattices and globe lanterns. A little further along on the same side of the street, on the corner of rue Pierre Leroux, stands **Fromagerie Quatrehomme** (p128). Run by the eponymous Marie, this place is famous across Paris for its comté fruité, beaufort and oozy st-marcellin – all dispensed with winning bonhomie.

Your basket will now be near to overflowing and the smell of the cheese will be making you hungry. It's time to head back into the 6th arrondissement and make for a picnic spot in the Jardin du Luxembourg. Turn round and cycle north back up rue de Sèvres, as far as rue St-Placide on the right, just before you reach Le Bon Marché. Shortly after you pass the St-Placide métro station, turn left into rue de Fleurus. You'll pass the men's and women's branches of the unbearably cool clothing store **APC** (p137), which stand opposite each other. And if you think you need more biscuits or another tart, pop into **Bread & Roses** (p135).

The **Jardin du Luxembourg** (p132) is ahead of you, on the far side of rue Guynemer. There's a Vélib station at 26 rue Guynemer, next to the park entrance. As is usual in Paris, the grass here is not for sitting on, let alone picnicking on. Instead, find a bench in the shade and indulge.

Paris by Area

Grand Palais

Champs-Elysées & Western Paris

The eighth arrondissement is all wealth and grandeur, and those qualities spill over into much of the 16th and the nearer parts of the 17th. Through the heart of this district runs the Champs-Elysées, the city's most iconic thoroughfare.

For all its historic associations, the 'Elysian Fields' underperformed for years, offering little other than fast-food joints and drab shops. But the area is now jumping again with new hotels and restaurants, luxury and concept stores, and renovations of old landmarks.

The western end of the Champs-Elysées is dominated by the **Arc de Triomphe** towering above place Charles-de-Gaulle, also known as L'Etoile. Built by Napoleon, the arch was modified to celebrate the Revolutionary armies. From the top, visitors can gaze over the square (commissioned later by Haussmann), with 12 avenues radiating out in all directions.

South of the arch, avenue Kléber leads to the monumental buildings of the panoramic Trocadéro.

Sights & museums

Arc de Triomphe

Pl Charles-de-Gaulle, 8th (01.55.37.73.77). M° Charles de Gaulle Etoile. **Open** *Oct-Mar* 10am-10.30pm daily. *Apr-Sept* 10am-11pm daily. **Admission** €9; free-€5 reductions. **Map** p58 B2 ❶
See box p62.

Bateaux-Mouches

Pont de l'Alma, 8th (01.42.25.96.10/ www.bateaux-mouches.fr). M° Alma-Marceau. **Tickets** €10; free-€5 reductions. **Map** p58 C4 ❷

If you're after a whirlwind tour of the sights and don't mind tourists and schoolchildren, this, the oldest cruise operation on the Seine, is a good option.

Cinéaqua

2 av des Nations Unies, 16th (01.40.69.23.23/www.cineaqua.com). M° Trocadéro. **Open** 10am-8pm daily. **Admission** €19.50; free-€15 reductions. **Map** p58 B5 ❸

Opened in 2006, this aquarium and three-screen cinema is a wonderful attraction and a key element in the renaissance of the once moribund Trocadéro. Many have baulked at the admission price, though.

Cité de l'Architecture et du Patrimoine

Palais de Chaillot, 1 pl du Trocadéro, 16th (01.58.51.52.00/www.citechaillot.fr). M° Trocadéro. **Open** 11am-7pm Mon, Wed, Fri-Sun; 11am-9pm Thur. **Admission** €8; free-€5 reductions. **Map** p58 A4 ❹

Opened in 2007 in the east wing of the Palais de Chaillot, this architecture and heritage museum impresses by its scale. The expansive ground floor is filled with life-size mock-ups of cathedral façades and heritage buildings, and interactive screens place the models in context. Upstairs, darkened rooms house full-scale copies of medieval and Renaissance murals and stained-glass windows. The highlight of the modern architecture section is the walk-in replica of an apartment from Le Corbusier's Cité Radieuse in Marseille. Temporary exhibitions are housed in the large basement area.

Event highlights Positions: portraits d'une nouvelle génération d'architectes chinois (until 31 Dec 2009)

Galerie-Musée Baccarat

11 pl des Etats-Unis, 16th (01.40.22.11.00/www.baccarat.fr). M° Boissière or Iéna. **Open** 10am-6pm Mon, Wed-Sat. **Admission** €7; free-€3.50 reductions. **Map** p58 B3 ❺

Philippe Starck has created a neo-rococo wonderland in the former mansion of the Vicomtesse de Noailles. See items by Georges Chevalier and Ettore Sottsass, services made for princes and maharajahs, and show-off items made for the great exhibitions of the 1800s.

Galeries Nationales du Grand Palais

3 av du Général-Eisenhower, 8th (01.44.13.17.17/reservations 08.92.68.46.94/www.grandpalais.fr). M° Champs-Elysées Clemenceau. **Open** 10am-8pm Mon, Thur-Sun; 10am-10pm Wed; pre-booking compulsory before 1pm. **Admission** *Before 1pm with reservation* €11.10. *After 1pm without reservation* €10; free-€8 reductions. **Map** p59 E4 ❻

Built for the 1900 Exposition Universelle, the Grand Palais was the work of three different architects. During World War II it accommodated Nazi tanks. In 1994 the glass-roofed central hall was closed when bits of metal started falling off. After major restoration, the Palais reopened in 2005 and now hosts major exhibitions.

Musée d'Art Moderne de la Ville de Paris

11 av du Président-Wilson, 16th (01.53.67.40.00/www.mam.paris.fr). M° Alma Marceau or Iéna. **Open** 10am-6pm Tue-Sun. **Admission** *Temporary exhibitions* €4.50-€9; free-€4.50 reductions. No credit cards. **Map** p58 B4 ❼

This monumental 1930s building houses the city's modern art collection. The museum is strong on the Cubists, Fauves, the Delaunays, Rouault, Soutine, Modigliani and van Dongen.

Musée National des Arts Asiatiques – Guimet

6 pl d'Iéna, 16th (01.56.52.53.00/www.museeguimet.fr). M° Iéna. **Open** 10am-5.45pm Mon, Wed-Sun (last entry 5.15pm). **Admission** €6; free-€4 reductions. **Map** p58 B4 ❽

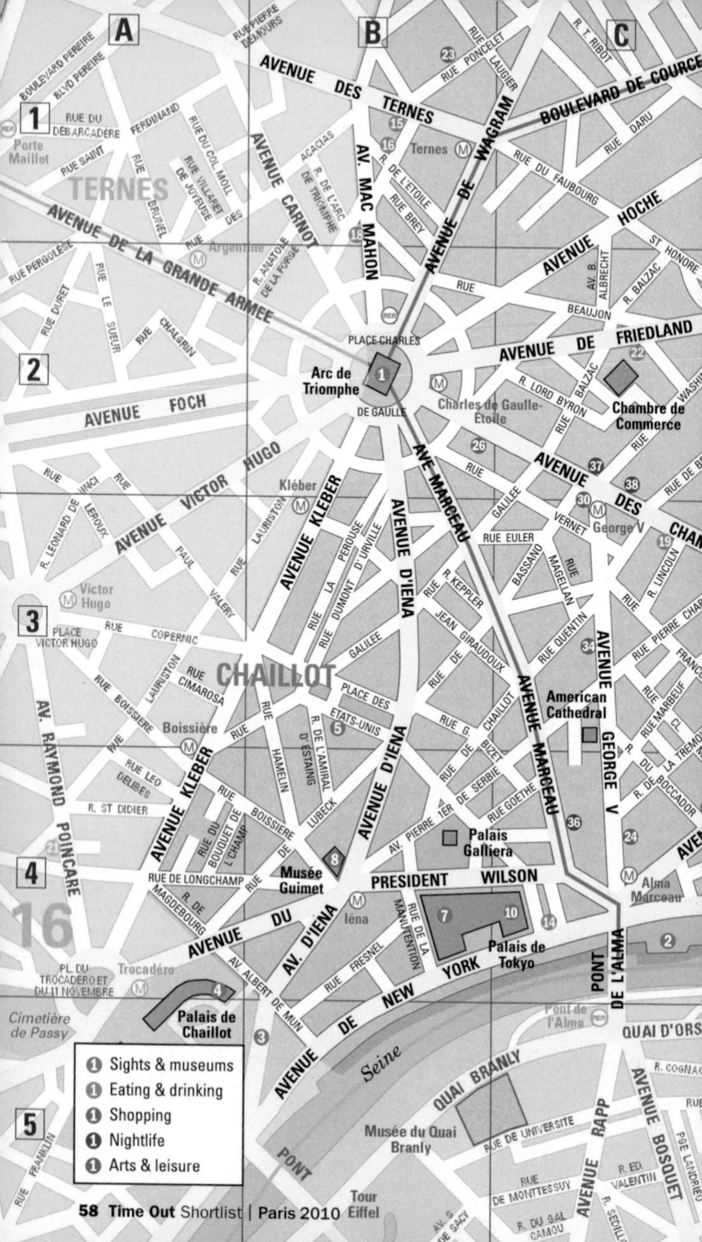
A
B
C
1
2
3
4
5
TERNES
CHAILLOT
16
Porte Maillot
Ternes
Argentine
Kléber
Victor Hugo
Boissière
Charles de Gaulle-Etoile
George V
Iéna
Trocadéro
Alma Marceau
Pont de l'Alma
Arc de Triomphe
Chambre de Commerce
American Cathedral
Palais Galliera
Musée Guimet
Palais de Tokyo
Palais de Chaillot
Musée du Quai Branly
Tour Eiffel
Cimetière de Passy
Seine
PLACE CHARLES DE GAULLE
PLACE VICTOR HUGO
PL. DU TROCADERO ET DU 11 NOVEMBRE
PLACE DES ETATS-UNIS
AVENUE DES TERNES
BOULEVARD DE COURCELLES
AVENUE DE WAGRAM
AVENUE HOCHE
AVENUE DE FRIEDLAND
AVENUE DE LA GRANDE ARMEE
AVENUE FOCH
AVENUE VICTOR HUGO
AVENUE KLEBER
AVENUE D'IENA
AVE MARCEAU
AVENUE MARCEAU
AVENUE GEORGE V
AVENUE DES CHAMPS
AVENUE CARNOT
AV. MAC MAHON
AV. RAYMOND POINCARE
AVENUE DU PRESIDENT WILSON
AVENUE DE NEW YORK
PONT DE L'ALMA
QUAI BRANLY
QUAI D'ORSAY
AVENUE RAPP
AVENUE BOSQUET
RUE DE L'UNIVERSITE
RUE DE MONTTESSUY
RUE DE LONGCHAMP
RUE DU FAUBOURG ST HONORE
RUE BEAUJON
RUE LORD BYRON
RUE BALZAC
RUE COPERNIC
RUE CIMAROSA
RUE BOISSIERE
RUE GALILEE
RUE LA PEROUSE
RUE DUMONT D'URVILLE
RUE DE CHAILLOT
RUE GOETHE
RUE EULER
RUE BASSANO
RUE VERNET
RUE LINCOLN
RUE PIERRE CHARRON
RUE MARBEUF
RUE DU BOCCADOR
RUE DE LA TREMOILLE
RUE QUENTIN BAUCHART
RUE HAMELIN
RUE LAURISTON
RUE DE LUBECK
RUE FRESNEL
RUE DE LA MANUTENTION
AV. ALBERT DE MUN
AV. PIERRE 1ER DE SERBIE
R. ST DIDIER
RUE LEO DELIBES
RUE DURET
RUE LE SUEUR
RUE CHALGRIN
RUE PERGOLESE
RUE DU DEBARCADERE
RUE SAINT FERDINAND
RUE PONCELET
RUE LAUGIER
R. T. RIBOT
RUE DARU
RUE BREY
R. DE L'ETOILE
R. DE L'ARC DE TRIOMPHE
BOULEVARD PEREIRE
BLVD PEREIRE
RUE PIERRE DEMOURS
RUE FRANKLIN
PONT
Sights & museums
Eating & drinking
Shopping
Nightlife
Arts & leisure

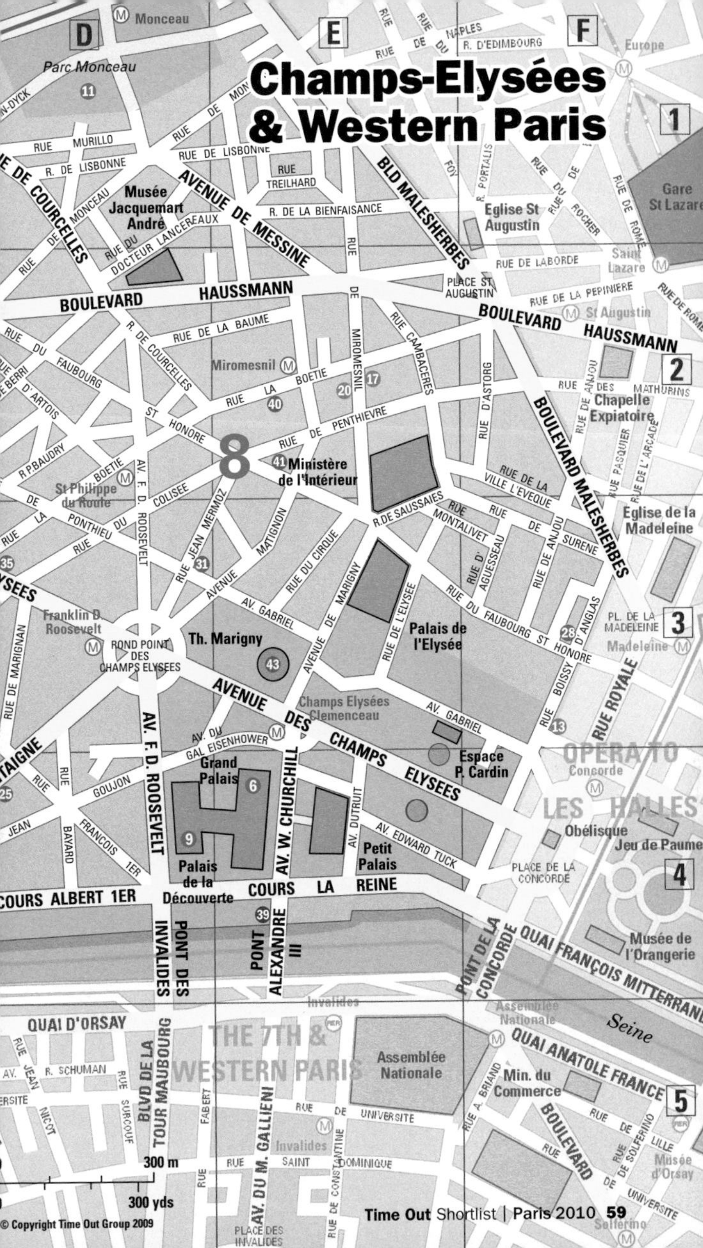

Champs-Elysées
& Western Paris
D
E
F
1
2
3
4
5
Monceau
Parc Monceau
Europe
Gare St Lazare
Musée Jacquemart André
Eglise St Augustin
Saint Lazare
St Augustin
Miromesnil
Chapelle Expiatoire
Ministère de l'Intérieur
St Philippe du Roule
Eglise de la Madeleine
Franklin D. Roosevelt
Th. Marigny
Palais de l'Elysée
Madeleine
Champs Elysées Clemenceau
Espace P. Cardin
Grand Palais
Petit Palais
Palais de la Découverte
OPERA TO LES HALLES
Concorde
Obélisque
Jeu de Paume
Musée de l'Orangerie
Seine
Invalides
THE 7TH & WESTERN PARIS
Assemblée Nationale
Min. du Commerce
Musée d'Orsay
Solférino
8
RUE DE NAPLES
R. D'EDIMBOURG
RUE MURILLO
R. DE LISBONNE
RUE DE LISBONNE
RUE DE COURCELLES
AVENUE DE MESSINE
RUE TREILHARD
R. DE LA BIENFAISANCE
BLD MALESHERBES
RUE DU DOCTEUR LANCEREAUX
RUE DE LABORDE
PLACE ST AUGUSTIN
RUE DE LA PEPINIERE
RUE DE ROME
RUE DU ROCHER
BOULEVARD HAUSSMANN
RUE DE LA BAUME
R. DE COURCELLES
RUE DU FAUBOURG ST HONORE
RUE LA BOETIE
RUE DE MIROMESNIL
RUE CAMBACERES
RUE D'ASTORG
RUE DES MATHURINS
RUE D'ANJOU
RUE PASQUIER
RUE DE L'ARCADE
RUE DE PENTHIEVRE
RUE DE LA VILLE L'EVEQUE
R. DE SAUSSAIES
RUE MONTALIVET
RUE DE SURENE
RUE D'AGUESSEAU
RUE DE L'ELYSEE
RUE BOISSY D'ANGLAS
RUE ROYALE
PL. DE LA MADELEINE
R. P. BAUDRY
RUE DE PONTHIEU
RUE DU COLISEE
AV. F. D. ROOSEVELT
RUE JEAN MERMOZ
AVENUE MATIGNON
RUE DU CIRQUE
AVENUE DE MARIGNY
AV. GABRIEL
ROND POINT DES CHAMPS ELYSEES
RUE DE MARIGNAN
AVENUE DES CHAMPS ELYSEES
AV. DU GAL EISENHOWER
RUE JEAN GOUJON
RUE BAYARD
RUE FRANCOIS 1ER
AV. W. CHURCHILL
AV. DUTRUIT
AV. EDWARD TUCK
PLACE DE LA CONCORDE
COURS ALBERT 1ER
COURS LA REINE
PONT DES INVALIDES
PONT ALEXANDRE III
PONT DE LA CONCORDE
QUAI FRANÇOIS MITTERRAND
QUAI D'ORSAY
QUAI ANATOLE FRANCE
RUE JEAN NICOT
AV. R. SCHUMAN
RUE SURCOUF
BLVD DE LA TOUR MAUBOURG
RUE FABERT
AV. DU M. GALLIENI
RUE DE L'UNIVERSITE
RUE DE CONSTANTINE
RUE SAINT DOMINIQUE
PLACE DES INVALIDES
RUE A. BRIAND
BOULEVARD
RUE DE SOLFERINO
RUE DE LILLE
300 m
300 yds

LIDO
CHAMPS-ELYSEES
PARIS
PHOTOS S. MATHÉ, P. VICTOR / ARTCOMART

Founded by industrialist Emile Guimet in 1889 to house his collection of Chinese and Japanese religious art, and later incorporating oriental collections from the Louvre, the museum has 45,000 objects from Neolithic times onwards, in a voyage across Asian religions and civilisations. Lower galleries focus on India and South-east Asia, centred on Hindu and Buddhist Khmer sculpture from Cambodia. Don't miss the Giant's Way, part of the entrance to a temple complex at Angkor Wat. Upstairs, Chinese antiquities include mysterious jade discs. Afghan glassware, Tibetan mandalas and Moghul jewellery also feature.
Event highlights Au pays du Dragon: arts sacrés du Bhoutan (6 Oct 2009-25 Jan 2010)

Palais de la Découverte

Av Franklin-D.-Roosevelt, 8th (01.56.43.20.21/www.palais-decouverte.fr). M° Champs-Elysées Clemenceau or Franklin D. Roosevelt. **Open** 9.30am-6pm Tue-Sat; 10am-7pm Sun (last entry 30mins before closing). **Admission** €7; free-€4.50 reductions. *Planetarium* €3.50. **Map** p59 D4 ⑨
This science museum houses designs dating from Leonardo da Vinci's time to the present day. Models, real apparatus and audio-visual material bring the displays to life, and exhibits cover astrophysics, astronomy, biology, chemistry, physics and earth sciences. The pertinent Planète Terre section highlights the latest developments in meteorology, and one room is dedicated to the sun. There are also shows at the Planetarium, and 'live' experiments take place at weekends and during school holidays.

Palais de Tokyo: Site de Création Contemporaine

13 av du Président-Wilson, 16th (01.47.23.54.01/www.palaisdetokyo.com). M° Alma Marceau or Iéna. **Open** noon-midnight Tue-Sun. **Admission** €6; free-€4.50 reductions. **Map** p58 C4 ⑩
When it opened in 2002, many thought the Palais' stripped-back interior was a design statement. In fact, it was a practical answer to tight finances. The 1937 building has now come into its own as an open-plan space with a skylit central hall, hosting exhibitions, shows and performances. Extended hours and a funky café have succeeded in drawing a younger audience, and the roll-call of artists is impressive (Pierre Joseph, Wang Du and others). The name dates to the 1937 Exposition Internationale, but is also a reminder of links with a new generation of artists from the Far East.

Parc Monceau

Bd de Courcelles, av Hoche, rue Monceau, 8th. M° Monceau. **Open** *Nov-Mar* 7am-8pm daily. *Apr-Oct* 7am-10pm daily. **Map** p59 D1 ⑪
Surrounded by grand *hôtels particuliers* and elegant Haussmannian apartments, Monceau is a favourite with well-dressed children and their nannies. It was laid out in the 18th century for the Duc de Chartres in the English style, with a lake, lawns and follies: an Egyptian pyramid, a Corinthian colonnade, Venetian bridge and sarcophagi.

Eating & drinking

Alain Ducasse au Plaza Athénée

Hôtel Plaza Athénée, 25 av Montaigne, 8th (01.53.67.65.00/www.alain-ducasse.com). M° Alma Marceau. **Open** 7.45-10.15pm Mon-Wed; 12.45-2.15pm, 7.45-10.15pm Thur, Fri. Closed mid July-mid Aug & 2wks Dec. **€€€€**. **Haute cuisine**. **Map** p58 C4 ⑫
The sheer glamour factor would be enough to recommend this restaurant, Alain Ducasse's most lofty Paris undertaking. The dining room ceiling drips with 10,000 crystals. An *amuse-bouche* of a single langoustine in a lemon cream with a touch of Iranian caviar starts the meal off beautifully, but other dishes can be inconsistent: a

Arch revival

The 50m (164ft) high **Arc de Triomphe** (p56), which dominates the western end of the Champs-Elysées, has long been one of the capital's quintessential landmarks, drawing in more than 1.5 million visitors a year in the process. It has been the focal point of many a high ceremony: Napoleon's remains were carried under it on their way to Les Invalides in 1840; French troops had their victory march through it at the end of World War I; France's Unknown Soldier was buried beneath it in 1921; Marshal Foch and Victor Hugo lay in state underneath it; and the annual Bastille Day military procession starts from here.

But until recently, the interior was far less impressive, having changed little since the 1930s. As Jean-Paul Ciret, director of cultural development for France's national monuments, put it: 'The way we were showing the Arc to visitors was not worthy of an important landmark. There was no light inside, and the ceiling was dirty.'

So in 2008, after a revamp by architect Christophe Girault and artist Maurice Benayouna, a new museum opened with interactive screens and multimedia displays allowing visitors to look at other famous arches throughout Europe and the world, as well as screens exploring the Arc's tumultuous 200-year history.

The story of the monument began in 1810, when the Arc was barely more than a set of foundations. But Napoleon wanted to impress his new (second) wife, Marie-Louise of Austria, when he brought her to Paris for the first time. Displaying a characteristic ability to think around a problem, he ordered an army of theatrical technicians to knock up a mock-up from timber and canvas, and just three weeks later the facsimile was ready to be admired by the happy couple.

Neither Marie-Louise nor Napoleon ever got to see the real thing: the stone version of the great monument was only finished in 1836.

part-raw/part-cooked salad of autumn fruit and veg in a sweet-and-sour dressing, or Breton lobster in an overwhelming sauce of apple, quince and spiced wine. Cheese is delicious, as is the *rum baba comme à Monte-Carlo*.

Les Ambassadeurs

Hôtel de Crillon, 10 pl de la Concorde, 8th (01.44.71.16.17/www.crillon.com). M° Concorde. **Open** 7-10.30am, 12.30-1.45pm, 7.30-9.45pm Tue-Sat; noon-3pm Sun. Closed 1st wk Jan & Aug. **€€€€**. **Haute cuisine**. **Map** p59 F3 ⓭

Since the arrival of chef Jean-François Piège, the experience of eating at Les Ambassadeurs has become sublime. In a main of Rossini-style bluefin tuna, a tube of foie gras is embedded in the tuna's raw centre, and crunchy-soft veal sweetbreads come with fresh morel mushrooms and tiny roast potatoes. A succession of bright ideas makes the meal memorable: bite-sized ice-creams arrive straight after the mains, followed by citrus-flavoured *madeleines* and pineapple macaroons.

Antoine

NEW *10 av de New York, 16th (01.40.70.19.28/www.antoine-paris.fr). M° Alma-Marceau or Trocadéro.* **Open** noon-2.45pm, 7.30-10.45pm daily. **€€€**. **Seafood**. **Map** p58 C4 ⓮

On the banks of the Seine, with tall bay windows overlooking the Eiffel Tower (albeit through trees), Antoine is Paris's newest shrine to the sea. Chic, moneyed crowds gather day and night to sample chef Mickaël Feval's perfect oysters and extravagant dishes like whole roasted lobster served with winter vegetables *en cocotte*, plump St-Jacques scallops with creamy purée, and wonderful vanilla millefeuille. The fixed-price lunch menu is excellent value.

Le Dada

12 av des Ternes, 17th (01.43.80.60.12). M° Ternes. **Open** 6am-2am Mon-Sat; 6am-10pm Sun. **Café**. **Map** p58 B1 ⓯

Perhaps the hippest café in this stuffy part of town, Le Dada is best known for its well-placed, sunny terrace. Inside, the wood-block carved tables and red walls provide a warm atmosphere for a crowd that tends towards the well-heeled, well-spoken and, well, loaded. That said, the atmosphere is friendly; if terracing is your thing, you could happily spend a summer's day here.

Flute l'Etoile

NEW *19 rue de l'Etoile, 17th (01.45.72.10.14/www.flutebar.com). M° Ternes.* **Open** 5pm-2am Tue-Sat; 6am-10pm Sun. **Champagne bar**. **Map** p58 B1 ⓰

With a menu of some 23 different champagnes and designer decor (slick wooden panelling, blue walls and red velvet), Paris's first champagne lounge certainly looks the part. Indeed the only indication that it's not French (it's American) is the sneaky appearance of a Californian sparkler on the list. For drinkers wishing to sample different vintages without buying a whole glass (from €9), the small tasting glasses (from €5) are a nice touch. And for anyone 'bored' by plain bubbly, cocktails such as champagne sangria and Rossini-Tini (champagne, raspberry juice, liqueur and Grey Goose vodka) make for a sophisticated alternative.

Granterroirs

30 rue de Miromesnil, 8th (01.47.42.18.18/www.granterroirs.com). M° Miromesnil. **Open** 9am-8pm Mon-Fri. *Food served* noon-3pm Mon-Fri. Closed 3wks Aug. **€€**. **Bistro**. **Map** p59 E2 ⓱

This *épicerie* with a difference is the perfect remedy for anyone for whom the word '*terroir*' conjures up visions of grease-soaked peasant food. Here, the walls heave with more than 600 enticing specialities from southern France, including Périgord foie gras, charcuterie from Aubrac and a fine selection of wines. Great gifts – but why not sample some of the goodies by

Ladurée

enjoying the midday *table d'hôte* feast? Come in early to ensure that you can choose from the five succulent *plats du jour* (such as marinated salmon with dill on a bed of warm potatoes).

Le Hide

NEW *10 rue du Général-Lanrezac, 17th (01.45.74.15.81/www.lehide.fr). M° Charles de Gaulle Etoile.* **Open** noon-3pm, 7.30-10.30pm Mon-Fri; 7.30-10.30pm Sat. **€€. Bistro. Map** p58 B1 ⑱

Ever since it opened, this snug bistro has been packed with a happy crowd who appreciate Japanese-born chef Hide Kobayashi's superb cooking and good-value prices. Expect dishes such as duck foie gras terrine with pear-and-thyme compôte to start, followed by tender faux-filet steak in a light foie gras sauce or skate wing with a *beurre noisette*. Desserts are excellent: perfect tarte tatin comes with crème fraîche from Normandy. Good, affordable wines explain the merriment.

Ladurée

75 av des Champs-Elysées, 8th (01.40.75.08.75/www.laduree.fr). M° Franklin D. Roosevelt or George V. **Open** 7.30am-12.30am daily. **€€. Café. Map** p58 C3 ⑲

Decadence permeates this elegant tearoom, from the 19th century-style interior and service to the labyrinthine corridors that lead to the toilets. While you bask in the warm glow of bygone wealth, indulge in tea, pastries (the pistachio pain au chocolat is heavenly) and, above all, the hot chocolate. It's a rich, bitter, velvety tar that will leave you in the requisite stupor for any lazy afternoon. The original branch at 16 rue Royale (8th, 01.42.60.21.79) is famed for its macaroons.

Maxan

37 rue de Miromesnil, 8th (01.42.65.78.60/www.rest-maxan.com). M° Miromesnil. **Open** noon-2.30pm Mon; noon-2.30pm, 7.30-10.30pm Tue-Fri; 7.30-10.30pm Sat. Closed Aug. **€€. Bistro. Map** p59 E2 ⑳

This is a welcome new-wave bistro in an area where eating options tend to be fashion haunts, grand tables or tourist traps. Owner-chef Laurent Zajac uses quality seasonal ingredients, giving them a personal spin in dishes such as scallops with curry spices and artichoke hearts, classic veal sweetbreads with wild asparagus, and an exotic take on *île flottante*. Popular with ministry of interior types at lunch, quieter by night.

La Table de Lauriston

129 rue de Lauriston, 16th (01.47.27.00.07). M° Trocadéro. **Open** noon-2.30pm, 7-10.30pm Mon-Fri; 7-10.30pm Sat. Closed 3wks Aug & 1wk Dec. **€€€. Bistro. Map** p58 A4 ㉑

Serge Barbey's dining room has a refreshingly feminine touch. The emphasis here is firmly on ingredients, expertly prepared to show off their freshness. In spring, stalks of asparagus from the Landes are trimmed to avoid any stringiness and served with the simplest *vinaigrette d'herbes*. More extravagant is *foie gras cuit au torchon*, in which the duck liver is wrapped in a cloth and poached in a bouillon. Skip the crème brûlée, which you could have anywhere, and order a dessert with attitude: the giant *baba au rhum*.

Taillevent

15 rue Lamennais, 8th (01.44.95.15.01/www.taillevent.com). M° George V. **Open** 12.15-1.30pm, 7.15-9.30pm Mon-Fri. Closed Aug. **€€€€. Haute cuisine. Map** p58 C2 ㉒

Prices here are not as shocking as in some restaurants at this level; there's a €70 lunch menu. *Rémoulade de coquilles St-Jacques* is a technical feat, with slices of raw, marinated scallop wrapped in a tube shape around a diced apple filling, encircled by a *rémoulade* sauce. An earthier and lip-smacking dish is the trademark *épeautre* – an ancient wheat – cooked 'like a risotto' with bone marrow, black truffle, whipped cream and parmesan, and topped with sautéed frog's legs.

Shopping

Alléosse

13 rue Poncelet, 17th (01.46.22.50.45/www.fromage-alleosse.com). M° Ternes. **Open** 9am-1pm, 4-7pm Tue-Thur; 9am-1pm, 4.30-7pm Fri, Sat. **Map** p58 B1 ㉓

People cross town for these cheeses – wonderful farmhouse camemberts, delicate st-marcellins, a choice of *chèvres* and several rarities.

Balenciaga

10 av George V, 8th (01.47.20.21.11/www.balenciaga.com). M° Alma Marceau or George V. **Open** 10am-7pm Mon-Sat. **Map** p58 C4 ㉔

The Spanish fashion house is ahead of Japanese and Belgian designers in the hip stakes. Floating fabrics contrast with dramatic cuts, producing a sophisticated style that the fashion *haut monde* can't wait to slip into.

Dior

26-30 av Montaigne, 8th (01.40.73.73.73/www.dior.com). M° Franklin D. Roosevelt. **Open** 10am-7pm Mon-Sat. **Map** p59 D4 ㉕

The Dior universe is here on avenue Montaigne, from the main prêt-à-porter store and jewellery, menswear and eyewear to Baby Dior, where rich infants are coochy-cooed by drooling assistants.

Drugstore Publicis

133 av des Champs-Elysées, 8th (01.44.43.79.00/www.publicisdrugstore.com). M° Charles de Gaulle Etoile. **Open** 8am-2am Mon-Fri; 10am-2am Sat, Sun. **Map** p58 B2 ㉖

A 1960s legend, Drugstore Publicis was clad with neon swirls by architect Michele Saee following a renovation in 2004; a glass-and-steel café stretches out on to the pavement. On the ground floor there's a newsagent, pharmacy, bookshop and upmarket deli full of quality olive oils and elegant biscuits. The basement is a macho take on Colette, keeping selected design items and lifestyle mags, and replacing high fashion with wines and a cigar cellar.

Fnac

74 av des Champs-Elysées, 8th (08.25.02.00.20/www.fnac.com). M° George V. **Open** 10am-midnight Mon-Sat; noon-midnight Sun. **Map** p58 C3 ㉗

LE66

Fnac is a supermarket of culture: books, DVDs, CDs, audio kit, computers and photographic equipment. Most branches – notably the enormous Forum des Halles one – stock everything; others specialise. All branches operate as a concert box office. This one stays open latest.

Givenchy

28 rue du Fbg-St-Honoré, 8th (01.42.68.31.00/www.givenchy.com). M° Madeleine or Concorde. **Open** 10am-7pm Mon-Sat. **Map** p59 F3 ㉘

In March 2008, Givenchy opened this new flagship Fbg-St-Honoré store for men's and women's prêt-à-porter and accessories. Designed by Jamie Fobert, who worked on Tate Modern, it incorporates surreal rooms within rooms – cut-out boxes filled with white, black or mahogany panelling – providing a contemporary art gallery setting for Givenchy's cutting-edge, sculptural and monochrome designs.

LE66

66 av des Champs-Elysées, 8th (01.53.53.33.96/www.myspace.com/lesoixantesix). M° George V. **Open** 11am-8pm daily. **Map** p59 D3 ㉙

Exchewing the glass cabinet approach of Colette, this fashion concept store is youthful and accessible, with an ever-changing selection of hip brands including Puma Black Label. Assistants, who are also the buyers and designers, make for a motivated team. The store takes the form of three transparent modules, the first a book and magazine store run by Black Book of the Palais de Tokyo, and the second two devoted to fashion. It even has its own vintage store, in collaboration with Come On Eline and Kiliwatch.

Louis Vuitton

101 av des Champs-Elysées, 8th (08.10.81.00.10/www.vuitton.com). M° George V. **Open** 10am-8pm Mon-Sat; 11am-7pm Sun. **Map** p58 C2 ㉚

The 'Promenade' flagship sets the tone for Vuitton's global image, from the 'bag bar', bookstore and new jewellery department to the women's and men's ready-to-wear. Contemporary art, videos by Tim White Sobieski and a pitch-black elevator by Olafur Eliasson complete the picture. Accessed by lift, the Espace Vuitton hosts temporary art exhibits – but the star of the show is the view over Paris.

Pietra Dura

NEW *6 rue de Ponthieu, 8th (01.45.63.18.18). M° Franklin Roosevelt.* **Open** noon-7pm Tue-Sat. **Map** p59 D3 31

Jewellery designer Carole Midy swapped a career in law for gold, silver and semi-precious stones, which she crafts into one-off pieces prized by fashion-conscious locals and celebrities such as Lenny Kravitz. Designs include chunky amethyst rings with gold threaded pearls, mix 'n' match quartz droplet earrings and neo-filigree amulet bracelets, all displayed like shimmering *bonbons*. Prices start at €800, but cheaper designs are available at the branch at 11 rue de la Tour, 16th.

Prada

10 av Montaigne, 8th (01.53.23.99.40/www.prada.com). M° Alma Marceau. **Open** 11am-7pm Mon; 10am-7pm Tue-Sat. **Map** p58 C4 32

The high priestess of European chic, Miuccia Prada's elegant stores pull in fashion followers of all ages. Handbags of choice are complemented by the coveted ready-to-wear range.

Sephora

70 av des Champs-Elysées, 8th (01.53.93.22.50/www.sephora.fr). M° Franklin D. Roosevelt. **Open** *Sept-June* 10am-midnight daily. *July, Aug* 10am-1.30am. **Map** p58 C3 33

The flagship of the cosmetic supermarket chain houses around 12,000 brands of scent and slap. Sephora Blanc (14 cour St-Emilion, 12th, 01.40.02.97.79) features beauty products in a minimalist interior.

Sony Style

NEW *39 av George V, 8th (www.boutiquegeorge5.fr). M° George V.* **Open** 10.30am-8pm Mon-Sat. **Map** p58 C3 34

Sony's first European concept store has hit Paris, bringing high-tech gadgets and zen decor together in an *hôtel particulier*. Phones, cameras, computers and Playstations are all here, and the latest innovations from Japan are beamed in on big screens to let you know what the future holds. The store also offers a range of personal services including free IT coaching in a swanky training suite and engraving to personalise your Vaio laptop.

Virgin Megastore

52-60 av des Champs-Elysées, 8th (01.49.53.50.00/www.virginmega.fr). M° Franklin D. Roosevelt. **Open** 10am-midnight Mon-Sat; noon-midnight Sun. **Map** p59 D3 35

The luxury of perusing CDs and DVDs till midnight makes this a choice spot, and the listening posts let you sample any CD. Tickets for concerts and sports events are available here too. This main branch has the best book selection.

Nightlife

Le Baron

6 av Marceau, 8th (01.47.20.04.01/www.clublebaron.com). M° Alma Marceau. **Open** times vary. **Admission** free. **Map** p58 C4 36

This small but supremely exclusive hangout for the international jet set used to be an upmarket brothel, and has the decor to prove it. It only holds 150, most of whom are regulars you'll need to befriend in order to get past the door. But if you manage to get in, you'll be rubbing shoulders with celebrities and super-glossy people.

Le Lido

116bis av des Champs-Elysées, 8th (01.40.76.56.10/www.lido.fr). M° Franklin D. Roosevelt or George V. **Lunch** 1pm. **Matinée** 3pm Tue, Sun (once a mth, dates vary). **Dinner** 7pm. **Shows** 9.30pm, 11.30pm daily. **Admission** *Matinée show* (incl champagne) €85. *Lunch & matinée show* (incl champagne) €125. *9.30pm show* (incl champagne) €100; €20 reductions. *11.30pm show* (incl champagne) €90; free under-12s. *Dinner & show* €140-€280; €30 reductions. **Map** p58 C2 37

PARIS BY AREA

This is the largest cabaret of all: high-tech touches optimise visibility, and chef Philippe Lacroix provides fabulous gourmet nosh. On stage, 60 Bluebell Girls slink around, shaking their boobs with panache. For a special treat, opt for the Premier service (€280) with free cloakroom, the best tables in the house and free water and coffee with your meal.

Queen

102 av des Champs-Elysées, 8th (01.53.89.08.90/www.queen.fr). M° George V. **Open** 11pm-5am Mon; midnight-6am Tue-Thur, Sun; midnight-8am Fri, Sat. **Admission** €15 Mon-Thur, Sun; €20 Fri, Sat. **Map** p58 C2 ㊳

Once the city's most fêted gay club and the only venue that could hold a torch to the Rex, with a roster of top local DJs holding court, Queen's star faded in the early noughties but is now starting to shine more brightly again. Last year it introduced more themed nights, and still packs 'em in seven nights a week.

Le Showcase

NEW *Underneath Pont Alexandre III, 8th (01.45.61.25.43/www.showcase.fr). M° Champs-Elysées-Clemenceau.* **Open** 10pm-dawn Fri, Sat; 11am-3pm Sun. Closed Aug. **Admission** free-€15. **Map** p59 E4 ㊴

A little too flash for some, but there's no doubting this brand new vaulted club by the Seine, and its Sous le Pont events – live performance followed by DJs – have been a big success story.

Arts & leisure

Salle Gaveau

45 rue La Boétie, 8th (01.49.53.05.07/www.sallegaveau.com). M° Miromesnil. **Box office** 10am-6pm Mon-Fri. **Admission** €10-€100. **Map** p59 E2 ㊵

Many of the small Paris orchestras have found refuge in the Salle Gaveau, but this delightful venue is underachieving, and the top-quality chamber music that used to be the core repertoire is a rarity – a concert by pianist Ivo Pogorelich was one of the few recent highlights.

Salle Pleyel

252 rue du Fbg-St-Honoré, 8th (01.42.56.13.13/www.sallepleyel.fr). M° Ternes. **Box office** noon-7pm Mon-Sat. *By phone* 11am-7pm Mon-Sat; 11am-5pm Sun. **Admission** €10-€160. **Map** p59 E2 ㊶

Home to the Orchestre de Paris, this restored concert hall looks splendid, but the acoustics are only partially successful. The hall has regained its prestigious status as the only venue dedicated to large-scale symphonic concerts in the capital until the completion of the new concert hall in 2012.

Event highlights Verdi's *Requiem* conducted by Daniel Barenboim (15 Nov 2009)

Théâtre des Champs-Elysées

15 av Montaigne, 8th (01.49.52.50.50/www.theatrechampselysees.fr). M° Alma Marceau. **Box office** 1-7pm Mon-Sat. *By phone* 10am-noon, 2-6pm Mon-Fri. **Admission** €5-€160. **Map** p58 C4 ㊷

This beautiful art nouveau theatre hosted the scandalous premiere of Stravinsky's *Le Sacre du Printemps* in 1913. It remains the favourite venue for visiting foreign orchestras.

Théâtre Marigny

Av de Marigny, 8th (01.53.96.70.30/www.theatremarigny.fr). M° Champs-Elysées Clemenceau or Franklin D. Roosevelt. **Box office** 11am-6.30pm Mon-Sat; 11am-3pm Sun. **Admission** €33-€51. **Map** p59 E3 ㊸

Théâtre Marigny is one of the most expensive nights out for theatregoers in Paris. But then not many other theatres can boast a location off the Champs-Elysées, a deluxe interior conceived by Charles Garnier, high-profile casts and an illustrious pedigree stretching back some 150 years.

Opéra to Les Halles

The swathe of the Right Bank between the Grands Boulevards and the Seine is, and has been for centuries, a commercial powerhouse. The two stock exchanges and the Banque de France are here, and so was the city's wholesale food market – until 1969, when it moved from Les Halles to the suburbs. For many observers, French and foreign, the demise of the market was an injury from which Paris could never recover; and there's no denying that the soulless shopping centre that took its place was no compensation for the loss of local colour and tradition that the market sellers had built up over centuries. But life and money-making march onwards: 40 years later, the area as a whole can match any other part of the city for shopping opportunities, and outdo most of them for art and history.

A short distance west of Les Halles is the **Louvre**, no longer the centre of French power though it still exerts considerable influence: first as a grandiose architectural ensemble, a palace within the city; and, second, as a symbol of the capital's cultural pre-eminence. Across rue de Rivoli from the Louvre stands the elegant **Palais-Royal**. After a stroll in its quiet gardens, it's hard to believe this was the starting point of the French Revolution. Today, its arcades house a mix of antiques dealers, philatelists and fashion showcases.

The city's business district is squeezed between the elegant calm of the Palais-Royal and shopping hub the Grands Boulevards.

Sights & museums

Eglise de la Madeleine

Pl de la Madeleine, 8th (01.44.51.69.00/www.eglise-lamadeleine.com). M° Concorde or Madeleine. **Open** 9am-7pm daily. **Map** p72 A2 ❶

The building of a church on this site began in 1764, and in 1806 Napoleon sent instructions from Poland for Barthélémy Vignon to design a 'Temple of Glory' dedicated to his Grand Army. After the emperor's fall, construction slowed and the building, by now a church again, was finally consecrated in 1845. The exterior is ringed by huge, fluted Corinthian columns, with a double row at the front, and a frieze of the Last Judgement just above the portico. Inside are giant domes, an organ and pseudo-Grecian side altars in a sea of multicoloured marble.

Forum des Halles

1st. M° Les Halles/RER Châtelet Les Halles. **Map** p73 E4 ❷

The labyrinthine mall and transport interchange extends three levels underground and includes the Ciné Cité multiplex cinema and the Forum des Images, as well as clothing chains, a branch of Fnac and the Forum des Créateurs, a section for young designers. Despite an open central courtyard, a sense of gloom prevails. All should change by 2012, with a new landscaping of the whole area.

Jardin des Tuileries

Rue de Rivoli, 1st. M° Concorde or Tuileries. **Open** 7.30am-7pm daily. **Map** p72 B4 ❸

Between the Louvre and place de la Concorde, the gravelled alleyways of these gardens have been a chic promenade ever since they opened to the public in the 16th century; and the popular mood persists with the funfair that sets up along the rue de Rivoli side in summer. André Le Nôtre created the prototypical French garden with terraces and central vista running down the *Grand Axe* through circular and hexagonal ponds. As part of Mitterrand's Grand Louvre project, sculptures such as Coysevox's winged horses were transferred to the Louvre and replaced by copies, and the Maillol sculptures were returned to the Jardins du Carrousel; a handful of modern sculptures have been added, including bronzes by Moore, Ernst, Giacometti, and Dubuffet's *Le Bel Costumé*.

Jeu de Paume

1 pl de la Concorde, 8th (01.47.03.12.50/ www.jeudepaume.org). M° Concorde. **Open** noon-9pm Tue; noon-7pm Wed-Fri; 10am-7pm Sat, Sun (last admission 30mins before closing). **Admission** €6; €3 reductions. **Map** p72 A3 ❹

The Centre National de la Photographie moved into this site in 2005. The building, which once served as a tennis court, has been divided into two white, almost hangar-like galleries. It is not an intimate space, but it works well for showcase retrospectives. A video art and cinema suite in the basement shows new digital installation work, as well as feature-length films made by artists.

Event highlights Federico Fellini (20 Oct 2009-3 Jan 2010)

Musée des Arts Décoratifs

107 rue de Rivoli, 1st (01.44.55.57.50/ www.lesartsdecoratifs.fr). M° Palais Royal Musée du Louvre or Pyramides. **Open** 11am-6pm Tue, Wed, Fri; 10am-6pm Sat, Sun. Closed some hols. **Admission** (with Musée de la Mode & Musée de la Publicité) €8; free-€6.50 reductions. **Map** p72 C4 ❺

Taken as a whole along with the Musée de la Mode et du Textile and Musée de la Publicité, this is one of the world's major collections of design and the decorative arts. The venue reopened in 2006 after a decade-long, €35-million restoration of the building and of 6,000 of the 150,000 items donated mainly by private collectors. The major focus here is French furniture and tableware, from extravagant carpets to delicate crystal and porcelain. Of most obvious attraction to the layman are the reconstructed period rooms, ten in all, showing how the other half lived from the late 1400s to the early 20th century.

Event highlights Dessiner le Design (22 Oct 2009-21 Feb 2010)

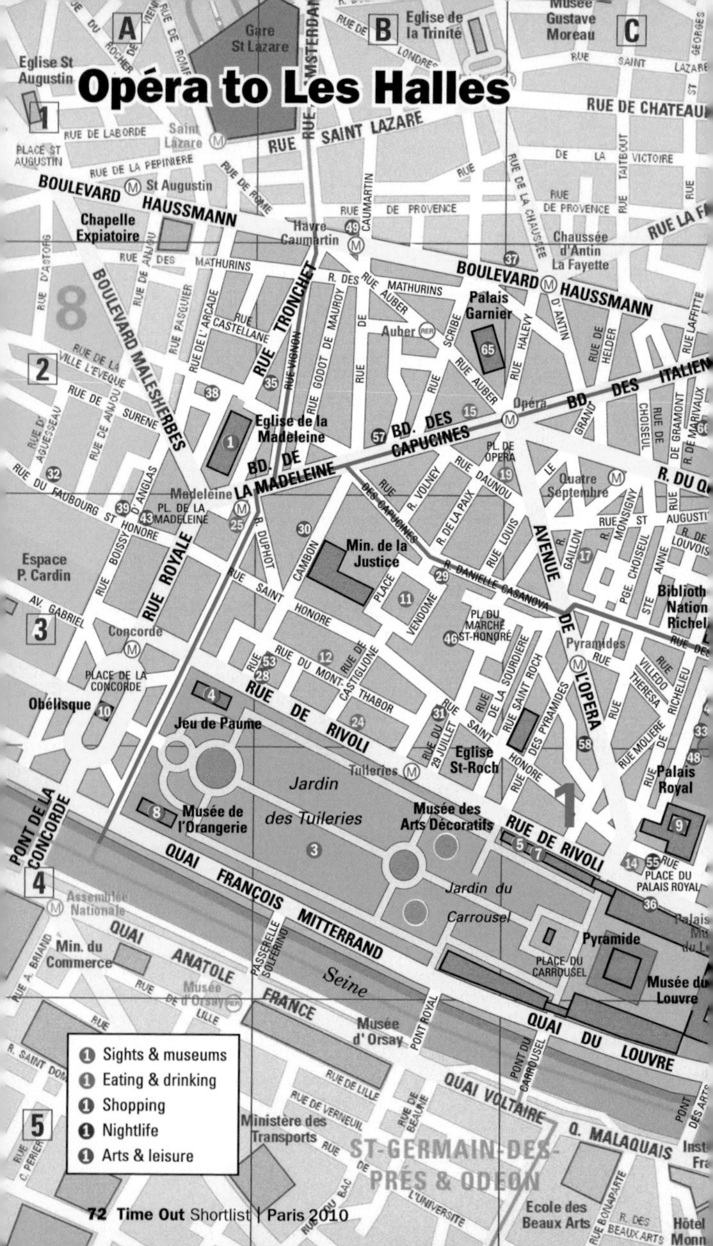
Opéra to Les Halles
A
B
C
1
2
3
4
5
8
Gare St Lazare
Eglise de la Trinité
Musée Gustave Moreau
Eglise St Augustin
Place St Augustin
Rue de Laborde
Saint Lazare
Rue Saint Lazare
Rue de Londres
Rue Saint Lazare
Rue de Chateaudun
Rue de la Victoire
Rue de Provence
Rue de la Pepinière
Boulevard Haussmann
St Augustin
Rue de Rome
Chapelle Expiatoire
Havre Caumartin
Rue Caumartin
Chaussée d'Antin La Fayette
Rue de la Chaussée d'Antin
Rue Taitbout
Rue des Mathurins
Rue d'Anjou
Rue Pasquier
Rue de l'Arcade
Rue Castellane
Rue Tronchet
Rue Vignon
Rue Godot de Mauroy
Rue Auber
Auber
Rue Scribe
Palais Garnier
Rue Halévy
Rue de Helder
Rue Laffitte
Boulevard Malesherbes
Rue de la Ville l'Evêque
Rue de Surène
Rue d'Aguesseau
Eglise de la Madeleine
Bd. de la Madeleine
Bd. des Capucines
Opéra
Bd des Italiens
Rue du Faubourg St Honoré
Rue Boissy d'Anglas
Pl. de la Madeleine
Madeleine
Rue Royale
Rue Duphot
Rue Cambon
Min. de la Justice
Rue des Capucines
R. Volney
R. de la Paix
Rue Daunou
Pl. de Opéra
Rue Louis le Grand
Quatre Septembre
Avenue de l'Opéra
Rue Gaillon
Rue Monsigny
Rue St Augustin
Pge. Choiseul
Rue Choiseul
Rue de Gramont
R. de Marivaux
Rue Ste Anne
R. de Louvois
Biblioth Nation Richel
Espace P. Cardin
Av. Gabriel
Concorde
Place de la Concorde
Obélisque
Rue Saint Honoré
Place Vendôme
R. Danielle Casanova
Pl. du Marché St-Honoré
Pyramides
Rue de la Sourdière
Rue Saint Roch
Rue des Pyramides
Rue Villedo
Rue Thérèsa
Rue Richelieu
Rue du Mont-Thabor
Rue de Castiglione
Rue de Rivoli
Jeu de Paume
Rue du 29 Juillet
Eglise St-Roch
Tuileries
Jardin des Tuileries
Musée de l'Orangerie
Musée des Arts Décoratifs
Rue Molière
Palais Royal
Place du Palais Royal
Jardin du Carrousel
Pont de la Concorde
Quai François Mitterrand
Passerelle Solférino
Pyramide
Place du Carrousel
Musée du Louvre
Assemblée Nationale
Quai Anatole France
Min. du Commerce
Rue A. Briand
Rue de Lille
Musée d'Orsay
Seine
Pont Royal
Quai du Louvre
Pont du Carrousel
Quai Voltaire
Q. Malaquais
Pont des Arts
R. Saint Dominique
Rue de Verneuil
Rue de Beaune
Ministère des Transports
Rue du Bac
Rue de l'Université
St-Germain-des-Prés & Odéon
Ecole des Beaux Arts
Rue Bonaparte
R. des Beaux Arts
Rue C. Perier
Sights & museums
Eating & drinking
Shopping
Nightlife
Arts & leisure

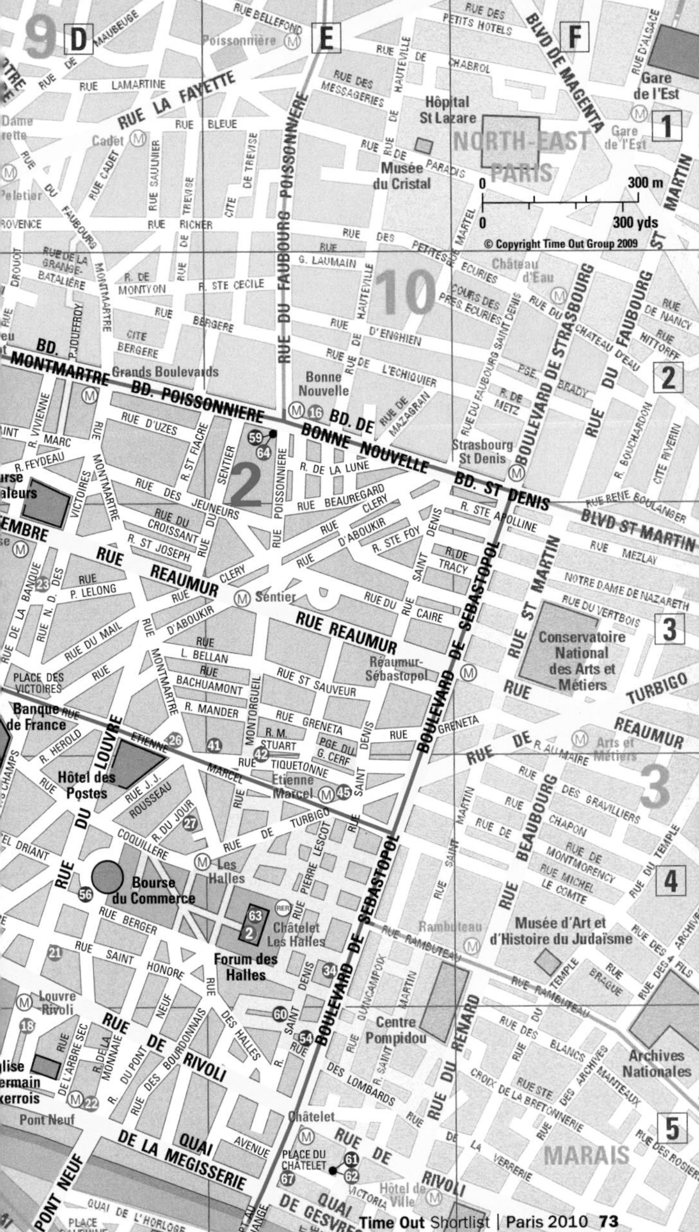
9
D
E
F
1
2
3
4
5
10
2
3
NORTH-EAST PARIS
MARAIS
0
300 m
0
300 yds
© Copyright Time Out Group 2009
RUE BELLEFOND
Poissonnière
RUE DES PETITS HOTELS
BLVD DE MAGENTA
RUE D'ALSACE
Gare de l'Est
RUE DE MAUBEUGE
RUE LAMARTINE
RUE LA FAYETTE
RUE BLEUE
Cadet
RUE CADET
RUE SAULNIER
RUE DE TREVISE
CITE DE TREVISE
RUE RICHER
RUE DU FAUBOURG POISSONNIERE
RUE DES MESSAGERIES
RUE DE HAUTEVILLE
RUE DE CHABROL
Hôpital St Lazare
RUE DE PARADIS
Musée du Cristal
RUE DES PETITES ECURIES
RUE MARTEL
G. LAUMAIN
Château d'Eau
COURS DES PETITES ECURIES
RUE DU CHATEAU D'EAU
BOULEVARD DE STRASBOURG
RUE DU FAUBOURG ST MARTIN
RUE DE NANCY
RUE HITTORFF
RUE DE LA GRANGE-BATALIERE
DROUOT
R. DE MONTYON
R. STE CECILE
RUE BERGERE
CITE BERGERE
P. JOUFFROY
RUE D'ENGHIEN
RUE DE L'ECHIQUIER
RUE DU FAUBOURG SAINT DENIS
PGE. BRADY
R. DE METZ
Grands Boulevards
BD. MONTMARTRE
BD. POISSONNIERE
Bonne Nouvelle
16
BD. DE BONNE NOUVELLE
RUE DE MAZAGRAN
Strasbourg St Denis
BD. ST DENIS
BLVD ST MARTIN
RUE RENE BOULANGER
R. BOUCHARDON
CITE RIVERIN
RUE VIVIENNE
RUE ST MARC
RUE D'UZES
R. FEYDEAU
RUE MONTMARTRE
R. ST FIACRE
RUE DU SENTIER
59
64
RUE POISSONNIERE
R. DE LA LUNE
RUE BEAUREGARD
RUE DES JEUNEURS
RUE DU CROISSANT
R. ST JOSEPH
RUE CLERY
RUE D'ABOUKIR
R. STE APOLLINE
R. STE FOY
R. DE TRACY
RUE SAINT DENIS
RUE MEZLAY
NOTRE DAME DE NAZARETH
RUE DU VERTBOIS
RUE REAUMUR
Sentier
RUE DU CAIRE
BOULEVARD DE SEBASTOPOL
RUE ST MARTIN
Conservatoire National des Arts et Métiers
RUE TURBIGO
RUE DES VICTOIRES
23
RUE N. D. DES VICTOIRES
RUE P. LELONG
RUE DE LA BANQUE
RUE DU MAIL
R. L. BELLAN
RUE BACHUAMONT
R. MANDER
RUE MONTORGUEIL
RUE ST SAUVEUR
Réaumur-Sébastopol
PLACE DES VICTOIRES
Banque de France
R. HEROLD
RUE DU LOUVRE
RUE ETIENNE MARCEL
26
41
42
R. M. STUART
PGE. DU G. CERF
RUE TIQUETONNE
RUE GRENETA
RUE DE REAUMUR
R. AU MAIRE
Arts et Métiers
Etienne Marcel
45
Hôtel des Postes
RUE J. J. ROUSSEAU
R. DU JOUR
27
RUE COQUILLERE
RUE DE TURBIGO
RUE PIERRE LESCOT
RUE DES GRAVILLIERS
RUE CHAPON
RUE DE MONTMORENCY
RUE MICHEL LE COMTE
RUE BEAUBOURG
RUE DU TEMPLE
Les Halles
Bourse du Commerce
56
RUE BERGER
63
2
RER
Châtelet Les Halles
Rambuteau
RUE RAMBUTEAU
Musée d'Art et d'Histoire du Judaïsme
RUE DES ARCHIVES
RUE DES 4 FILS
RUE BRAQUE
21
RUE SAINT HONORE
Forum des Halles
34
RUE QUINCAMPOIX
Louvre-Rivoli
18
RUE DE RIVOLI
RUE DES HALLES
60
54
Centre Pompidou
RUE DU RENARD
RUE DES BLANCS MANTEAUX
Archives Nationales
Eglise St Germain l'Auxerrois
RUE DE L'ARBRE SEC
R. DE LA MONNAIE
R. DU PONT NEUF
RUE DES BOURDONNAIS
DES LOMBARDS
RUE STE CROIX DE LA BRETONNERIE
22
Pont Neuf
Châtelet
RUE DE LA VERRERIE
RUE DES ROSIERS
QUAI DE LA MEGISSERIE
AVENUE VICTORIA
PLACE DU CHATELET
61
62
67
Hôtel de Ville
PONT NEUF
QUAI DE L'HORLOGE
PLACE DAUPHINE
PT AU CHANGE
QUAI DE GESVRES

Musée du Louvre

Musée du Louvre

Rue de Rivoli, 1st (01.40.20.50.50/ www.louvre.fr). M° Palais Royal Musée du Louvre. **Open** 9am-6pm Mon, Thur, Sat, Sun; 9am-10pm Wed, Fri. **Admission** €9; free-€6 reductions. **Map** p72 C5 ❻

Some 35,000 works of art and artefacts are on show, divided into eight departments and housed in three wings: Denon, Sully and Richelieu. Treasures from the Egyptians, Etruscans, Greeks and Romans each have their own galleries in the Denon and Sully wings, as do Middle Eastern and Islamic works of art. The first floor of Richelieu is taken up with European decorative arts from the Middle Ages up to the 19th century.

The main draw, though, is the painting and sculpture. Two glass-roofed sculpture courts contain the Marly horses on the ground floor of Richelieu, with French sculpture below and Italian Renaissance pieces in the Denon wing. The Grand Galerie and Salle de la Joconde (home to the *Mona Lisa*) run the length of Denon's first floor with French Romantic painting alongside. Dutch and French painting occupies the second floor of Richelieu and Sully. Mitterrand's Grand Louvre project expanded the museum two-fold, but the organisation and restoration of the Louvre are still very much a work in progress: check the website or lists in the Carrousel du Louvre to see which galleries are closed on certain days to avoid missing what you really want to see. Laminated panels found throughout provide a lively commentary, and the superb website is a technological feat unsurpassed by that of any of the world's major museums. Work continues on the new Islamic Arts department, which should open in 2010.

Musée de la Mode et du Textile

107 rue de Rivoli, 1st (01.44.55.57.50/ www.lesartsdecoratifs.fr). M° Palais Royal Musée du Louvre or Pyramides. **Open** *Exhibitions* 11am-6pm Tue-Fri; 10am-6pm Sat, Sun. **Admission** €8; free-€6.50 reductions. **Map** p72 C4 ❼

This municipal fashion museum holds Elsa Schiaparelli's entire archive and hosts exciting themed exhibitions. Dramatic black-walled rooms make a fine background to the clothes, and video screens and a cinema space show how the clothes move, as well as interviews with the creators.

Musée de l'Orangerie

Jardin des Tuileries, 1st (01.44.77. 80.07/www.musee-orangerie.fr). M° Concorde. **Open** 12.30-7pm Mon, Wed, Thur, Sat, Sun; 12.30-9pm Fri. **Admission** €6.50; free-€4.50 reductions. **Map** p72 A4 ❽

The long-delayed reopening of this Monet showcase finally took place in 2006, and the new look is utilitarian and fuss-free, with the museum's eight, tapestry-sized *Nymphéas* (water lilies) paintings housed in two plain oval rooms. They provide a simple backdrop for the ethereal romanticism of

Monet's works, painted late in his life. Downstairs, the Jean Walter and Paul Guillaume collection of Impressionism and the Ecole de Paris is a mixed bag of sweet-toothed Cézanne and Renoir portraits, with works by Modigliani, Rousseau, Matisse, Picasso and Derain.

Palais-Royal

Pl du Palais-Royal, 1st. M° Palais Royal Musée du Louvre. **Open** Gardens 7.30am-8.30pm daily. **Admission** free. **Map** p72 C4 ⑨

Built for Cardinal Richelieu by Jacques Lemercier, the building was once known as Palais Cardinal. Richelieu left it to Louis XIII, whose widow Anne d'Autriche preferred it to the Louvre and rechristened it when she moved in with her son, the young Louis XIV. In the 1780s the Duc d'Orléans enclosed the gardens in a three-storey peristyle and filled it with cafés, shops, theatres, sideshows and accommodation to raise money for rebuilding the burned-down opera. Daniel Buren's striped columns grace the main courtyard.

Place de la Concorde

1st/8th. M° Concorde. **Map** p72 A3 ⑩

This is the city's largest square, its grand east-west perspectives stretching from the Louvre to the Arc de Triomphe, and north-south from the Madeleine to the Assemblée Nationale across the Seine. Royal architect Gabriel designed it in the 1750s, along with the two colonnaded mansions astride rue Royale; the west one houses the chic Hôtel de Crillon and the Automobile Club de France, the other is the Naval Ministry. In 1792 the centre statue of Louis XV was replaced with the guillotine for Louis XVI, Marie-Antoinette and many more.

Place Vendôme

1st. M° Opéra or Tuileries. **Map** p72 B3 ⑪

Elegant place Vendôme got its name from a *hôtel particulier* built by the Duc de Vendôme that stood on the site.

Palais-Royal

Opened in 1699, the eight-sided square was conceived by Hardouin-Mansart to show off an equestrian statue of the Sun King, torn down in 1792 and replaced in 1806 by the Colonne de la Grande Armée. During the 1871 Commune this symbol of 'brute force and false glory' was pulled down; the present column is a replica. Today the square houses sparkling jewellers, top fashion houses and the justice ministry. At no.12, you can visit the Grand Salon where Chopin died in 1849; its fabulous allegorical decoration dates from 1777 and has been restored as part of a new museum above the jewellers Chaumet.

Eating & drinking

L'Ardoise

28 rue du Mont-Thabor, 1st (01.42.96.28.18/www.lardoise-paris.com). M° Concorde or Tuileries. **Open** noon-2.30pm, 6.30-11pm Tue-Sat; 6.30-11pm Sun. Closed 1st 3wks Aug. **€. Bistro. Map** p72 B3 ⑫

One of the city's finest modern bistros, L'Ardoise is regularly packed with gourmets eager to sample Pierre Jay's delicious cooking. A wise choice might be six oysters with warm chipolatas and pungent shallot dressing; equally attractive are a hare pie with an escalope of foie gras nestling in its centre. A lightly chilled, raspberry-scented Chinon, from a wine list arranged by price, is an ideal complement. Unusually, it's open on Sundays.

La Bourse ou la Vie

12 rue Vivienne, 2nd (01.42.60.08.83). M° Bourse. **Open** noon-10pm Mon-Fri. Closed 1wk Aug & 1wk Dec. **€€**. **Bistro**. **Map** p73 D3 ⓭

After a career as an architect, the round-spectacled owner of La Bourse ou la Vie has a new mission in life: to revive the dying art of the perfect *steak-frites*. The only decision you'll need to make is which cut of beef to order with your chips, unless you pick the cod. Choose between ultra-tender *coeur de filet* or a huge, surprisingly tender *bavette*. Rich, creamy pepper sauce is the speciality here, but the real surprise is the chips, which gain a distinctly animal flavour from the suet in which they are cooked.

Café Marly

93 rue de Rivoli, cour Napoléon, 1st (01.49.26.06.60). M° Palais Royal Musée du Louvre. **Open** 8am-2am daily. **€€**. **Café**. **Map** p72 B2 ⓮

A class act, this, as you might expect of a Costes café whose lofty, arcaded terrace overlooks the Louvre's glass pyramid. Reached through the passage Richelieu (the entrance for advance Louvre ticket holders), the prime location comes at a price: it's €6 for a Heineken – so you might as well splash out €12 on a chocolate martini or a Shark of vodka, lemonade and grenadine. Most wines are under €10 a glass, and everything is impeccably served by razor-sharp staff. Brasserie fare and sandwiches are on offer too.

Café de la Paix

12 bd des Capucines, 9th (01.40.07.36.36/www.cafedelapaix.fr). M° Opéra. **Open** 7am-midnight daily. **€€**. **Café**. **Map** p72 B2 ⓯

Lap up every detail – this is once-in-a-holiday stuff. Whether you're out on the historic terrace or looking up at the ornate stucco ceiling, you'll be sipping in the footsteps of the likes of Oscar Wilde, Josephine Baker, Emile Zola, and Bartholdi and the Franco-American Union (as they sketched out the Statue of Liberty). Let the immaculate staff bring you a kir (€12) or, for an afternoon treat, the vanilla mille-feuille – possibly the best in Paris.

De la Ville Café

34 bd de Bonne-Nouvelle, 10th (01.48.24.48.09/www.delavillecafe.com). M° Bonne Nouvelle. **Open** 11am-2am daily. **Bar**. **Map** p73 E2 ⓰

De la Ville has brought good news to Bonne-Nouvelle. A major expansion and refurbishment have upped the ante, bringing the Marais in-crowd to this otherwise ignored quarter. Inside, the distressed walls and industrial-baroque feel remain, but the curvy club section at the back has become very cool. A grand staircase leads to a first-floor lounge and exhibition space. The café was opened by the Café Charbon crew.

Drouant

18 rue Gaillon, 2nd (01.42.65.15.16/www.drouant.com). M° Pyramides or Quatre Septembre. **Open** noon-2.30pm, 7pm-midnight daily. **€€€**. **Brasserie**. **Map** p72 C3 ⓱

Star chef Antoine Westermann has whisked this landmark brasserie into the 21st century with bronze-coloured banquettes and butter-yellow fabrics. Westermann has dedicated this restaurant to the art of the hors d'oeuvre, in themed sets of four ranging from global (Thai beef salad with brightly coloured vegetables, coriander, and a sweet and spicy sauce) to nostalgic (silky leeks in vinaigrette). The bite-sized surprises

Café Marly

continue with the main course accompaniments – four of them for each dish – and multiple mini-desserts.

Le Fumoir

6 rue de l'Amiral-de-Coligny, 1st (01.42.92.00.24/www.lefumoir.fr). M° Louvre Rivoli. **Open** 11am-2am daily. Closed 2wks Aug. **Bar**. **Map** p73 D5 ⓲

This elegant bar facing the Louvre has become a local institution: neo-colonial fans whirr lazily and oil paintings adorn the walls. A sleek crowd sips martinis or reads papers at the mahogany bar (originally from a Chicago speakeasy), giving way to young professionals in the restaurant and pretty things in the library. It can feel a touch try-hard, but expertly mixed cocktails should take the edge off any evening.

Harry's New York Bar

5 rue Daunou, 2nd (01.42.61.71.14/www.harrys-bar.fr). M° Opéra. **Open** 10am-4am daily. **Bar**. **Map** p72 B2 ⓳

The city's most stylish American bar is beloved of expats, visitors and hard-drinking Parisians. The bartenders mix some of the most sophisticated cocktails in town, from the trademark bloody mary (invented here, so they say) to the *Pétrifiant*, an aptly named elixir of half a dozen spirits splashed into a beer mug. They can also whip up personalised creations that will have you swooning in the downstairs piano bar, where Gershwin composed *An American in Paris*.

Un Jour à Peyrassol

13 rue Vivienne, 2nd (01.42.60.12.92/www.peyrassol.com). M° Bourse. **Open** 12.30-2pm, 7.30-10pm Mon-Fri. Closed Aug & 1wk Dec. **€€**. **Brasserie**. **Map** p72 C3 ⓴

As anyone who has travelled around Provence will know, come winter the restaurants there go truffle-crazy. This chic little offshoot of the Commanderie de Peyrassol, a wine-producing castle in the Var, keeps up the game with its blackboard menu full of truffle treats. They can be eaten on toast, atop a baked potato, in scrambled eggs or in a rich, creamy sauce enveloping fluffy gnocchi. The natural complement is the Commanderie's wine – white, red and rosé AOC Côtes de Provence.

Kaï

18 rue du Louvre, 1st (01.40.15.01.99). M° Louvre Rivoli. **Open** noon-2pm, 7-10.30pm Tue-Sat; 7-10.30pm Sun. Closed 1wk Apr & 3wks Aug. **€€**. **Japanese**. **Map** p73 D4 ㉑

This Japanese restaurant has developed a following among fashionable diners. The 'Kai-style' sushi is a zesty take on a classic: marinated and lightly grilled yellowtail is pressed on to a roll of shiso-scented rice. Not to be outdone, the grilled aubergine with miso, seemingly simple, turns out to be a smoky, luscious experience. A main of breaded pork lacks the finesse and refinement of the starters, but is nonetheless satisfying.

Pedal power

The ups (and downs) of Vélib's first years.

The grey sit-up-and-beg bikes of the Vélib scheme are already such a familiar sight in Paris that it's hard to imagine the city without them. Dodging absent-minded *vélibistes* is now as firmly established a part of the pedestrian routine here as flirting or avoiding the *merde de chien*. Since Vélib was launched in July 2007, the 16,000 bikes in circulation have been hired some 42 million times.

Those are impressive figures, but the scheme hasn't been an unambiguous success, and what seemed at the beginning like teething problems have still to be solved. It soon became clear, for example, that demand at certain *stations* far outstripped supply. Anyone taking a bike into a busy entertainment district like the Bastille or Oberkampf on a Saturday night should be prepared to spend the best part of an hour circling the area looking for a free *borne* or rack.

A more intractable problem, though, has been that of theft and damage. In the first year, 3,000 bikes were stolen (some turning up in places as far flung as Romania and Morocco), and a similar number were damaged beyond repair.

But these difficulties haven't stopped mayor Delanoë from announcing the extension of the scheme to the *proche banlieue*, the suburbs immediately adjacent to the city, making good on his promise to cement the 'partnership' between Paris and its neighbours.

Kong

1 rue du Pont-Neuf, 1st (01.40.39.09.00/ www.kong.fr). M° Pont Neuf. **Open** noon-2am Mon-Thur, Sun; noon-3am Fri, Sat. **Bar**. **Map** p73 D5 ㉒

Set across the top two floors of the Kenzo building overlooking the Pont Neuf, this Philippe Starck-designed bar was once one of the city's hottest cocktail venues. But the bright, manga-inspired interior, decked out in a mishmash of neon and Hello Kitty, is looking past its quirky best. It's still fun to flirt with the too-beautiful-to-bartend staff and order an excellent Vodkatini, though it's not the place to come for a bargain. At weekends, there's a tiny dancing space.

Liza

14 rue de la Banque, 2nd (01.55.35.00.66/www.restaurant-liza.com). M° Bourse. **Open** 12.30-2pm, 8-10.30pm Mon-Thur; 12.30-2pm, 8-11pm Fri; 8-11pm Sat; noon-4pm Sun. **€€**. **Lebanese**. **Map** p73 D3 ㉓

Liza Soughayar's eaterie showcases the style and superb food of Beirut. Lentil, fried onion and orange salad is delicious, as are the *kebbe* (minced seasoned raw lamb) and grilled halloumi cheese with home-made apricot preserve. Main courses such as minced lamb with coriander-spiced spinach and rice are light, flavoursome and well presented. Try one of the excellent Lebanese wines, and finish with the halva ice-cream with carob molasses. Although there's no prix fixe menu at lunch, prices are cheaper at €17-€32.

Le Meurice

Hôtel Meurice, 228 rue de Rivoli, 1st (01.44.58.10.10/www.meuricehotel.com). M° Tuileries. **Open** 12.30-2pm, 7.30-10pm Mon-Fri. Closed 2wks Feb & Aug. **€€€€**. **Haute cuisine**. **Map** p72 B3 ㉔

Yannick Alléno, chef here since 2003, produces some glorious, if rather understated, dishes. Alléno has a light touch, teasing the flavour out of every leaf, frond, fin or fillet. Turbot is sealed in clay before cooking and then sauced with celery cream and a coulis of flat parsley, and Bresse chicken stuffed with foie gras and served with truffled *sarladais* potatoes is breathtakingly good. A fine cheese tray comes from Quatrehomme, and the pastry chef amazes with his signature millefeuille.

Senderens

9 pl de la Madeleine, 8th (01.42.65. 22.90/www.senderens.fr). M° Madeleine. **Open** noon-3pm, 7.30-11.30pm daily. Closed 3wks Aug. **€€€€. Haute cuisine**. **Map** p72 A3 ㉕

Alain Senderens reinvented his art nouveau institution (formerly Lucas Carton) a few years ago with a *Star Trek* interior and a mind-boggling fusion menu. Now, you might find dishes such as roast duck foie gras with a warm salad of black figs and liquorice powder, or monkfish steak with Spanish mussels and green curry sauce. Each dish comes with a suggested wine, whisky, sherry or punch.

Le Tambour

41 rue Montmartre, 2nd (01.42.33.06.90/http://restaurant letambour.com). M° Sentier. **Open** 6pm-6am daily. **Bar**. **Map** p73 D3 ㉖

The Tambour is a classic nighthawk's bar decked with vintage public transport paraphernalia, its slatted wooden banquettes and bus stop-sign bar stools occupied by chatty regulars who give the 24-hour clock their best shot. Neither tatty nor threatening, there's a long dining room memorable for its métro map from Stalingrad station.

Shopping

Agnès b

2, 3, 6 & 19 rue du Jour, 1st (men 01.42.33.04.13/women 01.45.08.56.56/ www.agnesb.com). M° Les Halles. **Open** *Oct-Apr* 10am-7pm Mon-Sat. *May-Sept* 10am-7.30pm Mon-Sat. **Map** p73 D4 ㉗

Agnès b rarely wavers from her design vision: pure lines in fine quality cotton, merino wool and silk. Best buys are shirts, pullovers and cardigans. Her mini-empire of men's, women's, children's, travel and sportswear shops is compact; see the website for details.

Alice Cadolle

4 rue Cambon, 1st (01.42.60.94.22/ www.cadolle.com). M° Concorde or Madeleine. **Open** 10am-1pm, 2-6.30pm Mon-Sat. Closed Aug. **Map** p72 B3 ㉘

Five generations of lingerie-makers are behind this boutique, founded by Hermine Cadolle, who claimed to be the inventor of the bra. Great-great-granddaughter Poupie Cadolle continues the tradition in a cosy space devoted to a luxury ready-to-wear line of bras, panties and corsets. For a special treat, Cadolle Couture (255 rue St-Honoré, 1st, 01.42.60.94.94) will create indulgent bespoke lingerie (by appointment only).

Boucheron

26 pl Vendôme, 1st (01.42.61.58.16/ www.boucheron.com). M° Opéra. **Open** 10.30am-7pm Mon-Sat. **Map** p72 B3 ㉙

Boucheron was the first to set up shop on place Vendôme, attracting celebrity custom from the nearby Ritz hotel. Owned by Gucci, the grand jeweller produces stunning pieces, using traditional motifs with new accents: take, for example, its fabulous chocolate-coloured gold watch.

Chanel

31 rue Cambon, 1st (01.42.86.28.00/ www.chanel.com). M° Concorde or Madeleine. **Open** 10am-7pm Mon-Sat. **Map** p72 B3 ㉚

Fashion legend Chanel has managed to stay relevant, thanks to Karl Lagerfeld. Coco opened her first boutique in this street, at no.21, in 1910, and the tradition continues in this elegant interior. Lagerfeld has been designing for Chanel since 1983, and keeps on revamping the classics – the little black dress and the Chanel suit – with great success.

Colette

213 rue St-Honoré, 1st (01.55.35.33.90/www.colette.fr). M° Pyramides or Tuileries. **Open** 11am-7pm Mon-Sat. **Map** p72 B3 31

The renowned and much-imitated one-stop concept and lifestyle store stationed a mobile 'superette' outside while it went into rehab in summer 2008. It is now back with the same highly eclectic selection of accessories, fashion, books, media, gadgets, and hair and beauty brands själ, Kiehl's and uslu airlines.

Comme des Garçons

54 rue du Fbg-St-Honoré, 8th (01.53.30.27.27). M° Concorde or Madeleine. **Open** 11am-7pm Mon-Sat. **Map** p72 A2 32

Rei Kawakubo's design ideas and revolutionary mix of materials have influenced fashions of the past two decades, and are showcased in this fibreglass store. Comme des Garçons Parfums (23 pl du Marché-St-Honoré, 1st, 01.47.03.15.03) provides a futuristic setting for the brand's fragrances.

Didier Ludot

20-24 galerie de Montpensier, 1st (01.42.96.06.56/www.didierludot.com). M° Palais Royal Musée du Louvre. **Open** 10.30am-7pm Mon-Sat. **Map** p72 C3 33

Didier Ludot's temples to vintage haute couture appear in Printemps, Harrods and New York's Barneys. The pieces are stunning: Dior, Molyneux, Balenciaga, Pucci, Féraud and Chanel, from the 1920s onwards. Ludot also curates exhibitions, using the shop windows around the Palais-Royal as a gallery. La Petite Robe Noire (125 galerie de Valois, 1st, 01.40.15.01.04) stocks Ludot's own line of vintage little black dresses.

Ekivok

39 bd de Sébastopol, 1st (01.42.21.98.71/www.ekivok.com). M° Les Halles/RER Châtelet Les Halles. **Open** 11am-7.30pm Mon-Sat. **Map** p73 E4 34

In Ekivok's graffiti-covered boutique you'll find labels such as Bullrot, Carhartt, Hardcore Session and Juicy Jazz for men, and Golddigga, Punky Fish, Skunk Funk, Emilie the Strange and Hardcore Session for women, plus a selection of Eastpak accessories.

Erès

2 rue Tronchet, 8th (01.47.42.28.82/ www.eres.fr). M° Madeleine. **Open** 10am-7pm Mon-Sat. **Map** p72 B2 35

Erès's beautifully cut swimwear has embraced a sexy '60s look with buttons on the low-cut briefs. The top and bottom can be purchased in different sizes, or you can buy one piece of a bikini.

La Galerie du Carrousel du Louvre

99 rue de Rivoli, 1st (01.43.16.47.10/ www.lecarrouseldulouvre.com). M° Palais Royal Musée du Louvre. **Open** 10am-8pm daily. **Map** p72 C4 36

This massive underground centre – open every day of the year – is home to more than 35 shops, mostly big-name chains vying for your attention and cash. The Petit Prince boutique and Réunion des Musées Nationaux shops are great for last-minute gifts.

Galeries Lafayette

40 bd Haussmann, 9th (01.42.82.34.56/fashion shows 01.42.82.30.25/fashion advice 01.42.82.35.50/www.galerieslafayette.com). M° Chaussée d'Antin/RER Auber. **Open** 9.30am-8pm Mon-Wed, Fri, Sat; 9.30am-9pm Thur. **Map** p72 C2 37

The store recently launched a massive renovation programme, with the opening in October 2008 of its Espace Luxe on the first floor, featuring luxury prêt-à-porter and accessories and nine avant-garde designers. The men's fashion space on the third floor, Lafayette Homme, has natty designer corners and a 'Club' area with internet access. On the first floor, Lafayette Gourmet has exotic foods, and a vast wine cellar.

Printemps p83

Lafayette Maison over the road has five floors of home furnishings and interior design products.

Hédiard

21 pl de la Madeleine, 8th (01.43.12.88.88/www.hediard.fr). M° Madeleine. **Open** 8.30am-9pm Mon-Sat. **Map** p72 A2 ㊳

Hédiard's charming shop dates back to 1880, when they were the first to introduce exotic foods to Paris, specialising in rare teas and coffees, spices, jams and candied fruits. Pop upstairs for a cuppa in the shop's posh tearoom.

Hermès

24 rue du Fbg-St-Honoré, 8th (01.40.17.47.17/www.hermes.com). M° Concorde or Madeleine. **Open** 10.30am-6.30pm Mon-Sat. **Map** p72 A3 ㊴

The fifth generation of the family directs the Hermès empire from this 1930s building. Originally – and still – a saddler, it is no also-ran in the fashion stakes, with Jean-Paul Gaultier at the reins. Most of its clients, however, are tourists after a horsey scarf.

Jean-Paul Gaultier

6 rue Vivienne, 2nd (01.42.86.05.05/ www.jeanpaulgaultier.com). M° Bourse. **Open** 10.30am-7pm Mon-Fri; 11am-7pm Sat. **Map** p73 D3 ㊵

Having celebrated his 30th year in the fashion business, Gaultier is still going strong. His boudoir boutique stocks men's and women's ready-to-wear and the reasonably priced JPG Jeans lines. The haute couture department (01.42.97.48.12) is by appointment.

Kiliwatch

64 rue Tiquetonne, 2nd (01.42.21. 17.37/http://espacekiliwatch.fr). M° Etienne Marcel. **Open** 2-7pm Mon; 11am-7.30pm Tue-Sat. **Map** p73 E3 ㊶

The trailblazer of the rue Etienne-Marcel revival is filled with hoodies, casual shirts and jeans. Brands include Gas, Edwin and Pepe Jeans.

Kokon To Zai

48 rue Tiquetonne, 2nd (01.42.36.92.41/www.kokontozai.co.uk). M° Etienne Marcel. **Open** 11.30am-7.30pm Mon-Sat. **Map** p73 E4 ㊷

Always a spot-on spotter of the latest creations, this tiny style emporium is sister to the Kokon To Zai in London. The neon-lit club feel of the mirrored interior matches the dark glamour of the designs. Unique pieces straight off the catwalk share space with creations by Marjan Peijoski, Noki, Raf Simons, Ziad Ghanem and new Norwegian designers.

Lanvin

22 rue du Fbg St-Honoré, 8th (01.44.71.31.73/www.lanvin.com). M° Concorde or Madeleine. **Open** 10am-7pm Mon-Sat. **Map** p72 A3 43

The couture house that began in the 1920s with Jeanne Lanvin has been reinvented by the indefatigable Albert Elbaz. In October 2007 he unveiled this, the revamped showroom that set new aesthetic standards for luxury fashion retailing. Lanvin has an exhibition room devoted to her in the Musée des Arts Décoratifs, and this apartment-boutique also incorporates original furniture from the Lanvin archive that has been restored. All this would be nothing, of course, if the clothes themselves were not exquisite.

Legrand Filles et Fils

1 rue de la Banque, 2nd (01.42.60.07.12/www.caves-legrand.com). M° Bourse. **Open** 11am-7pm Mon; 10am-7.30pm Tue-Fri; 10am-7pm Sat. Closed Mon in July & Aug. **Map** p73 D3 44

Fine wines, teas and *bonbons*, and a showroom for regular wine tastings.

Limi Feu

NEW *13 rue de Turbigo, 2nd (01.40.28.41.41/www.limifeu.com). M° Etienne Marcel.* **Open** 11am-7pm Tue-Sat (dates vary; calendar on the website). **Map** p73 E4 45

Still bearing the tattoos of her rebel past, Yohji Yamamoto's 33-year-old daughter wowed the fashion world with her 2007 runway show, using all Asian models. Her designs show the influence of the master, though she considers them more 'realistic', with practical details such as zip bags incorporated into the clothing. Hidden behind a discreet door, her HQ and showroom doubles as a boutique that is open for nine months of the year, excluding the periods leading up to the fashion shows.

Marc by Marc Jacobs

NEW *19 rue du Marché-Saint-Honoré, 1st (01.40.20.11.30/www.marcjacobs.com). M° Tuileries.* **Open** 9am-6pm Mon-Sat. **Map** p72 B3 46

The new store for Jacobs' casual, punky line has fashionistas clustering like bees round a honeypot, not least for the fabulously inexpensive accessories that make great gifts or add instant spice to a tired outfit. A skateboard table and giant pedalo in the form of a swan are the centrepieces of the store, which stocks men's and women's prêt-à-porter, shoes and special editions.

Marc Jacobs

56 galerie de Montpensier, 1st (01.55.35.02.60/www.marcjacobs.com). M° Palais Royal Musée du Louvre. **Open** 11am-8pm Mon-Sat. **Map** p72 C3 47

By choosing the Palais-Royal for his first signature boutique in Europe, Marc Jacobs brought new life – and an influx of fashionistas – to these elegant cloisters. Stocking womenswear, menswear, accessories and shoes, it has already become a place of pilgrimage for the designer's legion of admirers, who are snapping up his downtown New York style.

Martin Margiela

23 & 25bis rue de Montpensier, 1st (womenswear 01.40.15.07.55/ menswear 01.40.15.06.44/www.maisonmartinmargiela.com). M° Palais Royal Musée du Louvre. **Open** 11am-7pm Mon-Sat. **Map** p72 C4 48

The first Paris outlet for the JD Salinger of fashion is a pristine, white, unlabelled space. His collection for

PARIS BY AREA

women (Line 1) has a blank label but is recognisable by external white stitching. You'll also find Line 6 (women's basics) and Line 10 (menswear), plus accessories for men and women and shoes.

Printemps

64 bd Haussmann, 9th (01.42.82.50.00/www.printemps.com). M° Havre Caumartin/RER Auber. **Open** 9.35am-8pm Mon-Wed, Fri, Sat; 9.35am-10pm Thur. **Map** p72 B1 49

In the magnificently appointed Printemps you'll find everything you didn't even know you wanted and English-speaking assistants to help you find it. But fashion is where the store really excels; an entire floor is devoted to shoes, and the beauty department stocks more than 200 brands. In all, there are six floors of men's and women's fashion. In Printemps de la Mode, French designers Paul & Joe and APC sit alongside all the big international designers. The Fashion Loft offers a younger but equally stylish take on current trends. Along with furnishings, Printemps de la Maison stocks everything from everyday tableware to design classics. For fast refuelling, Printemps has a tearoom, sushi bar and Café Be, an Alain Ducasse bakery.

Robert Normand

NEW *149-150 galerie de Valois, 1st (www.robertnormand.com). M° Palais Royal Musée du Louvre.* **Open** 1-7pm Mon; 10.30am-7pm Tue-Sat. **Map** p72 C3 50

Normand is a new addition to the smart Palais-Royal. The 38-year-old designer, who has collaborated with Lanvin, Pucci and Christophe Lemaire, launched his own label in 2000 – a combination of pop art patterns with gangsta cuts, satin puffballs in peacock colours and blousons made of the kind of fabrics favoured by African potentates. The man is treading the line between madness and genius.

Salons du Palais-Royal Shiseido

Jardins du Palais-Royal, 142 galerie de Valois, 1st (01.49.27.09.09/www.salons-shiseido.com). M° Palais Royal Musée du Louvre. **Open** 10am-7pm Mon-Sat. **Map** p72 C3 51

Under the arcades of the Palais-Royal, Shiseido's perfumer Serge Lutens practises his aromatic arts. A former photographer at Paris *Vogue* and artistic director of make-up at Christian Dior, Lutens is a maestro of rare taste. Bottles of his concoctions – Tubéreuse Criminelle, Rahat Loukoum and Ambre Sultan – can be sampled by visitors. Look out for Fleurs d'Oranger, which the great man defines as the smell of happiness. Many of the perfumes are exclusive to the Salons; prices start at around €100.

Stella McCartney

NEW *114-121 galerie du Valois, Jardin du Palais-Royal, 1st (01.47.03.03.80/www.stellamccartney.com). M° Palais Royal Musée du Louvre.* **Open** 10.30am-7pm Mon-Sat. **Map** p72 C3 52

McCartney is crazy about the 'clash of history, fashion and contemporary art' at the Palais-Royal, where she has opened her sumptuous boutique overlooking the gardens. Thick carpets, maplewood and metal sculptures create a rarified setting for women's prêt-à-porter, bags, shoes, sunglasses, lingerie, perfume and skincare.

Yohji Yamamoto

NEW *4 rue Cambon, 1st (01.40.20.00.71 /www.yohjiyamamoto.co.jp). M° Concorde.* **Open** 10am-7pm Mon-Sat. **Map** p72 B3 53

Yohji Yamamoto has achieved his dream of having a flagship store on rue Cambon, which will forever be synonymous with Chanel. This temple to the creator is as impressive as those in New York and Antwerp, a pristine white gallery space designed by Sophie Hicks. Behind an origami-screen window mannequins clothed in his showpieces seem to float in the air. A grand staircase leads to womenswear on the first floor, while menswear is on the lower ground.

Nightlife

Au Duc des Lombards

42 rue des Lombards, 1st (01.42.33.22.88/www.ducdeslombards.com). M° Châtelet. **Open** *Concerts* 9pm Mon-Sat. Closed mid Aug. **Admission** €19-€25. **Map** p73 E5 54

Some of the capital's venerated jazz spots, like Le Bilboquet, have lost the fight for survival in recent years. But this one has endured, and attracts a high class of performer.

Le Cab

2 pl du Palais-Royal, 1st (01.58.62.56.25/www.cabaret.fr). M° Palais Royal Musée du Louvre. **Open** 11.30pm-5am Wed-Sat. *Restaurant* 7.30-11.30pm Tue-Sat. **Admission** free; €20 Thur-Sat. **Map** p72 C4 55

Le Cab is owned by the management behind Club Mix and Queen, and R&B and commercial house dominate the playlist. The doormen are tough, and if they don't like you, you won't get in (unless you've booked for dinner).

Chacha Club

NEW *47 rue Berger, 1st (01.40.13.12.12/www.chachaclub.fr). M° Châtelet.* **Open** 8pm-5am Mon-Sat. **Admission** varies. **Map** p73 D4 56

See box p85.

Olympia

28 bd des Capucines, 9th (08.92.68.33.68/www.olympiahall.com). M° Opéra. **Open** *Box office* 10am-9pm Mon-Sat; 10am-7pm Sun. *Concerts* times vary. **Map** p72 B2 57

The Beatles, Frank Sinatra, Jimi Hendrix and Edith Piaf have all performed here over the years; as did Jacques Brel, who recorded two fabled live albums here in the 1960s. Now it's mostly home to nostalgia and *variété*.

Le ParisParis

5 av de l'Opéra, 1st (01.42.60.64.45/www.leparisparis.com). M° Pyramides. **Open** 11pm-5am Tue-Sat. *Concerts* times vary. **Admission** free. **Map** p72 C3 58

This small, sweaty *boîte* has become a focus for 'cool' Paris. It's great, albeit pricey, once you're in, but you'll have to pass the door test first.

Rex

5 bd Poissonnière, 2nd (01.42.36.10.96/www.rexclub.com). M° Bonne Nouvelle. **Open** 11.30pm-6am Wed-Sat. **Admission** free-€15. **Map** p73 E2 59

The Rex's new sound system puts over 40 different sound configurations at the DJ's fingertips, and has proved to be a magnet for top turntable stars. Once associated with iconic techno pioneer Laurent Garnier, the Rex has stayed at the top of the Paris techno scene, and occupies an unassailable position as the city's serious club music venue.

Le Sunset/Le Sunside

60 rue des Lombards, 1st (Sunside 01.40.26.21.25/Sunset 01.40.26.46.60/www.sunset-sunside.com). M° Châtelet. **Open** *Concerts* 9pm, 10pm daily. **Admission** €8-€25. **Map** p73 E5 60

A split-personality venue, with Sunset dealing in electric groups and Sunside hosting acoustic performances. Their renown pulls in big jazz names from both sides of the Atlantic.

Théâtre du Châtelet

1 pl du Châtelet, 1st (information 01.40.28.28.00/booking 01.40.28.28.40/www.chatelet-theatre.com). M° Châtelet. **Open** times vary. **Admission** €16-€69. **Map** p73 E5 61

This venerable theatre and classic music hall has another life as a jazz and *chanson* venue – old- and new-school jazzers, from Stacey Kent to Jamie Cullum, appeared last year.

Roll up, roll up

Paris's fetishistic obsession with the cigarette has produced a new nightlife phenomenon: the *fumoir*. The **Chacha Club** (p84) is the first high-profile establishment to open one, and it forms just one of the sexy attributes of this hot haunt near Les Halles that is attracting a spectacularly good-looking clientele through its doors.

The anti-smoking laws make it possible to install a *fumoir* according to stringent regulations (no more than 20 per cent of the total surface area, ventilation in place and no staff to enter until an hour after the last smoker has gone home). The Chacha has done it very well – set between the dining room and the bar/club area, the *fumoir* is surrounded by windows so you can check out the company before you head inside.

At first, people enter gingerly, experiencing a Proustian moment of nostalgia: 'Ah yes, I remember when…'. As the night goes on, though, this den becomes the ultimate place for a spot of 'smirtation' – its cosy size gives you the perfect excuse to plonk yourself down next to an attractive stranger, and the atmosphere is heightened by the feeling that you are doing something illicit.

The Chacha is sure to be copied, as this place has caused the biggest storm of 2009. In the style of a private club, but with no membership requirement (only a trio of exacting 'physionomists' stand at the door), it combines restaurant, bar and club in a suite of intimate rooms with subdued lighting and seductive, 1930s-inspired decor. Upstairs is a music room where you can impress your pals by strumming the electric guitars or jamming on the keyboard, as well as a boudoir fitted out with a bath – the perfect place to pout.

Châtelet – Théâtre Musical de Paris

1 pl du Châtelet, 1st (01.40.28.28.40/ www.chatelet-theatre.com). M° Châtelet. **Box office** 11am-7pm daily. *By phone* 10am-7pm Mon-Sat. Closed July, Aug. **Admission** €10-€122.50. **Map** p73 E5 62

Jean-Luc Choplin has radically changed the programming of this bastion of Paris music making. An attempt to rediscover the theatre's popular roots has been achieved at the expense of traditional fine music subscribers. The 2008/09 season kicked off with an Elvis Costello operatic adventure – good fun, but hardly a Wagner Ring cycle.

Forum des Images

2 Grande Galerie, Porte St-Eustache, Forum des Halles, 1st (01.44.76.63.00/ www.forumdesimages.net). M° Les Halles. **Open** 1-9pm Tue-Sun. Closed 2wks Aug. **Admission** (per day) €4.50-€5.50. **Map** p73 D4 63

Opened in 1988, the Forum was conceived partly as a screening venue for old and little-known movies, and partly as an archive centre for every kind of moving picture featuring Paris; today the collection numbers over 6,500 documentaries, adverts, newsreels and films, from the work of the Lumière brothers to 21st-century reportage. They have all been painstakingly digitised.

Le Grand Rex

1 bd Poissonnière, 2nd (08.92.68.05.96/www.legrandrex.com). M° Bonne Nouvelle. **Admission** €7-€8.50. *Les Etoiles du Rex tour* €9.80; €8 reductions. **Map** p73 E2 64

With its wedding-cake exterior, fairytale interior and the largest auditorium in Europe (2,750 seats), this is one of the few cinemas that manages to upstage whatever it screens: no wonder it's a listed historic monument. Its blockbuster programming (usually in French) is suited to its vast, roll-down screen; it also hosts concerts and rowdy all-night compilation events.

Opéra National de Paris, Palais Garnier

Pl de l'Opéra, 9th (08.92.89.90.90/from abroad 01.72.29.35.35/www.opera deparis.fr). M° Opéra. **Box office** 10.30am-6.30pm Mon-Sat. *By phone* 9am-6pm Mon-Fri; 9am-1pm Sat. **Admission** €7-€172. **Map** p72 B2 65

The Palais Garnier, with its ornate, extravagant decor and ceiling by Marc Chagall, is the jewel in the crown of Paris music-making, as well as a glistening focal point for the Right Bank. The Opéra National often favours the high-tech Bastille for new productions, but the matchless acoustics of the Palais Garnier are superior to the new house.

Théâtre National de l'Opéra Comique

Pl Boieldieu, 2nd (08.25.01.01.23/ www.opera-comique.com). M° Richelieu Drouot. **Box office** 11am-7pm Mon-Sat; 11am-5pm Sun. *By phone* 11am-7pm Mon-Sat; 11am-5pm Sun. **Admission** €6-€115. **Map** p72 C2 66

Its promotion to national theatre status has brought this jewel box of a theatre back to life. Jérôme Deschamps' second season included Auber's *Fra Diavolo*, Rameau's *Zoroastre*, and the first Paris performances of *Lady Sarashina*, a new opera by Peter Eötvös.

Théâtre de la Ville

2 pl du Châtelet, 4th (01.42.74.22.77/ www.theatredelaville-paris.com). M° Châtelet. **Box office** 11am-7pm Mon; 11am-8pm Tue-Sat. **Admission** €12-€23. **Map** p73 E5 67

Programming features hip chamber music outfits such as the Kronos and Takács Quartets, Early Music pioneer Fabio Biondi, and soloists like pianist Aleksandar Madzar and tenor Werner Güra. The season spills over to performances at the Théâtre des Abbesses, which shares the same phone number.

Moulin Rouge p94

Montmartre & Pigalle

For such a young part of Paris – it was only annexed by the city in 1860 – Montmartre has astonishing renown, among foreigners as much as Frenchmen. It doesn't take much exploring before you realise that the fame and affection are deserved: the steep streets and staircases, the ghosts of some of the 19th and 20th centuries' greatest artists, and the present-day buzz of hip cafés and bars all produce a charm that even mass tourism can't obscure. The same can't be said of louche Pigalle at the bottom of the hill, with its sex shops and grime. Still, these days, many of the red lights are attached not to brothels but to hot music venues and nightspots.

Perched on a hill (or *butte*), Montmartre is the highest point in Paris, its tightly packed houses spiralling round the mound below the dome of **Sacré-Coeur**. Despite the many tourists, it's surprisingly easy to fall under the spell of this unabashedly romantic district. Climb quiet stairways, peer down narrow alleys and into ivy-covered houses and quiet squares, and explore streets such as rue des Abbesses, rue des Trois-Frères and rue des Martyrs, with their cafés, boutiques and bohemian residents.

Sights & museums

Cimetière de Montmartre

20 av Rachel, access by staircase from rue Caulaincourt, 18th (01.53.42.36.30). M° Blanche or Place de Clichy. **Open** *6 Nov-15 Mar* 8am-5.30pm Mon-Sat; 9am-5.30pm Sun & public hols. *16 Mar-5 Nov* 8am-6pm Mon-Sat; 9am-6pm Sun & public hols. **Admission** free. **Map** p89 A1 ❶

Truffaut, Nijinsky, Berlioz, Degas, Offenbach and German poet Heine are all buried here. So, too, are La Goulue, the first great cancan star and model for Toulouse-Lautrec, and the consumptive heroine Alphonsine Plessis, inspiration for Verdi's *La Traviata*. Flowers are still left on the grave of pop diva Dalida.

Cimetière de Montmartre p87

Musée d'Art Halle St-Pierre

2 rue Ronsard, 18th (01.42.58.72.89/ www.hallesaintpierre.org). M° Anvers. **Open** *Jan-July, Sept-Dec* 10am-6pm daily. *Aug* noon-6pm Mon-Fri. **Admission** €7; free-€5.50 reductions. **Map** p89 C2 ❷

The former market in the shadow of Sacré-Coeur specialises in *art brut*, *art outsider* and *art singulier* from its own and other collections.

Event highlights Peintures de Marie Morel (10 Sept 2009-7 Mar 2010)

Musée de l'Erotisme

72 bd de Clichy, 18th (01.42.58.28.73/ www.musee-erotisme.com). M° Blanche. **Open** 10am-2am daily. **Admission** €8; €6 reductions. **Map** p89 A2 ❸

Seven floors of erotic art and artefacts amassed by collectors Alain Plumey and Joseph Khalif. The first three run from first-century Peruvian phallic pottery through Etruscan fertility symbols to Yoni sculptures from Nepal; the fourth gives a history of Paris brothels; and the recently refurbished top floors host exhibitions of modern erotic art.

Musée Gustave Moreau

14 rue de La Rochefoucauld, 9th (01.48.74.38.50/www.musee-moreau.fr). M° Trinité. **Open** 10am-12.45pm, 2-5.15pm Mon, Wed-Sun. **Admission** €5; free-€3 reductions. **Map** p89 A4 ❹

This wonderful museum combines the private apartment of Symbolist painter Gustave Moreau (1825-98) with the vast gallery he built to display his work – set out as a museum by the painter himself. Downstairs shows his obsessive collector's nature with family portraits, Grand Tour souvenirs and a boudoir devoted to the object of his unrequited love, Alexandrine Durem. Upstairs is Moreau's fantasy realm, which plunders Greek mythology and biblical scenes for canvases filled with writhing maidens, trance-like visages, mystical beasts and strange plants. Don't miss the trippy masterpiece *Jupiter et Sémélé* on the second floor. Printed on boards you can carry around are the artist's lengthy, mad commentaries.

Musée de Montmartre

12 rue Cortot, 18th (01.49.25.89.37/ www.museedemontmartre.fr). M° Abbesses. **Open** 11am-6pm Wed-Sun. **Admission** €7; free-€5.50 reductions. **Map** p89 B1 ❺

At the back of a garden, this 17th-century manor displays the history of the hilltop, with rooms devoted to composer Gustave Charpentier and a tribute to the Lapin Agile cabaret, with Toulouse-Lautrec posters. There are paintings by Suzanne Valadon, who had a studio above the entrance, as did Renoir, Raoul Dufy and Maurice Utrillo.

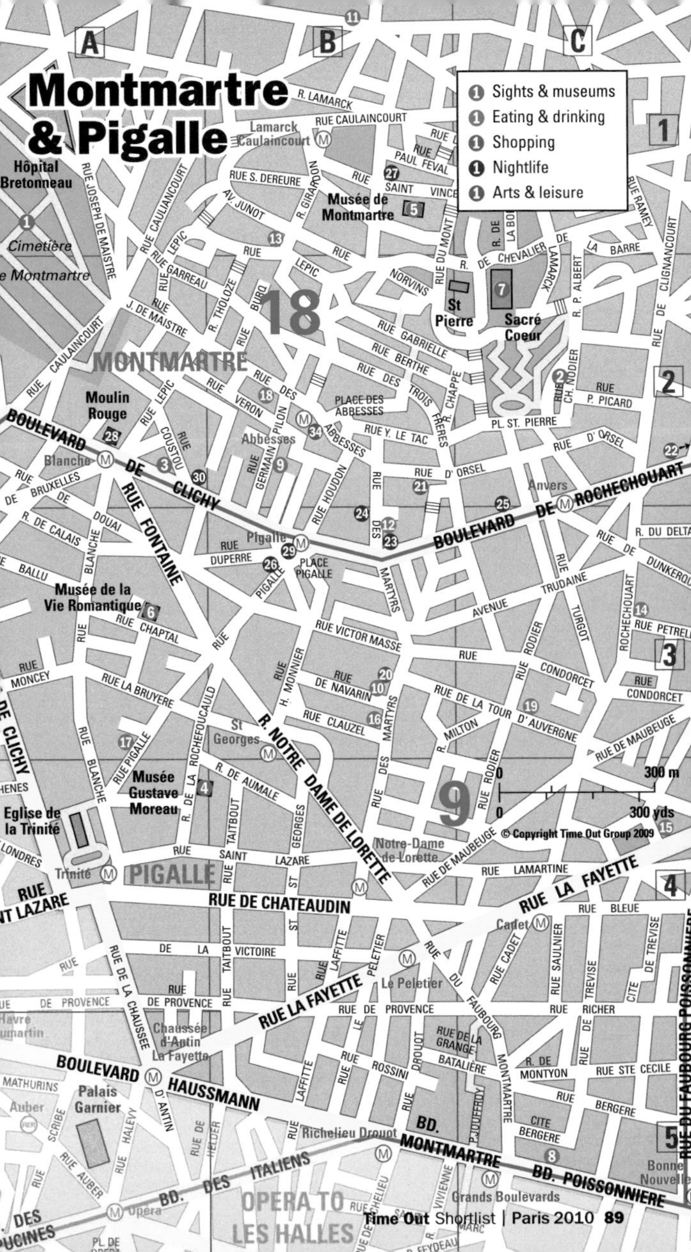
A
B
C
1
2
3
4
5
Montmartre & Pigalle
Sights & museums
Eating & drinking
Shopping
Nightlife
Arts & leisure
R. LAMARCK
RUE CAULAINCOURT
Lamarck Caulaincourt
Hôpital Bretonneau
Cimetière de Montmartre
RUE JOSEPH DE MAISTRE
RUE CAULAINCOURT
RUE S. DEREURE
AV. JUNOT
R. GIRARDON
Musée de Montmartre
PAUL FEVAL
RUE SAINT VINCENT
RUE RAMEY
RUE LEPIC
RUE GARREAU
RUE J. DE MAISTRE
R. THOLOZE
RUE BURQ
18
RUE NORVINS
RUE DU MONT
R. DE CHEVALIER DE LA BARRE
LAMARCK
R. P. ALBERT
RUE DE CLIGNANCOURT
St Pierre
Sacré Coeur
RUE GABRIELLE
RUE BERTHE
RUE DES TROIS FRERES
R. CHAPPE
RUE CH. NODIER
RUE P. PICARD
PL. ST. PIERRE
MONTMARTRE
Moulin Rouge
RUE VERON
PLACE DES ABBESSES
Abbesses
RUE Y. LE TAC
RUE D'ORSEL
BOULEVARD DE CLICHY
Blanche
RUE COUSTOU
RUE GERMAIN PILON
RUE HOUDON
RUE DES MARTYRS
Anvers
BOULEVARD DE ROCHECHOUART
RUE DE BRUXELLES
RUE DE DOUAI
R. DE CALAIS
RUE FONTAINE
RUE BLANCHE
Pigalle
PLACE PIGALLE
RUE DUPERRE
R. DU DELTA
RUE DE DUNKERQUE
RUE BALLU
Musée de la Vie Romantique
RUE CHAPTAL
AVENUE TRUDAINE
RUE TURGOT
RUE ROCHECHOUART
RUE PETRELLE
RUE VICTOR MASSE
RUE H. MONNIER
RUE DE NAVARIN
RUE RODIER
RUE CONDORCET
RUE MONCEY
RUE LA BRUYERE
RUE DE LA ROCHEFOUCAULD
RUE CLAUZEL
RUE DE LA TOUR D'AUVERGNE
R. MILTON
RUE DE MAUBEUGE
St Georges
R. NOTRE DAME DE LORETTE
RUE PIGALLE
Musée Gustave Moreau
R. DE AUMALE
300 m
300 yds
9
Eglise de la Trinité
RUE TAITBOUT
RUE ST GEORGES
© Copyright Time Out Group 2009
RUE SAINT LAZARE
Notre-Dame de Lorette
RUE LAMARTINE
RUE LA FAYETTE
Trinité
PIGALLE
RUE DE CHATEAUDIN
RUE BLEUE
Cadet
RUE DE LA VICTOIRE
RUE LAFFITTE
RUE LE PELETIER
RUE DU FAUBOURG MONTMARTRE
RUE CADET
RUE SAULNIER
RUE TREVISE
CITE DE TREVISE
RUE DU FAUBOURG POISSONNIERE
RUE DE LA CHAUSSEE D'ANTIN
RUE DE PROVENCE
Le Peletier
RUE RICHER
Havre Caumartin
Chaussée d'Antin La Fayette
RUE DE LA GRANGE BATALIÈRE
RUE ROSSINI
RUE DROUOT
R. DE MONTYON
RUE STE CECILE
BOULEVARD HAUSSMANN
MATHURINS
Palais Garnier
Auber
RUE BERGERE
CITE BERGERE
RUE SCRIBE
RUE HALEVY
RUE DU HELDER
Richelieu Drouot
BD. MONTMARTRE
BD. POISSONNIERE
P. JOUFFROY
Bonne Nouvelle
RUE AUBER
BD. DES ITALIENS
Grands Boulevards
RUE VIVIENNE
BD. DES CAPUCINES
Opéra
OPERA TO LES HALLES
PL. DE OPERA
RUE FEYDEAU

Musée de la Vie Romantique

Hôtel Scheffer-Renan, 16 rue Chaptal, 9th (01.55.31.95.67/www.vie-romantique.paris.fr). M° Blanche or St-Georges. **Open** 10am-6pm Tue-Sun. **Admission** free. *Exhibitions* €7; free-€3.50 reductions. **Map** p89 A3 ❻

When Dutch artist Ary Scheffer lived in this small villa, the area teemed with composers, writers and artists. Aurore Dupin, Baronne Dudevant (George Sand) was a guest at Scheffer's soirées, and many other great names crossed the threshold, including Chopin and Liszt. The museum is devoted to Sand, although the watercolours, lockets, jewels and plastercast of her right arm that she left behind reveal little of her ideas or affairs.

Sacré-Coeur

35 rue du Chevalier-de-la-Barre, 18th (01.53.41.89.00/www.sacre-coeur-montmartre.com). M° Abbesses or Anvers. **Open** *Basilica* 6am-10.30pm daily. *Crypt & dome* Winter 10am-5.45pm daily. Summer 9am-6.45pm daily. **Admission** free. *Crypt & dome* €5. **Map** p89 C2 ❼

Work on this enormous mock Romano-Byzantine edifice began in 1877. It was commissioned after the nation's defeat by Prussia in 1870, voted for by the Assemblée Nationale and built from public subscription. Finally completed in 1914, it was consecrated in 1919 – by which time a jumble of architects had succeeded Paul Abadie, winner of the original competition. The interior boasts lavish mosaics.

PARIS BY AREA

Eating & drinking

Le Brébant

32 bd Poissonnière, 9th (01.47.70.01.02). M° Grands Boulevards. **Open** 7.30am-6am daily. **Bar**. **Map** p89 C5 ❽

Proof that change has swept the Grands Boulevards comes in the form of this prominent, round-the-clock bar-bistro. There's a busy terrace below a colourful, stripy awning, and the split-level interior is all bare bulbs and wrought iron. Prices are steep, so push the boat out and opt for an expertly prepared fruit daiquiri, or a Bonne Nouvelle of Bombay Sapphire gin and Pisang Ambon. There are rarer bottled beers too – Monaco, Picon and sundry brews from Brabant.

Chez Toinette

20 rue Germain-Pilon, 18th (01.42.54.44.36). M° Abbesses or Pigalle. **Open** 7.30-11.30pm Mon-Sat. Closed last 3wks Aug. **€€**. **Bistro**. **Map** p89 B2 ❾

This stalwart purveyor of bistro fare behind the Théâtre de Montmartre has steadily upped its prices in line with its burgeoning success. However, the blackboard menu is still good value. As you squeeze into the seats, the amiable waiter describes each dish with pride, then presents an appetiser of olives, cherry tomatoes and crisp radishes. Of the starters, try the red-blooded wild boar terrine or the soufflé-like asparagus quiche. Carnivorous mains include *mignon de porc*, spring lamb and assorted steaks. Round it off with armagnac-steeped prunes.

Le Ch'ti Catalan

NEW *4 rue de Navarin, 9th (01.44.63.04.33). M° Notre-Dame-de-Lorette.* **Open** noon-3pm, 7.30-11pm Mon-Fri; 7.30-11pm Sat. **€**. **Bistro**. **Map** p89 B3 ❿

It's unconventional, to say the least, to pair ingredients such as endives, bacon and eel, commonly found in the north of France, with the sunny flavours of French Catalan cooking. But that's what two friends have done in this ochre-painted bistro. The amazing thing is, it works. *Anchoïade* – red peppers with tangy anchovies – is fresh and tasty; tender pork cheeks served in a casserole with melting white beans are succulent; and the *gueule noire* (black face) – crushed spice biscuits with crème fraîche and egg – refers to slang for miners in northern France.

La Divette de Montmartre

136 rue Marcadet, 18th (01.46.06.19.64). M° Lamarck Caulaincourt. **Open** 5pm-1am Mon-Sat; 5-11pm Sun. **Bar**. **Map** p89 B1 ⓫

Tucked away among Montmartre's hilly backstreets, this cavern of colourful nostalgia is run by Serge and serves as his *Recherche du temps perdu* in the shape of album covers, posters and table football. Beatles and Rolling Stones sleeves bedeck the bar, interrupted by *yé-yé* pop tat, St-Etienne football paraphernalia and an old red telephone box. On tap are Wieckse Witte, Afflighem, Pelforth and gossip from the days when Manu Chao were regulars. On Friday nights, come for live operetta, jazz, pop or whatever else takes Serge's fancy.

La Fourmi

74 rue des Martyrs, 18th (01.42.64.70.35). M° Pigalle. **Open** 8.30am-2am Mon-Thur; 8.30am-4am Fri, Sat; 10am-2am Sun. **Bar**. **Map** p89 B3 ⓬

Set on the cusp of the ninth and 18th arrondissements, La Fourmi is an old bistro that has been converted for today's tastes, with picture windows lighting the spacious, roughshod interior. The classic zinc bar counter is crowned by industrial lights, and an excellent music policy and cool clientele (although they'd have to go some to beat the bar staff) ensure a pile of flyers. As good a place as any to find out what's happening in town.

Le Moulin de la Galette

83 rue Lepic, 18th (01.46.06.84.77). M° Abbesses. **Open** noon-2.45pm, 7.30-11pm Tue-Fri. Closed Aug. €€€. **Bistro**. **Map** p89 B1 ⓭

The Butte Montmartre was once dotted with windmills, and this survivor houses a chic modern restaurant with a few tables in the cobbled courtyard. It's hard to imagine a more picturesque setting in Montmartre, but the kitchen makes an effort nonetheless with dishes such as foie gras with melting beetroot cooked in lemon balm and juniper or suckling pig alongside potato purée. Desserts, such as figs caramelised with muscovado sugar, look like a painter's *tableau*. If you're on a budget, stick to the set menus and order carefully from the wine list.

Pétrelle

34 rue Pétrelle, 9th (01.42.82 11.02). M° Anvers. **Open** 8-10pm Tue-Sat. Closed 4wks July/Aug & 1wk Dec. €€. **Bistro**. **Map** p89 C3 ⓮

Jean-Luc André is as inspired a decorator as he is a cook, and the quirky charm of his dining room has made it popular with fashion designers and film stars. But behind the style is some serious substance. André seeks out the best ingredients from local producers, and the quality shines through. The €29 no-choice menu is huge value (marinated sardines with tomato relish, rosemary-scented rabbit with roasted vegetables, deep purple poached figs) – or you can splash out with à la carte dishes such as tournedos Rossini.

Poussette Café

6 rue Pierre Sémard, 9th (01.78.10.49.00/www.lepoussettecafe.com). M° Cadet or Poissonnière. **Open** 10.30am-6.30pm Tue-Sat. No credit cards. €. **Café**. **Map** p89 C4 ⓯

Fed up with the impracticalities of pushing her pram (*poussette*) into the local café, mother of two Laurence Constant designed her own parent-friendly establishment. This upmarket *salon de thé* caters for the harassed parent (herbal teas, smoothies, quiches and salads) and demanding baby (purées, solids and cuddly toys). You can sign up for magic shows and parenting workshops via the café's website.

Rose Bakery

46 rue des Martyrs, 9th (01.42.82.12.80). M° Notre-Dame-de-Lorette. **Open** 9am-7pm Tue-Fri; 10am-5pm Sat, Sun. Closed 2wks Aug & 1wk Dec. €. **Café**. **Map** p89 B3 ⓰

This English-themed café run by a Franco-British couple stands out for the quality of its ingredients – organic or from small producers – as well as the too-good-to-be-true puddings. The DIY salad plate is crunchily satisfying, but the thin-crusted *pizzettes*, daily soups and occasional risottos are equally good. Don't expect much beyond scones in the morning except at weekends, when brunch is served.

Rouge Passion

NEW *14 rue Jean-Baptiste Pigalle, 9th (www.rouge-passion.fr). M° Pigalle or St Georges.* **Open** noon-3pm Mon; noon-3pm, 6pm-1am Tue-Fri; 6pm-1am Sat. **Wine bar. Map** p89 A3 17

Two bright upstarts (Anne and Sébastien) determined to make their mark on Paris's bar scene are behind this new venture. Offering a long list of wines (from just €3), free *assiettes apéros* (peanuts, olives and tapenades on toast) and decor that is satisfyingly vintage (red banquettes and beige walls), the formula is spot on. A small but mouthwatering selection of hot dishes, salads, cheese and *saucisson* platters help soak up *le vin* (set lunch menu €20, mains from €15). Look out for the wine tasting classes, given by a guest sommelier.

Le Sancerre

35 rue des Abbesses, 18th (01.42.58.08.20). M° Abbesses. **Open** 7am-2am Mon-Thur; 7am-4am Fri, Sat; 9am-2am Sun. **Bar. Map** p89 B2 18

This popular Montmartre institution is home to a frenzied mix of alcohol-fuelled transvestites, tourists, lovers and bobo (bohemian-bourgeois) locals, who all come for the cheap beer (under €4), trashy music and buzzy terrace. The decor inside is scruffy, the service slow and the food (omelettes, *steak-frites*) nothing special; yet there is something irresistibly refreshing about the no-frills approach that makes this bar stand out from the multitude of try-hard cafés in the area.

Spring

28 rue de la Tour d'Auvergne, 9th (01.45.96.05.72). M° Anvers or Cadet. **Open** 8.30pm Tue, Wed; 1pm & 8.30pm Thur, Fri. Closed Aug & 1wk Dec. **€€. Bistro. Map** p89 C3 19

Where do Michelin inspectors go on their day off? To Spring, where young American chef Daniel Rose has wowed the critics since opening this sleek 16-seat bistro a few years ago. He serves a no-choice four-course menu that changes every day according to what he finds at the place des Fêtes market. On a late spring day this might result in a velvety cauliflower soup, chunky octopus salad, poached guinea hen with root vegetables, and baked apple with french toast. Reserve well ahead.

Shopping

Arnaud Delmontel

39 rue des Martyrs, 9th (01.48.78.29.33/www.arnaud-delmontel.com). M° St-Georges. **Open** 7am-8.30pm Mon, Wed-Sun. No credit cards. **Map** p89 B3 20

With its crisp crust and chewy crumb shot through with irregular holes, Delmontel's Renaissance bread is one of the finest in Paris. He puts the same skill into his almond croissants and *tarte au citron à l'ancienne.*

Base One

47bis rue d'Orsel, 18th (01.73.75.37.10/www.baseoneshop.com). M° Anvers. **Open** 12.30-8pm Tue-Sat; 3.30-8pm Sun. Closed 2wks Aug. **Map** p89 B2 21

Clubland duo Princesse Léa and Jean-Louis Faverole squeeze items from little-known local and international designers, plus small, established brands (Fenchurch, Motel, Consortium) into their boutique.

Tati

4 bd de Rochechouart, 18th (01.55.29.52.20/www.tati.fr). M° Barbès Rochechouart. **Open** 10am-7pm Mon-Fri; 9.15am-7pm Sat. **Map** p89 C2 22

The rebirth of chanson

While 1930s Britain was revelling in Hollywood exports, France was whooping it up with its own answer to American culture: Le Music Hall. This form of cabaret (leagues away from the glitzy boob-wobbling of today) saw the rise of stars Charles Trenet, Edith Piaf and Maurice Chevalier, followed after World War II by Jacques Brel, Georges Brassens and Serge Gainsbourg, whose poetry and humour became the emblem of *chanson française*.

While *chanson* artists performed across the city, one small theatre, **Les Trois Baudets** (p94), launched more musical careers between 1947 and 1966 than anywhere else – Gainsbourg, Brel, Hénri Salvador and Brigitte Fontaine all performed there. But in 1967 the unthinkable occurred. The Trois Baudets closed, becoming an erotic cabaret, then a crumbling concert venue, before finally falling into disrepair in 1996. In 2001, after much lobbying (notably by Charles Aznavour) and the rise of the 'new' *chanson française* in the charts thanks to next-generation songwriters like Bénabar, Anaïs and Vincent Delerm, it was decided that Paris lacked a theatre entirely devoted to francophone music, and that Les Trois Baudets – the cradle of *chanson* – should be brought back to life.

Eight years on the makeover is spectacular. All dolled up in black and red, with a 250-seater theatre, an enviable sound system, two bars and a restaurant, it offers enough musical genres (rock, electro, folk and slam) to appeal to a wide range of fans. And for the artists themselves, getting such high-profile stage space is a treat indeed.

Expect to find anything from T-shirts to wedding dresses, as well as bargain children's clothes and household goods at this discount heaven.

Nightlife

La Cigale/La Boule Noire

120 bd de Rochechouart, 18th (01.49.25.81.75/www.lacigale.fr). M° Anvers or Pigalle. **Open** times vary. **Map** p89 B3 ㉓

The lovely, horseshoe-shaped theatre La Cigale is linked to more cosy venue La Boule Noire, good for catching cult-ish visiting acts.

Le Divan du Monde

75 rue des Martyrs, 18th (01.42.52.02.46/www.divandumonde.com). M° Abbesses or Pigalle. **Open** 8pm-2am Tue-Thur; 7.30pm-5am Fri, Sat. **Admission** €6-€30. **Map** p89 B3 ㉔

After a drink in the Fourmi opposite, pop over to the Divan for one-off parties and regular events. The upstairs specialises in VJ events, and downstairs holds dub, reggae, funk and world music club nights.

Elysée Montmartre

72 bd de Rochechouart, 18th (01.44.92.45.36/www.elyseemontmartre.com). M° Anvers. **Open** midnight-6am Fri, Sat. **Admission** €10-€15. **Map** p89 C2 ㉕

A gig venue and club, the Elysée hosts big nights by outside promoters, such as Open House, Panik and Nightfever.

Folies Pigalle

11 pl Pigalle, 9th (01.48.78.55.25/www.folies-pigalle.com). M° Pigalle. **Open** midnight-dawn Mon-Thur; midnight-noon Fri, Sat; 6pm-midnight Sun. **Admission** €20 (incl 1 drink); €7 Sun eve. **Map** p89 B3 ㉖

The racy Folies Pigalle's programme includes everything from dancehall and hip hop to techno and electro, go-go dancers, striptease and Paris's only transsexual spectacle.

Au Lapin Agile

22 rue des Saules, 18th (01.46.06.85.87/www.au-lapin-agile.com). M° Lamarck Caulaincourt. **Shows** 9pm-2am Tue-Sun. **Admission** Show (incl 1 drink) €24; €17 reductions (except Sat & public hols). No credit cards. **Map** p89 B1 ㉗

The prices have gone up, tourists outnumber the locals and they sell their own compilation CDs these days, but that's all that seems to have changed since this quaint, pink bar first opened its doors in 1860.

Moulin Rouge

82 bd de Clichy, 18th (01.53.09.82.82/www.moulin-rouge.com). M° Blanche. **Dinner** 7pm. **Shows** 9pm, 11pm daily. **Admission** *9pm show* (incl champagne) €99. *11pm show* (incl champagne) €89. *Dinner & show* €145-€175. **Map** p89 A2 ㉘

Toulouse-Lautrec posters, glittery lampposts and fake trees lend tacky charm to this revue, while 60 Doriss dancers cavort with faultless synchronisation. Costumes are flamboyant and the *entr'acte* acts funny. The downer is the space, with tables packed in. There's also a twice-monthly matinée.

Nouvelle Athènes

9 pl Pigalle, 9th (01.49.70.03.99). M° Pigalle. **Open** 10am-2am Mon-Sat. **Concerts** 10.30pm Tue-Sat. **Admission** varies. **Map** p89 B3 ㉙

Nouvelle Athènes has a weight of history behind it. It was the café in Degas' *L'Absinthe*, a striptease joint frequented by the Nazis and Liberation troops, then rock venue New Moon, before burning down in 2004. The place has been resurrected as Pigalle's first jazz venue for decades.

Les Trois Baudets

64 bd de Clichy, 18th (01.42.62.33.33/www.lestroisbaudets.com). M° Blanche. **Open** times vary. **Admission** €12-€15. **Map** p89 A2 ㉚

See box p93.

Point Ephémère p99

North-east Paris

Traditionally, the area north and north-east of place de la République was a staunchly proletarian district, shot through by the Canal St-Martin that brought raw goods and rough barges into the city. Many streets around here are still tatty and dingy, but others, especially those near the canal, have been fashionable for at least ten years. Gentrification as such is not much in evidence – unless you take the rise in rents as an index, in which case it's rampant. But to the visitor, unconcerned by property prices, this part of Paris has much to offer: there's a palpable buzz and strong sense of authenticity on streets such as rue du Fbg-St-Denis.

Sights & museums

Canauxrama

13 quai de la Loire, 19th (01.42.39.15.00/01.42.39.11.24/ www.canauxrama.fr). **Tickets** €15; free-€8 reductions. **Map** p97 C1 ❶

If the Seine palls, then take a trip up the city's second waterway, the Canal St-Martin. The tree-lined canal is a pretty and characterful sight, and the trip even goes underground for a stretch, where the tunnel walls are enlivened by a light show.

Gare du Nord

Rue de Dunkerque, 10th (08.91.36.20. 20). M° Gare du Nord. **Map** p97 A2 ❷

The grandest of the great 19th-century train stations (and Eurostar terminal since 1994) was designed by Hittorff between 1861 and 1864. The stone façade, with Ionic capitals and statues representing towns served by the station, hides a vast iron-and-glass vault.

Musée de la Musique

Cité de la Musique, 221 av Jean-Jaurès, 19th (01.44.84.45.00/www.cite-musique.fr). M° Porte de Pantin. **Open** noon-6pm Tue-Sat; 10am-6pm Sun. **Admission** €8; free-€6.40 reductions. **Map** p97 E1 ❸

See box p99.

Musée de la Musique p95

Parc des Buttes-Chaumont

Rue Botzaris, rue Manin, rue de Crimée, 19th. M° Buttes Chaumont. **Open** *Oct-Apr* 7am-8.15pm daily. *May, mid Aug-Sept* 7am-9.15pm daily. *June-mid Aug* 7am-10.15pm daily. **Map** p97 E2 ④

This lovely park, with its meandering paths and vertical cliffs, was designed by Adolphe Alphand for Haussmann in the 1860s. A bridge (cheerfully named the Pont des Suicides) crosses the lake to an island crowned by a mini-temple.

Eating & drinking

Bar Ourcq

68 quai de la Loire, 19th (01.42.40. 12.26). M° Laumière. **Open** 3pm-midnight Wed, Thur; 3pm-2am Fri, Sat; 3-10pm Sun. *Summer* 5-9.30pm Wed-Fri, Sun; 3pm-2am Sat. No credit cards. **Bar. Map** p97 D1 ⑤

This was one of the first hip joints to hit the Canal de l'Ourcq, with an embankment broad enough to accommodate *pétanque* games (ask at the bar) and a cluster of deckchairs. The cabin-like interior is cosy, and drinks are listed in a hit parade of prices, starting with €2.40 for a *demi* or glass of red. Pastas at €8, exhibitions and a regular DJ spot keep the cool clientele sated. Closed on rainy weekdays in summer.

A la Bière

104 av Simon-Bolivar, 19th (01.42.39. 83.25). M° Colonel Fabien. **Open** noon-3pm, 7pm-1.30am daily. **€. Brasserie. Map** p97 D2 ⑥

A la Bière looks like one of those nondescript corner brasseries with noisy pop music, but what makes it stand out is an amazingly good-value prix fixe full of fine bistro favourites. Starters of thinly sliced pig's cheek with a nice French dressing on the salad, and a home-made rabbit terrine exceed expectations. Mains live up to what's gone before: charcoal-grilled entrecôte with hand-cut chips, and Lyonnais sausages with potatoes drenched in olive oil, garlic and parsley. This is one of the few bargains left in Paris – let's hope it stays that way.

Chez Jeanette

47 rue du Fbg-St Denis, 10th (01.47.70.30.89). M° Château d'Eau or Strasbourg St-Denis. **Open** 8am-2am daily. **€. Café. Map** p97 A3 ⑦

When she sold her café back in March 2007, Jeanette handed over to the young team from Chez Justine. Now the awful 1940s lights, tobacco-stained wallpaper depicting the Moulin Rouge and PVC-covered banquettes have been rewarded with a Fooding prize for decor, and the café is fast becoming one

North-east Paris

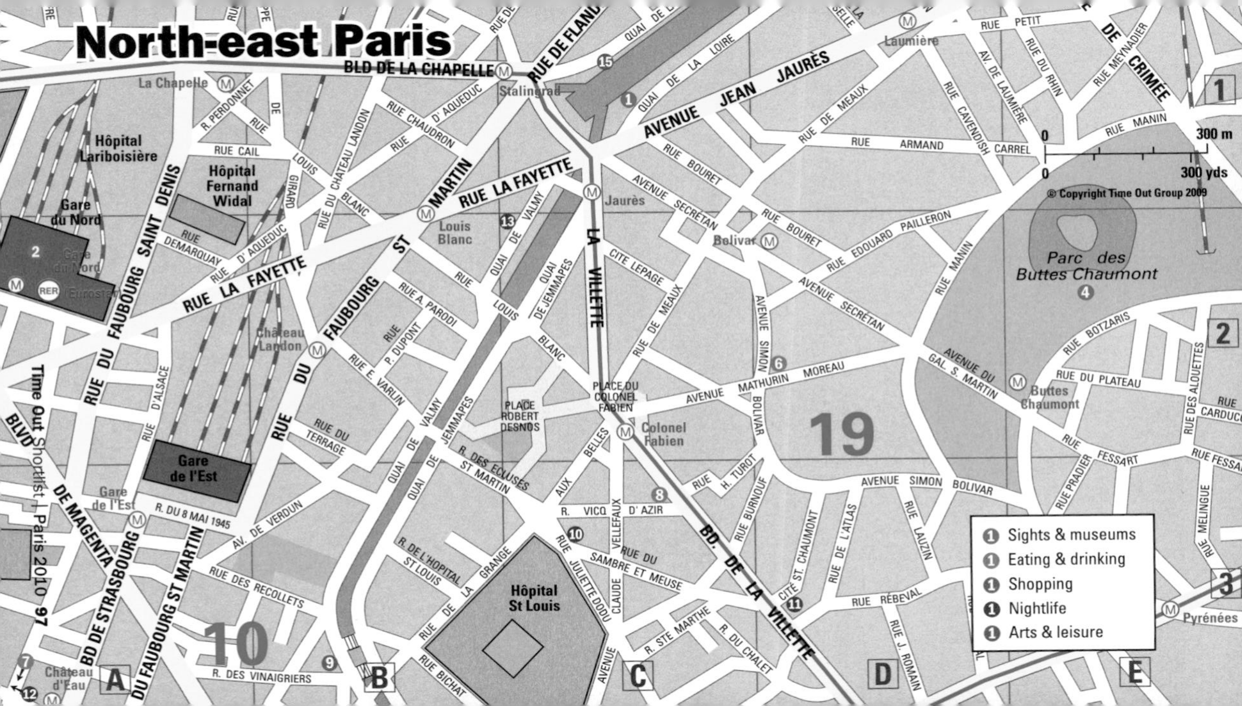

Antoine et Lili

of Paris's hippest spots for an aperitif. There's a *plat du jour* at lunch and plates of cheese and charcuterie at night; at 8pm, the fluorescent lights go off and candlelight takes over.

L'Ile Enchantée/ Wash Bar

NEW *65 bd de la Villette, 10th (01.42.01.67.99/www.washbar-lg.com). M° Colonel Fabien.* **Open** 8am-2am Mon-Fri; 5pm-2am Sat. *Wash Bar* 10am-8pm Mon-Fri; 4-8pm Sat. **Bar**. **Map** p97 C3 ❽

This house/electro DJ bar has made the bizarre decision to turn its entire first floor over to Korean conglomerate LG, which has installed the Wash Bar. Grab a cocktail (€6.50) downstairs in the retro-chic bar, then head upstairs to your choice of zones. There's the 'bureau' (surf the net), the 'lounge' (watch TV) or the 'launderette' – a high-tech installation of LG's latest washing machines, all free to use. It's the only excuse to get your knickers off in the bobo HQ that is the Canal St-Martin.

Shopping

Antoine et Lili

95 quai de Valmy, 10th (01.40.37.41.55/www.antoineetlili.com). M° Jacques Bonsergent. **Open** 11am-7pm Mon, Sun; 11am-8pm Tue-Fri; 10am-8pm Sat. **Map** p97 B3 ❾

Antoine et Lili's fuchsia-pink, custard-yellow and apple-green shopfronts, reflected in the Canal St-Martin, are a new raver's dream. The designer's clothes, often in wraparound styles, adapt to all sizes and shapes. The Canal St-Martin 'village' comprises womenswear, a kitsch home decoration boutique and childrenswear.

Nightlife

Baxo

NEW *21 rue Juliette Dodu, 10th (01.42.02.99.71/www.baxo.fr). M° Colonel Fabien.* **Open** 9am-3pm, 7pm-2am Mon-Fri; 5pm-2am Sat, Sun. **Admission** free. **Map** p97 C3 ❿

Baxo is a spanking new hybrid venue that triples as a restaurant, bar and DJ lounge for an übercool clientele. Friday nights are reserved for resident DJs, while Saturdays feature live bands and guest splicers. The food is satisfyingly innovative.

Café Chéri(e)

44 bd de la Villette, 19th (01.42.02.02.05). M° Belleville. **Open** 8am-2am daily. **Admission** free. **Map** p97 D3 ⓫

A popular DJ bar, especially in summer, when fashionistas flock to the terrace. Live music is played from Thursdays to Saturdays after 10pm. Expect anything from DJ Jet Boy's electro punk to rock, funk, hip hop, rare groove, indie, dance, jazz, and '80s classics.

New Morning

7-9 rue des Petites-Ecuries, 10th (01.45.23.51.41/www.newmorning.com). **Concerts** 9pm daily. **Admission** €15-€21. **Map** p97 A3 ⓬

One of the best places for the latest cutting-edge jazz exponents, with a policy that also embraces *chanson*, blues, world and sophisticated pop.

Point Ephémère

200 quai de Valmy, 10th (01.40.34.02.48/www.pointephemere.org). Mº Jaurès or Louis Blanc. **Open** noon-2am daily. **Concerts** 8.30pm daily. **Map** p97 C2 ⑬

This converted warehouse is a classy affair, bringing together up-and-coming local rock, jazz and world gigs with a decent restaurant, dance and recording studios and exhibitions.

Arts & leisure

Hammam Med Centre

43-45 rue Petit, 19th (01.42.02.31.05/www.hammammed.com). Mº Ourcq. **Open** *Women* 11am-10pm Mon-Fri; 9am-7pm Sun. *Mixed (swimwear required)* 10am-9pm Sat. **Map** p97 E1 ⑭

This hammam is hard to beat – spotless mosaic-tiled surroundings, flowered sarongs and a relaxing pool. The exotic 'Forfait florale' option (€139) will have you enveloped in rose petals and massaged with *huile d'Argan* from Morocco, while the more simple hammam and *gommage* followed by mint tea and pastries is €39. Plan to spend a few hours here, as the soft-voiced staff take things at their own pace.

MK2

14 quai de la Seine, 19th (08.92.69.84.84/www.mk2.fr). Mº Stalingrad. **Open** times vary. **Admission** €9.90; €5.90-€7.20 reductions. **Map** p97 C1 ⑮

MK2's mini multiplex on the quai de la Loire was seen as a key factor in the social rise of what had previously been a scuzzy part of town. Now the chain has opened another multiplex across the water – with a boat taking punters from one to the other. Programming is as innovative and international as at other MK2s in the city.

Perfect pitch

The Musée de la Musique is sounding better than ever.

Ever since opening in 1997, the Cité de la Musique complex at Parc de la Villette has earned a reputation for cutting-edge innovation – and its recently revamped **Musée de la Musique** (p95) is no exception.

The museum's collection is composed of some remarkable restored instruments from the old Conservatoire, scale models of opera houses and concert halls, and music-inspired artworks. But it's the museum's much-imitated use of sound that has put it on the map. Throughout the day, concerts are organised on stages inside the museum space, while an individual audio guide allows visitors to hear excerpts from the collection's different instruments simply by approaching a display. As part of the recent renovation, the audio guides have been updated, giving visitors the choice of three different sound-based tours (including one for the disabled). Extra sound samples have also been recorded using instruments from the collection, many of which date from the 17th and 18th century.

Another major objective of the revamp has been to give more importance to 20th-century and world music. Exhibits now include jazz ace Django Reinhardt's guitar, Stéphane Grappelli's violin and Frank Zappa's modular synthesiser, and future plans include a section dedicated to pop music.

Espace Claude Berri

The Marais & Eastern Paris

Beaubourg and its eastern neighbour the Marais are a chunk of town largely untouched by Haussmann, which means lots of small streets in which to get lost and – to a degree – a sense of old Paris. The clean-up operation begun in the Marais in the 1960s by culture minister André Malraux did much to primp and preserve the old buildings. However, although much of the fabric is ancient, the people and the activities are resolutely fashionable and exuberant. This, famously, is the city's gay quarter, but it's just as popular with other inclinations – museums, boutiques, bars and restaurants abound, and the crowds, particularly at the weekends, can be oppressive. Come with time, and money, to spare.

A little further east is the edgy Oberkampf district, home to some of the city's best bars and a nightlife hub for the last decade.

Sights & museums

Atelier Brancusi

Piazza Beaubourg, 4th (01.44.78.12.33/ www.centrepompidou.fr). M° Hôtel de Ville or Rambuteau. **Open** 2-6pm Mon, Wed-Sun. **Admission** free. **Map** p102 A2 ❶

When Constantin Brancusi died in 1957, he left his studio and its contents to the state, and it was later moved and rebuilt by the Centre Pompidou. His fragile works in wood and plaster, the endless columns and streamlined bird forms show how Brancusi revolutionised sculpture.

Centre Pompidou (Musée National d'Art Moderne)

Rue St-Martin, 4th (01.44.78.12.33/ www.centrepompidou.fr). M° Hôtel de Ville or Rambuteau. **Open** 11am-9pm (last entry 8pm) Mon, Wed-Sun (until 11pm some exhibitions); 11am-

11pm Thur. **Admission** *Museum & exhibitions* €10-€12; free-€8 reductions. **Map** p102 A2 ❷
The primary colours, exposed pipes and air ducts make this one of the best-known sights in Paris. The Centre Pompidou (or 'Beaubourg') holds the largest collection of modern art in Europe, rivalled only in its breadth and quality by MOMA in New York. For the main collection, buy tickets on the ground floor and take the escalators to level four for post-1960s art. Level five spans 1905 to 1960. Masterful ensembles let you see the span of Matisse's career on canvas and in bronze, the variety of Picasso's invention, and the development of cubic orphism by Sonia and Robert Delaunay. Others on the hits list include Braque, Duchamp, Mondrian, Malevich, Kandinsky, Dalí, Giacometti, Ernst, Miró, Calder, Magritte, Rothko and Pollock.

Level four houses post-'60s art. Its thematic rooms concentrate on the career of one artist or focus on movements such as Anti-form or *arte povera*. Recent acquisitions line the central corridor, and at the far end you can find architecture and design. Video art and installations by the likes of Mathieu Mercier and Dominique Gonzalez-Foerster are in a room given over to *nouvelle création*.

Cimetière du Père-Lachaise

Bd de Ménilmontant, 20th (01.55.25.82.10). M° Père-Lachaise. **Open** *6 Nov-15 Mar* 8am-5.30pm Mon-Fri; 8.30am-5.30pm Sat; 9am-5.30pm Sun. *16 Mar-5 Nov* 8am-6pm Mon-Fri; 8.30am-6pm Sat; 9am-6pm Sun & hols. **Map** p103 F2 ❸
Père-Lachaise is the celebrity cemetery – it has almost anyone French, talented and dead that you care to mention. Not even French, for that matter. Creed and nationality have never prevented entry: you just had to have lived or died in Paris or have an allotted space in a family tomb. Finding a particular grave can be tricky. Requests for information from the entry guards will be met with a shrug, so buy a €2 map from the hawkers at the Père-Lachaise métro entrance or from shops nearby. Highlights include Chopin's medallion portrait and the muse of Music, famous neighbours La Fontaine and Molière, who knew each other in real life and now share the same fenced-off plot, and Victor Noir. This journalist, shot by Napoleon's cousin Prince Pierre, rests underneath a bronze likeness, its groin rubbed so often by women hoping to conceive that it gleams.

Espace Claude Berri

NEW *8 rue Rambuteau, 3rd (01.44.54.88.50). M° Rambuteau.* **Open** 11am-1pm, 2-7pm Tue-Sat. Closed Aug. **Admission** free. **Map** p102 A2 ❹
Claude Berri, who died in January 2009, was best known as one of France's most successful film directors and producers, but he also made a name for himself in another field: the world of contemporary art. The aim of this space is to alternate themed exhibitions of works from Berri's private collection with solo shows organised around artists, critics or gallery owners.

Hôtel de Sully

62 rue St-Antoine, 4th (01.42.74.47.75). M° St-Paul. **Open** noon-6.30pm Tue-Fri; 10am-6.30pm Sat, Sun. **Admission** €5; €2.50 reductions. **Map** p102 C4 ❺
With the Jeu de Paume, the former Patrimoine Photographique forms part of the two-site home for the Centre National de la Photographie.

Hôtel de Ville

29 rue de Rivoli, 4th (01.42.76.40.40/www.paris.fr). M° Hôtel de Ville. **Open** 10am-7pm Mon-Sat. Tours by appointment only. **Map** p102 A3 ❻
The palatial, multi-purpose Hôtel de Ville is the heart of the city administration, and a place in which to entertain visiting dignitaries. Free exhibitions

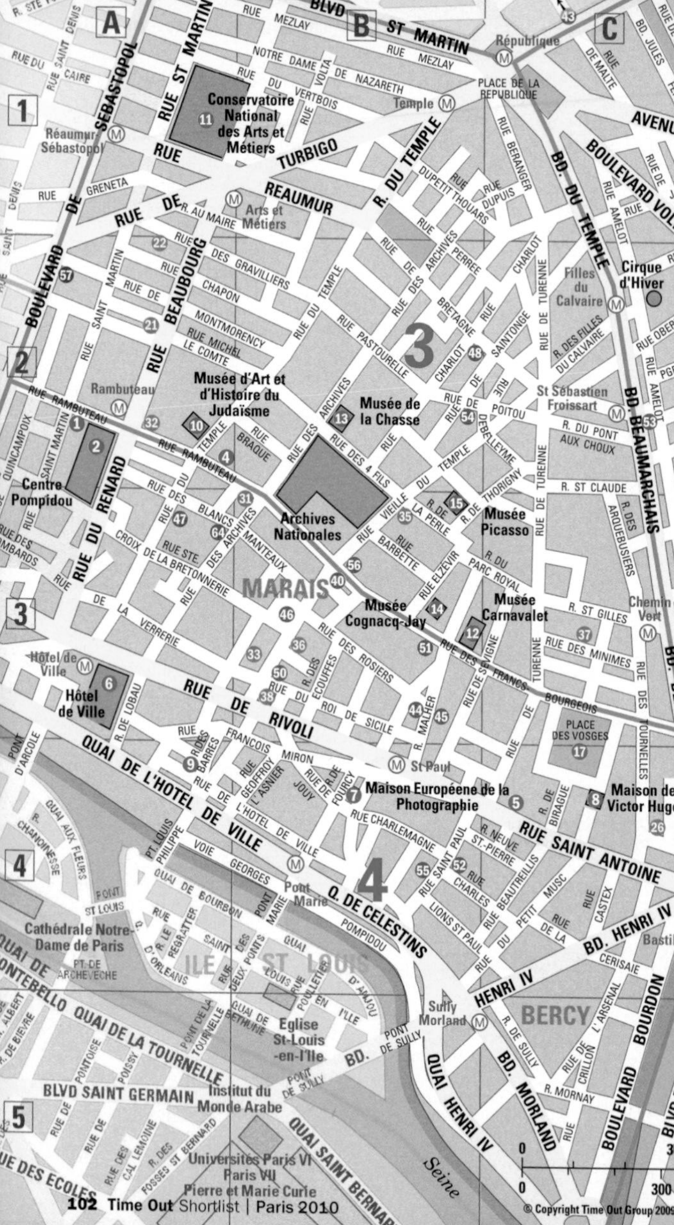
A
B
C
1
2
3
4
5
R. STE FOY
RUE DU CAIRE
RUE SAINT DENIS
BOULEVARD DE SEBASTOPOL
RUE ST MARTIN
BLVD ST MARTIN
RUE MEZLAY
RUE NOTRE DAME DE NAZARETH
RUE DU VERTBOIS
RUE VOLTA
République
PLACE DE LA REPUBLIQUE
Temple
RUE DE MALTE
BD. JULES FERRY
AVENUE
BOULEVARD VOLTAIRE
Conservatoire National des Arts et Métiers
Réaumur-Sébastopol
RUE TURBIGO
RUE GRENETA
RUE REAUMUR
Arts et Métiers
R. AU MAIRE
R. DU TEMPLE
RUE DUPETIT THOUARS
RUE DUPUIS
RUE BERANGER
BD. DU TEMPLE
RUE AMELOT
RUE DE BEAUBOURG
RUE DES GRAVILLIERS
RUE CHAPON
RUE DE MONTMORENCY
RUE MICHEL LE COMTE
RUE DES ARCHIVES
RUE PERREE
RUE CHARLOT
RUE DE BRETAGNE
RUE DE SAINTONGE
RUE DE TURENNE
Filles du Calvaire
Cirque d'Hiver
R. DES FILLES DU CALVAIRE
RUE OBERKAMPF
RUE PASTOURELLE
3
Musée d'Art et d'Histoire du Judaïsme
Musée de la Chasse
Rambuteau
RUE RAMBUTEAU
RUE DE POITOU
RUE DEBELLEYME
St Sébastien Froissart
R. DU PONT AUX CHOUX
BD. BEAUMARCHAIS
RUE QUINCAMPOIX
RUE SAINT MARTIN
Centre Pompidou
RUE DU RENARD
RUE DU TEMPLE
RUE BRAQUE
RUE DES 4 FILS
R. DE THORIGNY
R. ST CLAUDE
R. DES ARQUEBUSIERS
RUE DES BLANCS MANTEAUX
Archives Nationales
RUE VIEILLE DU TEMPLE
R. DE LA PERLE
Musée Picasso
RUE DES LOMBARDS
RUE STE. CROIX DE LA BRETONNERIE
RUE BARBETTE
RUE ELZEVIR
R. DU PARC ROYAL
MARAIS
Musée Cognacq-Jay
Musée Carnavalet
R. ST GILLES
Chemin Vert
RUE DE LA VERRERIE
RUE DES ROSIERS
RUE DES FRANCS BOURGEOIS
RUE DES MINIMES
RUE DES TOURNELLES
Hôtel de Ville
RUE DE RIVOLI
R. DE LOBAU
RUE DU ROI DE SICILE
R. DES ECOUFFES
RUE MALHER
RUE DE SEVIGNE
PLACE DES VOSGES
PONT D'ARCOLE
QUAI DE L'HOTEL DE VILLE
R. DES BARRES
RUE FRANCOIS MIRON
St Paul
RUE GEOFFROY L'ASNIER
RUE DE JOUY
R. DE FOURCY
Maison Européene de la Photographie
R. DE BIRAGUE
Maison de Victor Hugo
QUAI AUX FLEURS
R. CHANOINESSE
RUE CHARLEMAGNE
RUE SAINT PAUL
R. NEUVE ST.-PIERRE
RUE SAINT ANTOINE
PT. LOUIS PHILIPPE
VOIE GEORGES POMPIDOU
4
Pont Marie
Q. DE CELESTINS
RUE CHARLES
RUE BEAUTREILLIS
RUE DU PETIT MUSC
RUE CASTEX
RUE DE LA CERISAIE
BD. HENRI IV
Bastille
PONT ST LOUIS
QUAI DE BOURBON
RUE LIONS ST PAUL
Cathédrale Notre-Dame de Paris
PT. DE ARCHEVECHE
ILE ST LOUIS
RUE LE REGRATTIER
RUE SAINT LOUIS EN L'ILE
RUE DES DEUX PONTS
RUE POULLETIER
QUAI D'ANJOU
QUAI D'ORLEANS
QUAI DE MONTEBELLO
QUAI DE LA TOURNELLE
QUAI DE BETHUNE
Eglise St-Louis -en-l'Ile
PONT DE SULLY
Sully Morland
BERCY
R. DE SULLY
RUE DE L'ARSENAL
RUE DE CRILLON
BOULEVARD BOURDON
R. MORNAY
BD. MORLAND
QUAI HENRI IV
BLVD SAINT GERMAIN
Institut du Monde Arabe
RUE DE PONTOISE
RUE DE POISSY
RUE DES FOSSES ST BERNARD
RUE DU CAL LEMOINE
RUE DE BIEVRE
RUE DES ECOLES
QUAI SAINT BERNARD
Universites Paris VI Paris VII Pierre et Marie Curie
Seine
0
300
© Copyright Time Out Group 2009

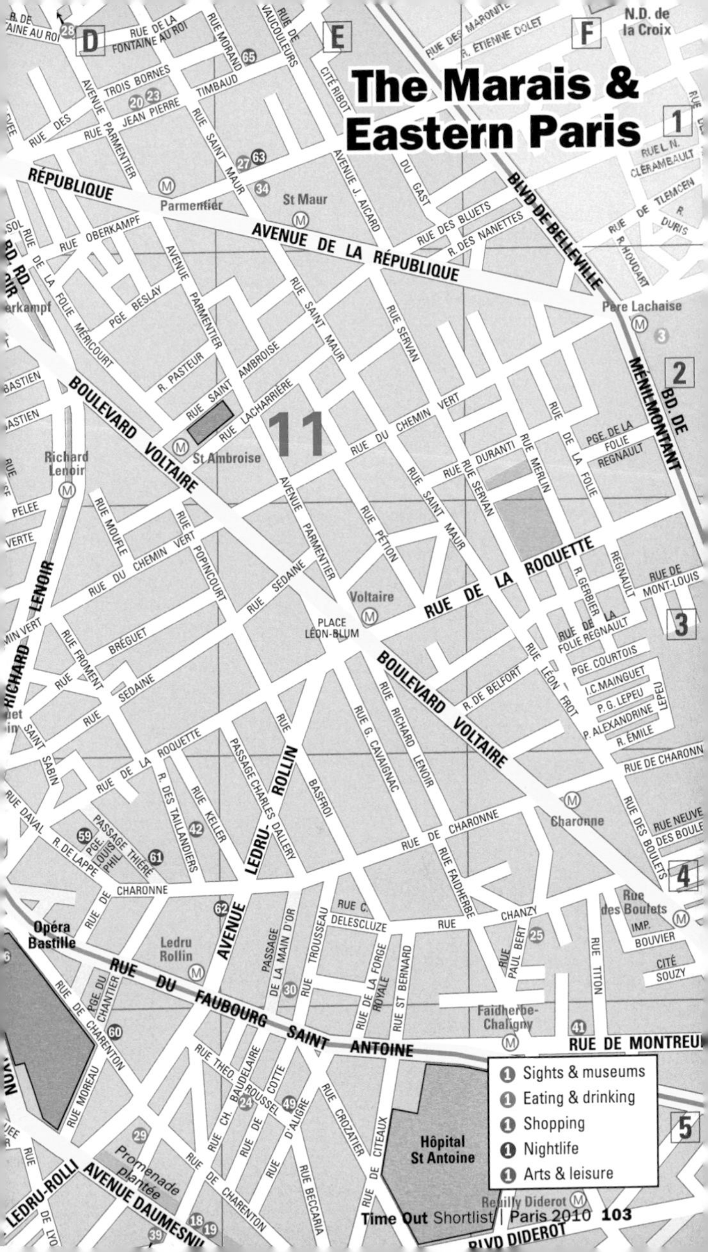
The Marais & Eastern Paris
D
E
F
1
2
3
4
5
11
N.D. de la Croix
Rue de la Fontaine au Roi
Rue Morand
Rue de Vaucouleurs
Cité Ribot
Rue des Maronites
R. Étienne Dolet
Rue des Trois Bornes
Rue Jean Pierre Timbaud
Avenue Parmentier
Rue Saint Maur
Avenue J. Aicard
Rue du Gast
Rue L. N. Clérambault
Rue de Tlemcen
R. Duris
R. Houdart
Blvd de Belleville
Rue des Bluets
R. des Nanettes
République
Parmentier
St Maur
Avenue de la République
Rue Oberkampf
Rue de la Folie Méricourt
Pge Beslay
Rue Servan
Père Lachaise
Bd. de Ménilmontant
R. Pasteur
Rue Saint Ambroise
Rue Lacharrière
St Ambroise
Rue du Chemin Vert
Rue Duranti
Rue Merlin
Rue de la Folie Regnault
Pge. de la Folie Regnault
Richard Lenoir
Boulevard Voltaire
Rue Moufle
Rue Popincourt
Rue Pétion
Rue de la Roquette
R. Gerbier
Rue de Mont-Louis
Voltaire
Place Léon-Blum
Rue Sedaine
Bréguet
Rue Froment
Rue Léon Frot
R. de Belfort
Pge. Courtois
I.C. Mainguet
P. G. Lepeu
P. Alexandrine
R. Émile
Lepeu
Rue Richard Lenoir
Rue G. Cavaignac
Rue Basfroi
Passage Charles Dallery
Ledru-Rollin
R. des Taillandiers
Rue Keller
Rue Saint Sabin
Rue Daval
R. de Lappe
Passage Thiéré
Pge. Louis Phil.
Rue de Charonne
Charonne
Rue des Boulets
Rue Neuve des Boulets
Rue Faidherbe
Rue Chanzy
Rue Paul Bert
Rue des Boulets
Imp. Bouvier
Cité Souzy
Rue Titon
Rue C. Delescluze
Opéra Bastille
Ledru Rollin
Avenue Ledru-Rollin
Passage de la Main d'Or
Rue Trousseau
Rue de la Forge Royale
Rue St Bernard
Faidherbe-Chaligny
Rue du Faubourg Saint Antoine
Rue de Montreuil
Pge. du Chantier
Rue de Charenton
Rue Moreau
Rue Théo. Roussel
Rue Ch. Baudelaire
Rue de Cotte
Rue d'Aligre
Rue Crozatier
Rue de Cîteaux
Rue Beccaria
Hôpital St Antoine
Promenade plantée
Avenue Daumesnil
Reuilly Diderot
Blvd Diderot
Sights & museums
Eating & drinking
Shopping
Nightlife
Arts & leisure

are held in the Salon d'Accueil (10am-6pm Mon-Fri). The rest of the building, accessible by weekly tours (book in advance), has parquet floors, marble statues and painted ceilings.

Maison Européenne de la Photographie

5-7 rue de Fourcy, 4th (01.44.78.75.00/ www.mep-fr.org). M° St-Paul. **Open** 11am-7.30pm Wed-Sun. **Admission** €6; free-€3 reductions. Map p102 B4 ❼

Probably the capital's best photography exhibition space, hosting retrospectives by Larry Clark and Martine Barrat, along with work by emerging photographers. The building, an airy mansion with a modern extension, contains a huge permanent collection.

Maison de Victor Hugo

Hôtel de Rohan-Guéménée, 6 pl des Vosges, 4th (01.42.72.10.16/www. musee-hugo.paris.fr). M° Bastille or St-Paul. **Open** 10am-6pm Tue-Sun. **Admission** free. *Exhibitions* prices vary. **Map** p102 C4 ❽

Victor Hugo lived here from 1833 to 1848, and today the house is a museum devoted to the life and work of the great man. On display are his first editions, nearly 500 drawings and, more bizarrely, Hugo's home-made furniture.

Le Mémorial de la Shoah

17 rue Geoffroy-l'Asnier, 4th (01.42.77.44.72/www.memorialdela shoah.org). M° Pont Marie or St-Paul. **Open** 10am-6pm Mon-Wed, Fri-Sun; 10am-10pm Thur. *Research centre* 10am-5.30pm Mon-Wed, Fri, Sun; 10am-7.30pm Thur. **Admission** free. **Map** p102 A4 ❾

Airport-style security checks mean queues, but don't let that put you off: the Mémorial du Martyr Juif Inconnu is an impressively presented and moving memorial to the Holocaust. Enter via the Wall of Names, where limestone slabs are engraved with the first and last names of each of the 76,000 Jews deported from France from 1942 to 1944 with, as an inscription reminds the visitor, the say-so of the Vichy government. The excoriation continues in the basement-level exhibition, which documents the plight of French and European Jews through photographs, texts, films and individual stories.

Musée d'Art et d'Histoire du Judaïsme

Hôtel de St-Aignan, 71 rue du Temple, 3rd (01.53.01.86.60/www.mahj.org). M° Rambuteau. **Open** 11am-6pm Mon-Fri; 10am-6pm Sun. Closed Jewish hols. **Admission** €6.80; free-€4.50 reductions. **Map** p102 A2 ❿

Set in a Marais mansion, this museum sprang from the collection of a private association formed in 1948 to safeguard Jewish heritage after the Holocaust. Displays illustrate ceremonies, rites and learning, and show how styles were adapted across the globe through examples of Jewish decorative arts. Photographic portraits of modern French Jews, each of whom tells his or her own story on the audio soundtrack, bring a contemporary edge. The Holocaust is marked by Boris Taslitzky's stark sketches from Buchenwald and Christian Boltanski's courtyard memorial to the Jews who lived in the building in 1939, 13 of whom died in the camps.

Event highlights Joseph Roth: L'Exil à Paris 1933-1939 (until 27 Sept 2009)

Musée des Arts et Métiers

60 rue Réaumur, 3rd (01.53.01.82.00/ www.arts-et-metiers.net). M° Arts et Métiers. **Open** 10am-6pm Tue, Wed, Fri-Sun; 10am-9.30pm Thur. **Admission** €6.50; free-€4.50 reductions. **Map** p102 A1 ⓫

Europe's oldest science museum was founded in 1794 by the constitutional bishop Henri Grégoire. Housed in the former Benedictine priory of St-Martin-des-Champs, it became a museum proper in 1819; it's a fascinating, well laid out and vast collection of treasures. Here are beautiful astrolabes, celestial spheres, barometers, clocks, some of Pascal's calculating devices, the Lumière brothers' cinematograph, an enormous 1938 TV set, and still larger exhibits like Cugnot's 1770 'Fardier' (the first ever powered vehicle) and Clément Ader's steam-powered Avion 3. The visit concludes in the chapel, which contains old cars, a scale model of the Statue of Liberty, the monoplane in which Blériot crossed the Channel in 1909, and a Foucault pendulum.

Musée Carnavalet

23 rue de Sévigné, 3rd (01.44.59.58.58/www.carnavalet.paris.fr). M° St-Paul. **Open** 10am-6pm Tue-Sun. **Admission** free. *Exhibitions* €7; free-€5.50 reductions. **Map** p102 B3 ⓬
Here, 140 rooms depict the history of Paris, from pre-Roman Gaul to the 20th century. Original 16th-century rooms house Renaissance collections, with portraits by Clouet and furniture and pictures relating to the Wars of Religion. The first floor covers the period up to 1789 and neighbouring Hôtel Le Peletier de St-Fargeau covers the period from 1789 onwards. Displays relating to 1789 detail that year's convoluted politics and bloodshed, with prints and memorabilia, including a chunk of the Bastille. There are items belonging to Napoleon, a cradle given by the city to Napoleon III, and a reconstruction of Proust's bedroom.
Event highlights La Révolution Française à Paris – Trésors cachés du Musée Carnavalet (until 3 Jan 2010)

Musée de la Chasse et de la Nature

Hôtel Guénégaud, 62 rue des Archives, 3rd (01.53.01.92.40/www.chassenature.org). M° Rambuteau. **Open** 11am-6pm Tue-Sun. **Admission** €6; free-€4.50 reductions. **Map** p102 B2 ⓭
A two-year overhaul turned the three-floor hunting museum from a musty old-timer into something really rather special. When it reopened in 2007, it had kept the layout and proportions of

Solid rock

Welcome to Paris's most rock 'n' roll district.

Ten years ago, the area around Bastille was dominated by funky, Latin-tinged club sounds. The sole outpost of rock culture was **Le Pop In** (105 rue Amelot, 11th), an eccentric English pub-meets-indie club on the edge of the 11th, but hugely influential on what has been happening in the Bastille since. With a dance area that made you feel like you were having a party in someone's garage, it set the tone with a largely anglophone, rock-leaning musical policy.

The first bar to follow Le Pop In's lead was **Planète Mars** (21 rue Keller, 11th) in 2004, this time with a location right in the heart of Bastille. It rapidly became a favoured haunt for musicians, and thus the territory for Paris's most rock 'n' roll district was staked out. Two streets along from that, on passage Thière, you can now find **La Mécanique Ondulatoire** (p115), a three-level bar with singles on the wall and a concert room downstairs. The co-owner, Pascale Biville, says: 'The principle idea was to open a rock bar. We found the building charming – only afterwards did we find out there were these other rock bars in the area.' Five minutes away in passage Josset, though, Remi Tettiravou of **Le Motel** (p115) makes no bones about the choice of location. 'We're here because it's the 11th, absolutely. It has become *the* area for people who are into rock.'

Musée National Picasso

the two adjoining 17th-century mansions it occupies, but many of its new exhibits and settings seem more suited to an art gallery than a museum. The history of hunting and man's larger relationship with the natural world are examined in things like a quirky series of wooden cabinets devoted to the owl, wolf, boar and stag, each equipped with a bleached skull, small drawers you can open to reveal droppings and footprint casts, and a binocular eyepiece you can peer into for footage of the animal in the wild. A cleverly simple mirrored box contains a stuffed hen that is replicated into infinity on every side; and a stuffed fox is set curled up on a Louis XVI chair.

Musée Cognacq-Jay

Hôtel Donon, 8 rue Elzévir, 3rd (01.40.27.07.21/www.paris.fr/musees). M° St-Paul. **Open** 10am-6pm Tue-Sun. **Admission** free. **Map** p102 B3 ⑭

This museum houses a collection put together in the early 1900s by La Samaritaine founder Ernest Cognacq and his wife Marie-Louise Jay. They stuck mainly to 18th-century French works, focusing on artists such as Watteau, Fragonard, Boucher, Greuze and pastellist Quentin de la Tour, though some English artists (Reynolds, Romney, Lawrence) and Dutch and Flemish names (an early Rembrandt, Ruysdael, Rubens), plus Canalettos and Guardis, have managed to slip in. Pictures are displayed in panelled rooms with furniture, porcelain, tapestries and sculpture of the same period.

Musée National Picasso

Hôtel Salé, 5 rue de Thorigny, 3rd (01.42.71.25.21/www.musee-picasso.fr). M° Chemin Vert or St-Paul. **Open** *Oct-Mar* 9.30am-5.30pm Mon, Wed-Sun. *Apr-Sept* 9.30am-6pm Mon, Wed-Sun. **Admission** €6.50; free-€4.50 reductions. *Exhibitions* prices vary. **Map** p102 B3 ⑮

Picasso's paintings, sculptures, collages, drawings and ceramics are shown off in style here. Many of the 'greatest hits' hang in other state-owned Paris museums, but to get a feeling for Picasso's artistic development this is the best resource in the city. From a haunting, blue-period self-portrait and rough studies for the *Demoiselles d'Avignon*, the collection moves to Picasso's Cubist and classical phases, the surreal *Nude in an Armchair* and portraits of his abundant lovers, in particular Marie-Thérèse and Dora Maar. A covered sculpture garden displays pieces that sat around Picasso's studio until his death.

Place de la Bastille

4th/11th/12th. M° Bastille. **Map** p102 C4 ⑯

Nothing remains of the prison that, on 14 July 1789, was stormed by revolutionary forces. Parts of the foundations can be seen in the métro. The Colonne de Juillet, topped by a gilded *génie* of Liberty, is a monument to Parisians who fell during the revolutions of July 1830 and 1848.

Place des Vosges

4th. M° St-Paul. **Map** p102 C4 ⑰

Paris's first planned square was commissioned in 1605 by Henri IV and inaugurated by his son Louis XIII in 1612. With harmonious red-brick and stone arcaded façades and pitched slate roofs, it differs from the later pomp of the Bourbons. Laid out symmetrically with carriageways through the taller Pavillon de la Reine on the north side and Pavillon du Roi on the south, the other lots were sold off as concessions to royal officials and nobles. It was called place Royale prior to the Napoleonic Wars, when the Vosges was the first region of France to pay its war taxes. Mme de Sévigné, salon hostess and letter-writer, was born at no.1bis in 1626. At that time the garden hosted duels and trysts.

La Promenade Plantée

Av Daumesnil, 12th. M° Gare de Lyon or Ledru-Rollin. **Map** p103 D5 ⑱

The railway tracks atop the Viaduc des Arts were replaced in the late 1980s by a promenade planted with roses, shrubs and rosemary. It continues at ground level through the Jardin de Reuilly and the Jardin Charles Péguy on to the Bois de Vincennes.

Le Viaduc des Arts

15-121 av Daumesnil, 12th (www.viaduc-des-arts.com). M° Gare de Lyon or Ledru-Rollin. Map p103 D5 ⑲

Glass-fronted workshops in the arches beneath the Promenade Plantée provide showrooms for furniture and fashion designers, picture-frame gilders, tapestry restorers, porcelain decorators, and chandelier, violin and flute makers. Design industry body VIA holds exhibitions of work at Nos.29-35.

Eating & drinking

L'Alimentation Générale

64 rue Jean-Pierre-Timbaud, 11th (01.43.55.42.50/www.alimentation-generale.net). M° Parmentier. **Open** 5pm-2am Wed, Thur, Sun; 5pm-4am Fri, Sat. **Bar**. **Map** p103 D1 ⑳

The 'Grocery Store' is rue Jean-Pierre-Timbaud's answer to La Mercerie: it, too, is a big old space filled with junk. Cupboards of kitsch china and lampshades made from kitchen sponges are an inspired touch. The beer is equally well chosen – Flag, Sagres, Picon and Orval by the bottle – and the unusual €8 house cocktail involves basil and figs. DJs rock the joint: expect a €5 cover price for big names or bands (including open-mic nights). Oh yes – and it has the most brazen toilet walls this side of town.

L'Ambassade d'Auvergne

22 rue du Grenier-St-Lazare, 3rd (01.42.72.31.22/www.ambassade-auvergne.com). M° Arts et Métiers. **Open** noon-2pm, 7.30-10pm daily. €. **Bistro**. **Map** p102 A2 ㉑

This rustic *auberge* is a fitting embassy for the hearty fare of central France. An order of cured ham comes as two hefty, plate-filling slices, and the salad bowl is chock-full of green lentils cooked in goose fat, studded with bacon and shallots. The *rôti d'agneau* arrives as a pot of melting chunks of lamb in a rich, meaty sauce with a helping of tender white beans. Dishes arrive with the flagship *aligot*, the creamy, elastic mash-and-cheese concoction. Of the regional wines (Chanturgue, Boudes, Madargues), the fruity AOC Marcillac makes a worthy partner.

Andy Whaloo

69 rue des Gravilliers, 3rd (01.42.71. 20.38). M° Arts et Métiers. **Open** 5.30pm-2am Tue-Sat. **Bar**.
Map p102 A2 ㉒

Andy Whaloo, created by the people behind its neighbour 404 and London's Momo and Sketch, is Arabic for 'I have nothing'. Bijou? This place brings new meaning to the word. The formidably fashionable crowd fights for coveted 'seats' on upturned paint cans; from head to toe, it's a beautifully designed venue, crammed with Moroccan artefacts and a spice rack of colours. It's quiet early on, with a surge around 9pm, and the atmosphere heats up as the night gets longer.

Au P'tit Garage

63 rue Jean-Pierre-Timbaud, 11th (01.48.07.08.12). M° Parmentier.
Open 6pm-2am daily. **Bar**.
Map p103 D1 ㉓

This quite marvellous rock 'n' roll bar is the pick of the bunch on rue Jean-Pierre-Timbaud. Not that the owners have fitted it with Americana or waitresses on rollerskates; the L'il Garage is as basic as the real car-fit business a few doors down. Stuffing bursts out of the bar stools and salvaged chairs accompany wobbly tables of ill-matched colours. Regulars cluster around the twin decks at the bar, as music-savvy Frenchettes giggle and gossip at the back.

Le Baron Rouge

1 rue Théophile-Roussel, 12th (01.43.43.14.32). M° Ledru-Rollin.
Open 10am-3pm, 5-10pm Tue-Thur; 10am-10pm Fri, Sat; 10am-3pm Sun.
Bar. **Map** p103 E5 ㉔

It sells wine, certainly – great barrels of the stuff are piled high and sold by the glass at very reasonable prices. But the Red Baron is not just a wine bar – more a local chat room, where regulars congregate to yak over their *vin*, along with a few draught beers and perhaps a snack of sausages or oysters. Despite its lack of seating (there are only four tables), it's a popular pre-dinner spot, so arrive early and don't expect much elbow room; drinkers often spill out on to the pavement.

Le Bistrot Paul Bert

18 rue Paul-Bert, 11th (01.43.72. 24.01). M° Charonne or Faidherbe Chaligny. **Open** noon-2pm, 7.30-11pm Tue-Thur; noon-2pm, 7.30-11.30pm Fri, Sat. Closed Aug. **€€**. **Bistro**.
Map p103 F4 ㉕

This heart-warming bistro gets it right almost down to the last crumb. A starter salad of *ris de veau* illustrates the point, with lightly browned veal sweetbreads perched on a bed of green beans and baby carrots with a sauce of sherry vinegar and deglazed cooking juices. A roast shoulder of suckling pig and a thick steak with a raft of golden, thick-cut *frites* look inviting indeed. Desserts are superb too, including what may well be the best *île flottante* in Paris. If you're in the area at lunchtime, bear in mind that the prix fixe menu is remarkable value.

Bofinger

5-7 rue de la Bastille, 4th (01.42.72. 87.82/www.bofingerparis.com). M° Bastille. **Open** noon-3pm, 6.30pm-12.30am Mon-Fri; noon-12.30am Sat, Sun. **€€**. **Brasserie**. **Map** p102 C4 ㉖

Bofinger draws big crowds for its authentic art nouveau setting and its brasserie atmosphere. Downstairs is the prettiest place in which to eat, but the upstairs room is air-conditioned. An à la carte selection might start with plump, garlicky snails or a well-made langoustine terrine, followed by an intensely seasoned salmon tartare, a generous (if unremarkable) cod steak, or calf's liver accompanied by cooked melon. Alternatively, you could have

PARIS BY AREA

the foolproof brasserie meal of oysters and fillet steak, followed by a pungent plate of munster cheese and bowl of cumin, washed down by the fine Gigondas at €35.50 a bottle.

Café Charbon

109 rue Oberkampf, 11th (01.43.57.55.13/www.nouveaucasino.net). M° Ménilmontant or Parmentier. **Open** 9am-2am Mon-Thur, Sun; 9am-4am Fri, Sat. **Bar**. **Map** p103 E1 27

The bar contained within this beautifully restored belle époque building sparked the Oberkampf nightlife boom. Its booths, mirrors and adventurous music policy put trendy locals at ease, capturing the essence of café culture spanning each end of the 20th century. After more than 15 years, the formula still works – and is copied by nearby bars.

Le Chateaubriand

129 av Parmentier, 11th (01.43.57.45.95). M° Goncourt. **Open** noon-2pm, 8-11pm Tue-Fri; 8-11pm Sat. Closed 3wks Aug, 1wk Dec. **€€€**. **Bistro**. **Map** p103 D1 28

Self-taught Basque chef Iñaki Aizpitarte runs this stylish bistro. Come at dinner to try the cooking at its most adventurous, as a much simpler (albeit cheaper) menu is served at lunch. Dishes have been deconstructed down to their very essence and put back together again. You'll understand if you try starters such as chunky steak tartare garnished with a quail's egg or asparagus with tahini foam and little splinters of sesame-seed brittle. The cooking's not always so cerebral – Aizpitarte's goat's cheese with stewed apple jam is brilliant.

L'Encrier

55 rue Traversière, 12th (01.44.68.08.16). M° Gare de Lyon or Ledru-Rollin. **Open** noon-2.15pm, 7.30-11pm Mon-Fri; 7.30-11pm Sat. Closed Aug & Christmas wk. **€**. **Bistro**. **Map** p103 D5 29

Through the door and past the velvet curtain, you find yourself face to face with the kitchen – and a crowd of locals, many of whom seem to know the charming boss personally. Start with fried rabbit kidneys on a bed of salad dressed with raspberry vinegar, an original and wholly successful combination, and follow with goose *magret* with honey – a welcome change from the usual duck version and served with crunchy, thinly sliced sautéed potatoes. To end, share a chocolate cake, or try the popular profiteroles. The Chinon is a classy red.

Le Fanfaron

6 rue de la Main-d'Or, 11th (01.49.23.41.14). M° Ledru-Rollin. **Open** 6pm-2am Mon-Sat. Closed 2wks Aug. No credit cards. **Bar**. **Map** p103 E4 30

On a small backstreet, Le Fanfaron (named after Dino Risi's 1962 movie) is the favoured haunt for musically inclined retro dudes. Owner Xavier's enviable collection of rare film soundtracks, the cheap (€2.70) beer and crackle of needle on vinyl pack in the punters. The decor is kitsch-cool, with Stones and Iggy memorabilia, second-hand furniture and '60s movie posters. There are reasonably priced goat's cheese and *saucisson* bar snacks too.

Le Gaigne

12 rue Pecquay, 4th (01.44.59.86.72/www.restaurantlegaigne.fr). M° Rambuteau. **Open** 12.15-2.30pm, 7.30-10.30pm Mon, Wed, Thur; 12.15-2.30pm, 7.30-11pm Fri, Sat; 7.30-10.30pm Sun. **€€**. **Bistro**. **Map** p102 B3 31

It's a familiar story: young chef with haute cuisine credentials opens a small bistro in an out-of-the-way street. Here, the restaurant is even tinier than usual with only 20 seats and the cooking is unusually inventive. Chef Mickaël Gaignon worked with Pierre Gagnaire, and it shows in dishes such as *l'oeuf bio* – three open eggshells filled with creamed spinach, carrot and celeriac –

or roast monkfish with broccoli purée and a redcurrant emulsion. The dining room is pleasantly modern and staff are eager to please.

Le Hangar

12 impasse Berthaud, 3rd (01.42.74. 55.44). M° Rambuteau. **Open** noon-2.30pm, 7.30-11pm Tue-Sat. Closed Aug. €. No credit cards. **Bistro**. **Map** p102 A2 32

It's worth making the effort to find this bistro by the Centre Pompidou, with its terrace tucked away in a hidden alley and excellent cooking. A bowl of tapenade and toast is supplied to keep you going while choosing from the comprehensive *carte*. It yields, for starters, tasty and grease-free *rillettes de lapereau* (rabbit) alongside perfectly balanced pumpkin and chestnut soup. Main courses include pan-fried foie gras on a smooth potato purée made with olive oil.

Lizard Lounge

18 rue du Bourg-Tibourg, 4th (01.42.72.81.34/www.cheapblonde. com). M° Hôtel de Ville. **Open** noon-2am daily. **Bar**. **Map** p102 B3 33

An anglophone favourite deep in the Marais, this loud and lively (hetero) pick-up joint provides lager in pints (€6), plus cocktails (€7) and a viewing platform for beer-goggled oglers. Bare brick and polished woodwork are offset by the occasional lizard and a housey soundtrack. Bargain boozing (cocktails €5) kicks off at 5pm; from 8pm to 10pm there's another happy hour in the sweaty cellar bar; on Mondays it lasts all day. A weekend brunch of bacon, sausages and eggs benedict caters to the homesick.

La Mercerie

98 rue Oberkampf, 11th (01.43.38. 81.30/www.lamercerie.net). M° Parmentier. **Open** 5pm-2am daily. **Bar**. **Map** p103 E1 34

Opposite the Charbon and infinitely more grungy, the spacious Mercerie has bare walls (bare everything, in fact) and room for the usual Oberkampf shenanigans of death-wish drinking against a backdrop of loud, eclectic music. A DJ programme is lipsticked on the back bar mirror. Happy hour is from 7pm to 9pm, so you can cane the house vodkas (apricot, mango, honey) and still have enough euros to finish the job. The back area, with its tea lights, provides intimacy if that's where your evening's headed.

La Perle

78 rue Vieille-du-Temple, 3rd (01.42.72.69.93). M° Chemin Vert or St-Paul. **Open** 6am-2am Mon-Fri; 8am-2am Sat, Sun. **Bar**. **Map** p102 B3 35

With an old locomotive over the bar and sleek rows of grey chairs, the Pearl achieves a rare balance between all-day and late-night venue, and also has a good hetero/homo mix. It feels like a neighbourhood bar; labourers and screenwriters rub elbows with young dandies, keeping one eye on the mirror and an ear on the electro-rock.

Le Petit Fer à Cheval

30 rue Vieille-du-Temple, 4th (01.42.72.47.47/www.cafeine.com). M° St-Paul. **Open** 9am-2am daily. **Bar**. **Map** p102 B3 36

Even a miniature Shetland pony would be pushed to squeeze his hoof into this *fer à cheval* (horseshoe) – this adorable little café has one of France's smallest bars. Tucked in behind the glassy façade is a friendly dining room lined with reclaimed métro benches; if you want scenery, the tables out front overlook the bustle of rue Vieille-du-Temple. In business for more than 100 years, the café enjoyed a retro makeover by Xavier Denamur in the 1990s, and today sports vintage film posters with an ornate mirror backdrop.

Le Petit Marché

9 rue de Béarn, 3rd (01.42.72.06.67). M° Chemin Vert. **Open** noon-3pm, 7.30pm-midnight Mon-Fri; noon-4pm Sat, Sun. €€. **Bistro**. **Map** p102 C3 37

Petit Marché's menu is short and modern with Asian touches. Raw tuna is flash-fried in sesame seeds and served with a Thai sauce, making for a refreshing starter; crispy-coated deep-fried king prawns have a similar oriental lightness. The main vegetarian risotto is rich in basil, coriander, cream and green beans. Pan-fried scallops with lime are precision-cooked and accompanied by a good purée and more beans. There's a short wine list.

Stolly's

16 rue Cloche-Perce, 4th (01.42.76.06.76/www.cheapblonde.com). M° Hôtel de Ville or St-Paul. **Open** 4.30pm-2am daily. **Bar**. **Map** p102 B3 38

This seen-it-all drinking den has been serving a mainly anglophone crowd for nights immemorial. The staff make the place what it is, and a summer terrace eases libation, as do the long happy hours; but don't expect anyone at Stolly's to faff about with food.

Le Train Bleu

Gare de Lyon, pl Louis-Armand, 12th (01.43.43.09.06/www.le-train-bleu.com). M° Gare de Lyon. **Open** 11.30am-3pm, 7-11pm daily. **€€**. **Brasserie**. **Map** p103 D5 39

This listed dining room – with vintage frescoes and big oak benches – exudes a pleasant air of expectation. Don't expect cutting-edge cooking, but rather fine renderings of French classics. Lobster served on walnut oil-dressed salad leaves is a generous, beautifully prepared starter. Mains of veal chop topped with a cap of cheese, and *sandre* (pike-perch) with a 'risotto' of *crozettes* are also pleasant. A few reasonably priced wines would be welcome.

Le Train Bleu

Shopping

A-poc

47 rue des Francs-Bourgeois, 4th (01.44.54.07.05). M° Rambuteau or St-Paul. **Open** 11am-7pm Mon-Sat. Closed 3wks Aug. **Map** p102 B3 40

The unusual name is an acronym for 'A Piece of Cloth', and Issey Miyake's lab-style boutique takes a highly conceptual approach to fashion. Alongside ready-to-wear cotton Lycra ensembles are rolls of wool jersey cut *sur mesure*; Miyake's assistants will be happy to advise. Miyake's original shop (3 pl des Vosges, 4th, 01.48.87.01.86) is now home to the creations of Naoki Takizawa, protégé of the master.

L'Autre Boulange

43 rue de Montreuil, 11th (01.43.72.86.04). M° Faidherbe Chaligny or Nation. **Open** 7.30am-1.30pm, 3.30-7.30pm Tue-Sat. Closed Aug. **Map** p103 F5 41

Michel Cousin bakes up to 23 types of organic loaf in his wood-fired oven – varieties include the *flutiot* (rye bread with raisins, walnuts and hazelnuts), the *sarment de Bourgogne* (sourdough and a little rye) and a spiced cornmeal bread.

Chain reaction

Goldenberg's

On a Saturday night on rue des Ecoffes in the Marais the open door of the Synagogue Beith Yossef reveals a tiny group of people – just enough to make up the requisite ten needed for the Jewish rite – praying together. It is one of the last remnants of the old Jewish 'pletzl', or little square, that offered the beginnings of a new life for more than 20,000 Ashkenazi Jews escaping the pogroms between 1881 and 1914. But prayer, and even activism, have not been enough to save this historic area from the march of globalisation. Round the corner is rue des Rosiers, where tempers have been flaring for the past two years about the imminent arrival of chain stores COS (Collection of Style, the high-end brand from H&M) and Max Mara.

Both are moving into emblematic buildings: H&M a historic old hammam that had already been saved from McDonald's (though it has been the Capellini furniture store for 20 years without complaints), and Max Mara the restaurant Jo Goldenberg, which still bears the bullet holes from the 1982 terrorist attack that left six people dead and 22 injured. Locals from the association Quartier des Rosiers have organised vocal protests outside Goldenberg's, while trying to halt H&M on the grounds of illegal construction work; and Jack Lang and Green party deputy Martine Billard have got involved in what has become a political battle.

In the other corner is 4th arrondissement Mayor Dominique Bertinotti. She did stick her neck out against McDonald's, and has opposed an H&M on the Champs-Elysées, but with price tags in the range of Goldenberg's €1.3 million, she says preemptive purchases were out of the question. Market forces, maybe, but as more small businesses go bust, the big chains are in an even more powerful position to take over and destroy what's left of Paris's individuality.

Come On Eline

16-18 rue des Taillandiers, 11th (01.43.38.12.11). M° Ledru-Rollin. **Open** *Sept-July* 11am-8.30pm Mon-Fri; 2-8pm Sun. *Aug* 2-8pm Mon-Fri. **Map** p103 D4 42

The owners of this three-floor vintage wonderland have an eye for what's funky, from cowboy gear to 1960s debutantes frocks. The stock is in good condition, but prices are high.

Du Pain et des Idées

NEW *34 rue Yves Toudic, 10th (01.42.40.44.52/www.dupainetdesidees.com). M° Jacques Bonsergent.* **Open** 6.45am-8pm Mon-Fri. No credit cards. **Map** p102 C1 43

Christophe Vasseur won the Gault-Millau prize for Best Bakery last year. Among his specialities are Le Rabelais – *pain brioché* with saffron, honey and nuts; and Le Pagnol aux Pommes, a bread studded with royal gala apple (with its skin on), raisins and orange flower water.

L'Eclaireur

3ter rue des Rosiers, 4th (01.48.87.10.22/www.leclaireur.com). M° St-Paul. **Open** 11am-7pm Mon-Sat. **Map** p102 B3 44

Housed in a dandified warehouse, L'Eclaireur stocks designs by Comme des Garçons, Martin Margiela, Dries van Noten, Carpe Diem and Junya Watanabe. Among its exclusive finds, check out smocks by Finnish designer Jasmin Santanen. At the secretive rue Hérold branch you have to ring the doorbell to enter. A new space in rue Boissy d'Anglas, near Concorde, sells chic fashions for men and women.

L'Eclaireur Homme

12 rue Malher, 4th (01.44.54.22.11/www.leclaireur.com). M° St-Paul. **Open** 11am-7pm Mon-Sat. **Map** p102 B3 45

Amid the exposed ducts of this old printworks you'll find items by Prada, Comme des Garçons, Dries van Noten and Martin Margiela. The star is Italian Stone Island, whose radical clothing features parkas with a steel shell to counteract pollution.

Free 'P' Star

8 rue Ste-Croix-de-la-Bretonnerie, 4th (01.42.76.03.72). M° St-Paul. **Open** noon-11pm Mon-Sat; 2-10pm Sun. **Map** p102 B3 46

Late-night shopping is fun at this Aladdin's cave of retro glitz, ex-army wear and glad rags that has provided fancy dress for many a Paris party.

I Love My Blender

36 rue du Temple, 3rd (01.42.77.50.32/www.ilovemyblender.fr). M° Hôtel de Ville. **Open** 10am-7.30pm Tue-Sat. **Map** p102 A3 47

Christophe Persouyre left a career in advertising to share his passion for English and American literature: all the books he stocks were penned in English, and here you can find their mother-tongue and translated versions.

Julien, Caviste

50 rue Charlot, 3rd (01.42.72.00.94). M° Filles du Calvaire. **Open** 9am-1.30pm, 3.30-7.30pm Tue-Sat; 10.30am-1.30pm Sun. Closed 3rd wk Aug. **Map** p102 B2 48

Julien promotes the small producers he has discovered, and often holds wine tastings on Saturdays.

Moisan

5 pl d'Aligre, 12th (01.43.45.46.60). M° Ledru-Rollin. **Open** 7am-8pm Tue-Sat; 7am-2pm Sun. No credit cards. **Map** p103 E5 49

Moisan's organic bread, *viennoiseries* and rustic tarts are outstanding. At this branch, situated by the market, there's always a healthy queue.

Nodus

22 rue Vieille-du-Temple, 4th (01.42.77.07.96/www.nodus-boutique.com). M° Hôtel de Ville or St-Paul. **Open** 10.45am-2pm, 3-7.30pm Mon-Sat; 1-7.30pm Sun. **Map** p102 B3 50

Under the wooden beams of this cosy men's shirt specialist are rows of striped, checked and plain dress shirts, stylish silk ties with subtle designs, and silver-plated crystal cufflinks.

Paris-Musées

29bis rue des Francs-Bourgeois, 4th (01.42.74.13.02). M° St-Paul. **Open** 2-7pm Mon; 11am-1pm, 2-7pm Tue-Fri; 11am-7pm Sat; noon-7.30pm Sun. **Map** p102 B3 51

Run by the museum federation, this shop sells reproduction lamps and ceramics from local museums.

Red Wheelbarrow

22 rue St-Paul, 4th (01.48.04.75.08/ www.theredwheelbarrow.com). M° St Paul. **Open** 10am-6pm Mon; 10am-7pm Tue-Sat; 2-6pm Sun. **Map** p102 B4 52

Penelope Fletcher Le Masson and Abigail Altman run this friendly literary bookshop in the Marais, which also has an excellent children's section.

Robopolis

107 bd Beaumarchais, 3rd (01.44.78. 01.18/www.robopolis.com). M° Filles du Calvaire. **Open** 11am-1pm, 2-7pm Tue-Sat. **Map** p102 C2 53

This is the only store in the country devoted entirely to our friends electric, and as such it attracts gizmo-lovers of all ages. It's as much a showroom as a shop, with displays including dancing humanoids, white iPod rabbits that sing and read, and even robot vacuum cleaners. Models such as Roboreptile and Meccano's 'build-your-own' robot sit at the top of kids' (and big kids') Christmas lists.

Shine

15 rue de Poitou, 3rd (01.48.05.80.10). M° Filles du Calvaire. **Open** 11am-7.30pm Mon-Sat. **Map** p102 B2 54

See By Chloe, Marc by Marc Jacobs and Acne Jeans, plus Repetto shoes and Véronique Branquino, are among the goodies in this glossy showcase.

Le Village St-Paul

Rue St-Paul, rue Charlemagne & quai des Célestins, 4th. M° St-Paul. **Open** 10am-7pm Mon-Sat. No credit cards. **Map** p102 B4 55

This colony of antiques sellers, housed in small, linking courtyards, is a source of retro furniture, kitchenware and wine gadgets.

Zadig & Voltaire

42 rue des Francs-Bourgeois, 3rd (01.44.54.00.60/www.zadig-et-voltaire.com). M° Hôtel de Ville or St-Paul. **Open** 10.30am-7.30pm Mon-Sat; 1.30-7.30pm Sun. **Map** p102 B3 56

Zadig &Voltaire's relaxed, urban collection is a winner. Popular separates include cotton tops, shirts and faded jeans; its winter range of cashmere jumpers is superb. The more upmarket Zadig & Voltaire De Luxe store is at 18 rue François 1er (01.40.70.97.89).

Nightlife

Les Bains Douches

7 rue du Bourg-l'Abbé, 3rd (01.48.87.01.80/www.lesbainsdouches. net). M° Etienne Marcel. **Open** midnight-6am Wed-Sun (restaurant from 8pm). **Admission** €10-€20. **Map** p102 A2 57

Les Bains Douches rather lost its way in the 1990s, relying on its reputation to pull in tourists. This all changed recently, and now local star DJs like Busy P and international names such as Erol Alkan grace its decks once more. The clientele is increasingly, but not exclusively, gay.

Le Bataclan

50 bd Voltaire, 11th (01.43.14.00.30/ www.le-bataclan.com). M° Oberkampf. **Open** times vary. No credit cards. **Map** p103 D2 58

Established in 1864, this highly distinctive venue is still standing after the odd facelift, and remains admirably discerning in its booking of rock, world, jazz and hip hop acts.

Café de la Danse

5 passage Louis-Phillipe, 11th (01.47.00.57.59/www.myspace.com/cafedeladanse). M° Bastille. **Open** times vary. Closed July, Aug. No credit cards. **Map** p103 D4 59

Pristine sound and a rarefied ideal of pop and rock perfection typify this former dancehall. It's largely seated, but there's still room to shake a tailfeather.

Le China

NEW *50 rue de Charenton, 12th (01.43.46.08.09/www.lechina.eu). M° Bastille or Ledru-Rollin.* **Open** 5pm-2am daily. **Map** p103 D5 60

Le China is a carbon copy of its predecessor the China Club, which closed in 2007, wooing jazz and cocktail lovers with decor reminiscent of a 1930s Shanghai gentleman's club, an impressively long bar famed for its Singapore slings, and a reel of live music in the basement. For a touch of glamour sink into a Chesterfield sofa and try some of the top-notch Cantonese cuisine.

La Mécanique Ondulatoire

8 passage Thière, 11th (01.43.55.16.74/www.lamecond.com). M° Bastille or Ledru Rollin. **Open** 6pm-2am Mon-Sat. Concerts from 8pm Tue-Sat. **Admission** €3-€6. **Map** p103 D4 61

See box p105.

Le Motel

8 passage Josset, 11th (01.58.30.88.52/www.myspace.com/lemotel). M° Ledru Rollin. **Open** 6pm-2am Tue-Sun. Closed Aug. **Map** p103 E4 62

See box p105.

Nouveau Casino

109 rue Oberkampf, 11th (01.43.57.57.40/www.nouveaucasino.net). M° Parmentier. **Open** midnight-5am Wed-Sat. **Admission** €5 before 1am, €10 after. **Map** p103 E1 63

Nouveau Casino is a concert venue that also hosts some of the city's liveliest club nights. Local collectives, international names and record labels, such as Versatile, regularly host nights here; it's well worth checking the website for one-offs and after-parties.

Arts & leisure

Les Bains du Marais

31-33 rue des Blancs-Manteaux, 4th (01.44.61.02.02/www.lesbainsdumarais.com). M° St-Paul. **Open** *Men* 10am-11pm Thur; 10am-8pm Fri. *Women* 11am-8pm Mon; 10am-11pm Tue; 10am-7pm Wed. *Mixed (swimwear required)* 7-11pm Wed; 10am-8pm Sat; 10am-11pm Sun. Closed Aug. **Map** p102 A3 64

This hammam and spa mixes the modern and traditional (lounging beds and mint tea). Facials, waxing and essential oil massages (€70) are also available. The hammam is €35.

Maison des Métallos

94 rue Jean-Pierre Timbaud, 11th (01.48.05.88.27/www.maisondesmetallos.org). M° Parmentier or Couronnes. **Map** p103 E1 65

After serving over a century as a focal point for working-class activities, the Maison des Métallos reopened as a cutting-edge cultural showcase for contemporary artists. The venue offers up an ambitious multicultural programme of concerts, dance, film screenings, exhibitions, and popular debates.

Opéra National de Paris, Bastille

Pl de la Bastille, 12th (08.92.89.90.90/from abroad 01.72.29.35.35/www.operadeparis.fr). M° Bastille. **Box office** (130 rue de Lyon, 12th) 10.30am-6.30pm Mon-Sat. *By phone* 9am-6pm Mon-Fri; 9am-1pm Sat. **Admission** €5-€196. **Map** p103 D4 66

Restoration work is finally under way on this modern building everyone loves to hate. On the music front, director Gerard Mortier has introduced cutting-edge dramatic values, but disappointed those who enjoy spectacular singing and lavish period costumes.

La Conciergerie p119

The Seine & Islands

The Seine

For much of the 19th and 20th centuries, the Seine was barely given a second thought by anyone who wasn't working on it or driving along its quayside roads. But in 1994, UNESCO added 12 kilometres of Paris riverbank to its World Heritage register. Floating venues such as Batofar became super-trendy; and in the last ten years, it's been one new Seine-side attraction after another.

It's at its best in summer. Port de Javel and Jardin Tino-Rossi become open-air dancehalls; and there's the jamboree of Paris-Plage, Mayor Delanoë's city beach that brings sand, palm trees, loungers and free entertainment to both sides of the Seine. And, of course, there's a wealth of boat tours.

What's more, the river itself is cleaning up its act. The crackdown on pollution had a big symbolic payoff in August 2008, when, for the first time since records began, a sea trout was caught in the Seine on the western outskirts of the city.

Sights & museums

Vedettes du Pont-Neuf

Square du Vert-Galant, 1st (01.46.33.98.38/01.43.29.86.19/ www.vedettesdupontneuf.com). M° Pont Neuf. **Tickets** €12; free-€6 reductions. **Map** p117 B1 ❶

The hour-long cruise takes in all the big sights, from the Eiffel Tower to Notre-Dame. You can sit inside just a foot or two above water level or outside on the top deck – where you may get drenched by pranksters throwing water from bridges as you pass underneath.

The bridges

From the honeyed arches of the oldest, the Pont Neuf, to the swooping lines of the newest, the

The Seine & Islands

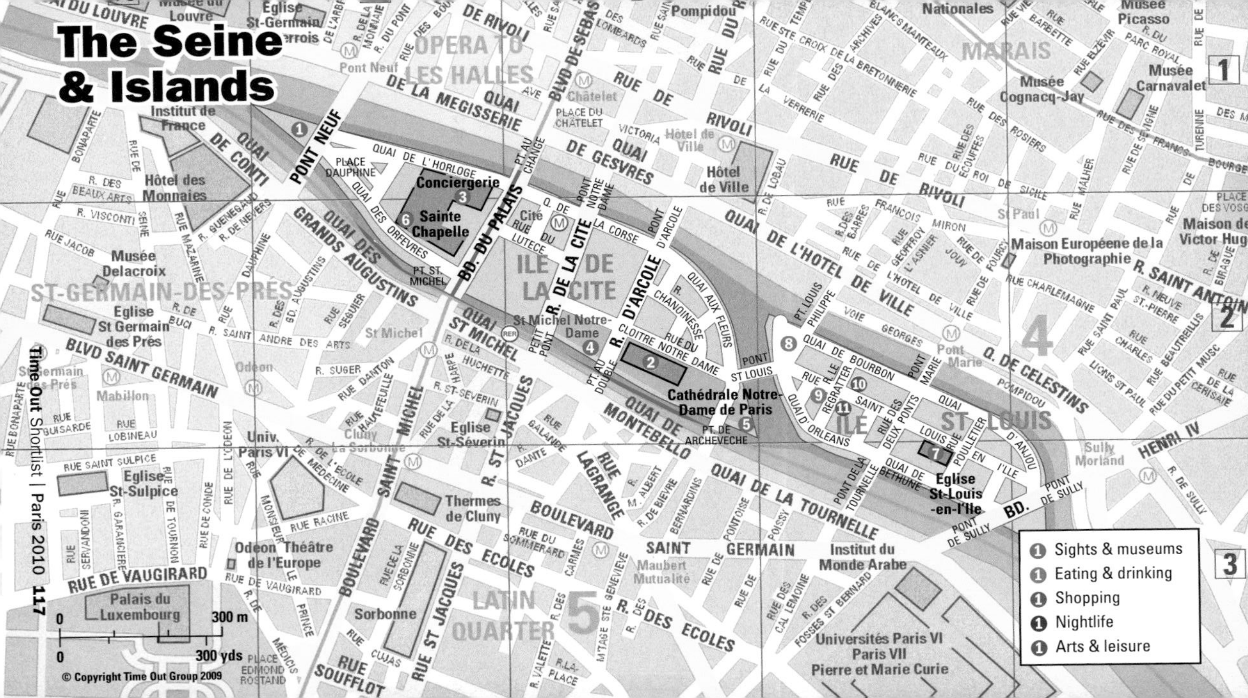

Vedettes du Pont-Neuf p116

Passerelle Simone-de-Beauvoir, the city's 37 bridges are among the best-known landmarks in the city, and enjoy some of its best views.

Over the years the city's *ponts* have been bombed, bashed by buses and boats, weather-beaten and even trampled to destruction: in 1634, the Pont St-Louis collapsed under the weight of a religious procession.

The 19th century was boom time for bridge-building: 21 were built in all, including the city's first steel, iron and suspension bridges. The Pont de la Concorde used up what was left of the Bastille after the storming of 1789; the romantic Pont des Arts was the capital's first solely pedestrian crossing (built in 1803 and rebuilt in the 1980s). The most glitteringly exuberant bridge is the Pont Alexandre III, with its bronze and glass, garlanding and gilded embellishments. More practical is the Pont de l'Alma, with its Zouave statue that has long been a flood monitor: when the statue's toes get wet, the state raises the flood alert and starts to close the quayside roads; when he's up to his ankles in Seine, it's no longer possible to navigate the river by boat. This offers some indication of how devastating the great 1910 flood was, when the plucky Zouave disappeared up to his neck – as did parts of central Paris.

The city's newest crossing, the Passerelle Simone-de-Beauvoir, is a walkway linking the Bibliothèque Nationale to the Parc de Bercy in the 12th arrondissement.

Ile de la Cité

The Ile de la Cité is where Paris was born around 250 BC, when the Parisii, a tribe of Celtic Gauls, founded a settlement on this convenient bridging point of the Seine. Romans, Merovingians and Capetians followed, in what became a centre of political and religious power right into the Middle Ages: royal authority at one end, around the Capetian palace; the Church at the other, by **Notre-Dame**.

Perhaps the most charming spot on the island is the western tip, where Pont Neuf spans the Seine. Despite its name, it is in fact the oldest bridge in Paris. Its arches are lined with grimacing faces, said to be modelled on some of the courtiers of Henri III. Down the steps is leafy square du Vert-Galant. In the centre of the bridge is an equestrian statue of Henri IV; the original went up in 1635, was melted down to make cannons during the Revolution, and replaced in 1818.

Sights & museums

Cathédrale Notre-Dame de Paris

Pl du Parvis-Notre-Dame, 4th (01.42. 34.56.10/www.cathedraledeparis.com). M° Cité/RER St-Michel Notre-Dame.

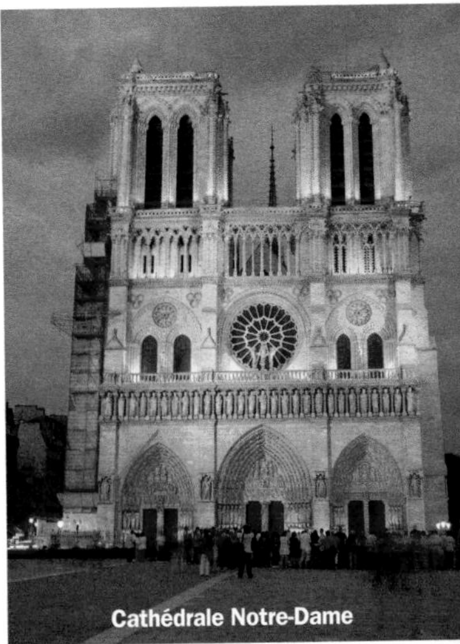

Cathédrale Notre-Dame

Open 8am-6.45pm Mon-Fri; 8am-7.15pm Sat, Sun. *Towers* Apr-Sept 10am-6.30pm daily (*June, Aug* until 11pm Sat, Sun). Oct-Mar 10am-5.30pm daily. **Admission** free. *Towers* €7.50; free-€4.80 reductions. **Map** p117 C2 ❷
Notre-Dame was constructed between 1163 and 1334, and the amount of time and money spent on it reflected the city's growing prestige. The west front remains a high point of Gothic art for the balanced proportions of its twin towers and rose window, and the three doorways with their rows of saints and sculpted tympanums: the *Last Judgement* (centre), *Life of the Virgin* (left) and *Life of St Anne* (right). Inside, take a moment to admire the long nave with its solid foliate capitals and high altar with a marble *Pietà* by Coustou.

To truly appreciate the masonry, climb up the towers. The route runs up the north tower and down the south. Between the two you get a close-up view of the gallery of chimeras – the fantastic birds and hybrid beasts designed by Viollet-le-Duc along the balustrade. After a detour to see the Bourdon (the massive bell), a staircase leads to the top of the south tower.

La Conciergerie

2 bd du Palais, 1st (01.53.40.60.80). M° Cité/RER St-Michel Notre-Dame.
Open *Mar-Oct* 9.30am-6pm daily. *Nov-Feb* 9am-5pm daily. **Admission** €6.50; free-€4.50 reductions. *With Sainte-Chapelle* €10; €8 reductions. **Map** p117 B1 ❸
The Conciergerie looks every inch the forbidding medieval fortress. However, much of the façade was added in the 1850s, long after Marie-Antoinette, Danton and Robespierre had been imprisoned here. The visit takes you through the Salle des Gardes, the medieval kitchens with their four huge chimneys, and the Salle des Gens d'Armes, a vaulted Gothic hall built between 1301 and 1315. After the royals moved to the Louvre, the fortress became a prison under the watch of the Concierge. The wealthy had private cells with their own furniture, which

they paid for; others had to make do with straw beds. A list of Revolutionary prisoners, including a hairdresser, shows that not all victims were nobles. In Marie-Antoinette's cell, the Chapelle des Girondins, are her crucifix, some portraits and a guillotine blade.

La Crypte Archéologique

Pl Jean-Paul II, 4th (01.55.42.50.10). M° Cité/RER St-Michel Notre-Dame. **Open** 10am-6pm Tue-Sun. **Admission** €3.30; free-€2.20 reductions.
Map p117 C2 ❹
Hidden under the forecourt in front of the cathedral is a large void that contains bits and pieces of Roman quaysides, ramparts and hypocausts, medieval cellars, shops and pavements, the foundations of the Eglise Ste-Geneviève-des-Ardens (the church where Geneviève's remains were stored during the Norman invasions), an 18th-century foundling hospital and a 19th-century sewer. It's not easy to work out which wall, column or staircase is which – but you do get a vivid sense of the layers of history piled one atop another during 16 centuries.

PARIS BY AREA

Mémorial des Martyrs de la Déportation

Sq de l'Ile de France, 4th (01.46.33.87.56). M° Cité/RER Châtelet or St-Michel Notre-Dame. **Open** *Oct-Mar* 10am-noon, 2-5pm daily. *Apr-Sept* 10am-noon, 2-7pm daily. **Admission** free. **Map** p117 C2 ❺
This tribute to the 200,000 Jews, Communists, homosexuals and *résistants* deported to concentration camps from France in World War II stands on the eastern tip of the island. A blind staircase descends to river level, where chambers are lined with tiny lights and the walls are inscribed with verse. A barred window looks on to the Seine.

Sainte-Chapelle

6 bd du Palais, 1st (01.53.40.60.97). M° Cité/RER St-Michel Notre-Dame. **Open** *Mar-Oct* 9.30am-6pm daily. *Nov-Feb* 9am-5pm daily. **Admission** €7.50; free-€4.80 reductions. *With Conciergerie* €10; €8 reductions.
Map p117 B2 ❻
Devout King Louis IX (St Louis, 1226-70) had a hobby of accumulating holy relics (and children: he fathered 11). In the 1240s he bought what was advertised as the Crown of Thorns, and ordered Pierre de Montreuil to design a shrine. The result was the exquisite Flamboyant Gothic Sainte-Chapelle. With 15m (49ft) windows, the upper level, intended for the royal family and the canons, appears to consist almost entirely of stained glass. The windows depict hundreds of scenes from the Old and New Testaments, culminating with the Apocalypse in the rose window.

Ile St-Louis

The Ile St-Louis is one of the most exclusive residential addresses in the city. Delightfully unspoiled, it has fine architecture, narrow streets and pretty views from the tree-lined quays, and still retains the air of a tranquil backwater, curiously removed from city life.

Rue St-Louis-en-l'Ile – lined with fine historic buildings that now house gift shops and gourmet food stores (many open on Sunday), quaint tearooms, stone-walled bars, restaurants and hotels – runs the length of the island. At the western end there are great views of the buttresses of Notre-Dame from the terraces of the Brasserie de l'Ile St-Louis and the Flore en l'Ile café.

Sights & museums

Eglise St-Louis-en-l'Ile

19bis rue St-Louis-en-l'Ile, 4th (01.46.34.11.60/www.saintlouisenlile.com). M° Pont Marie. **Open** 9am-noon, 3-7pm Tue-Sun. **Map** p117 D3 ❼
The island's church was built between 1664 and 1765, following plans by Louis Le Vau and later completed by

Brasserie de l'Ile St-Louis

Gabriel Le Duc. The interior boasts Corinthian columns and a sunburst over the altar, and sometimes hosts classical music concerts.

Eating & drinking

Brasserie de l'Ile St-Louis

55 quai de Bourbon, 4th (01.43.54.02.59). M° Pont Marie. **Open** noon-midnight Mon, Tue, Thur-Sun. Closed Aug. €. **Brasserie**. **Map** p117 D2 ❽

Happily, this old-fashioned brasserie soldiers on while exotic juice bars on the Ile St-Louis come and go. The terrace has one of the best summer views in Paris and is invariably packed; the dining room exudes shabby chic. Nicotined walls make for an authentic Paris mood, though nothing here is gastronomically gripping: a well-dressed *frisée aux lardons*, perhaps, or a pan of warming tripe.

Mon Vieil Ami

69 rue St-Louis-en-l'Ile, 4th (01.40.46.01.35/www.mon-vieil-ami.com). M° Pont Marie. **Open** noon-2.30pm, 7-11.30pm Wed-Sun. Closed 3wks Jan & 1st 3wks Aug. €€. **Bistro**. **Map** p117 D2 ❾

Antoine Westermann from the Buerehiesel in Strasbourg has created a true foodie destination here. Starters such as tartare of finely diced raw vegetables with sautéed baby squid on top impress with their deft seasoning. Typical of the mains is a casserole of roast duck with caramelised turnips and couscous. Even the classic room has been successfully refreshed.

Shopping

Arche de Noé

70 rue St-Louis-en-l'Ile, 4th (01.46.34.61.60). M° Pont Marie. **Open** 10.30am-7pm daily. **Map** p117 D2 ❿

'Noah's Ark' is a great place for Christmas shopping, with traditional wooden toys from eastern Europe, games, jigsaws and finger puppets.

L'Occitane

55 rue St-Louis-en-l'Ile, 4th (01.40.46.81.71/www.loccitane.com). M° Pont Marie. **Open** 10.30am-7.30pm daily. **Map** p117 D2 ⓫

The many branches of this popular Provençal chain offer natural beauty products in neat packaging. Soap rules, along with essential oils and perfumes.

PARIS BY AREA

Musée du Quai Branly p126

The 7th & Western Paris

The buttoned-up seventh arrondissement is the Paris of the establishment: it's home to the French parliament, the Assemblée Nationale, several French ministries and foreign embassies, the Ecole Militaire and the headquarters of UNESCO. Much of it is rather formal and lacking in soul, with few visitor-friendly cultural and historic attractions. However, the attractions that do occupy this lofty district are big hitters: the **Musée d'Orsay**, **Les Invalides** and the **Eiffel Tower**.

Near to St-Germain-des-Prés is the cosy Faubourg St-Germain, with its historic mansions and upmarket shops. Further west is the 15th arrondissement, with its predominantly residential buildings done in a suprisingly broad array of styles.

Sights & museums

Les Egouts de Paris

Opposite 93 quai d'Orsay, by Pont de l'Alma, 7th (01.53.68.27.81). M° Alma Marceau/RER Pont de l'Alma. **Open** 11am-4pm (until 5pm May-Sept) Wed-Sat. Closed 3wks Jan. **Admission** €4.20; free-€3.40 reductions. No credit cards. **Map** p123 B1 ❶

For centuries the main source of drinking water in Paris was the Seine, which was also the main sewer. Construction of an underground sewerage system began at the time of Napoleon. Today the Egouts de Paris constitutes a smelly museum; each sewer in the 2,100km (1,305-mile) system is marked with a replica of the street sign above.

Eiffel Tower

Champ de Mars, 7th (01.44.11.23.45/ recorded information 01.44.11.23.23/ www.tour-eiffel.fr). M° Bir-Hakeim/

The 7th & Western Paris

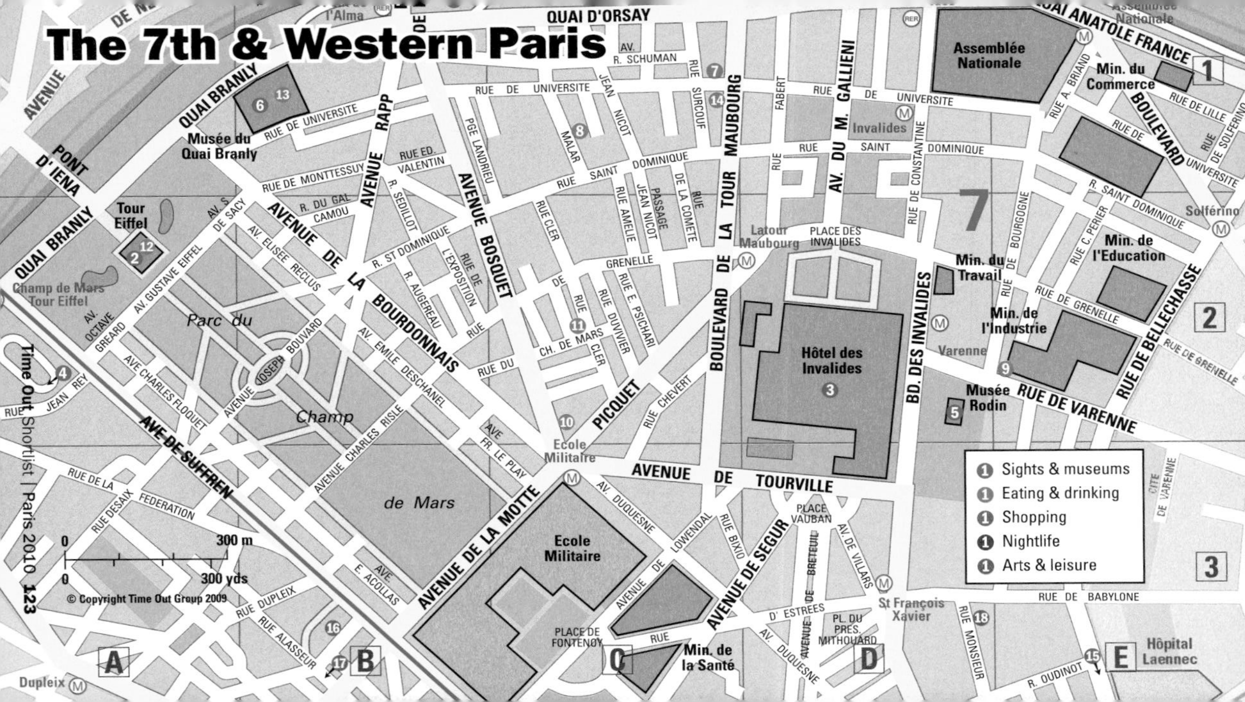

RER Champ de Mars Tour Eiffel. **Open** *13 June-Aug* 9am-12.45am daily. *Sept-12 June* 9.30am-11.45pm daily. **Admission** *By stairs* (1st & 2nd levels, Sept-mid June 9.30am-6pm, mid June-Aug 9am-midnight) €4; €3.10 reductions. *By lift* (1st level) €4.80; €2.50 reductions; (2nd level) €7.80; €4.30 reductions; (3rd level) €12; free-€6.70 reductions. **Map** p123 A2 ❷

No building better symbolises Paris than the Tour Eiffel. The radical cast-iron tower was built for the 1889 World Fair and the centenary of the 1789 Revolution by engineer Gustave Eiffel. Construction took more than two years and used some 18,000 pieces of metal and 2,500,000 rivets. The 300m (984ft) tower stands on four massive concrete piles; it was the tallest structure in the world until overtaken by New York's Empire State Building in the 1930s. Vintage double-decker lifts ply their way up and down; you can walk as far as the second level. There are souvenir shops, an exhibition space, café and even a post office on the first and second levels. At the top (third level), there's Eiffel's cosy salon and a viewing platform with panels pointing out what to see. Views can reach 65km (40 miles) on a good day. At night, for ten minutes on the hour, 20,000 flashbulbs attached to the tower provide a stunning effect.

Musée National Rodin p126

Les Invalides & Musée de l'Armée

Esplanade des Invalides, 7th (01.44. 42.38.77/www.invalides.org). M° La Tour-Maubourg or Les Invalides. **Open** *Apr-Sept* 10am-6pm daily. *Oct-Mar* 10am-5pm daily. Closed 1st Mon of mth. **Admission** *Musée de l'Armée & Eglise du Dôme* €8; free-€6 reductions. **Map** p123 D2 ❸

Topped by its gilded dome, the Hôtel des Invalides was (and in part still is) a hospital. Commissioned by Louis XIV for wounded soldiers, it once housed up to 6,000 invalids. Behind lines of cannons and bullet-shaped yews, the main (northern) façade has a relief of Louis XIV and the Sun King's sunburst. Wander through the main courtyard and you'll see grandiose two-storey arcades and a statue of Napoleon glaring down from the end. The complex contains two churches – or, rather, a sort of double church: the Eglise St-Louis was for the soldiers, the Eglise du Dôme for the king. An opening behind the altar connects the two.

The Invalides complex also houses the enormous Musée de l'Armée. Even if militaria are not your thing, the building is a splendour, and there's some fine portraiture. The Antique Armour wing is packed full of armour and weapons that look as good as new. The Plans-Reliefs section is a collection of gorgeous 18th- and 19th-century scale models of French cities, used for military strategy; also here is a 17th-century model of Mont St-Michel, made by a monk from playing cards. The World War I rooms are moving, with the conflict brought into focus by uniforms, paintings, a scale model of a

See things differently

Alternative ways to check out the sights.

Fancy seeing the city of lights in a new, erm, light? From eccentric themed visits to touring on novel forms of transport, there is a host of alternative trips on offer.

Several companies offer an insider's guide to the city. At www.parisiendunjour.org, Paris residents take visitors around their neighbourhood, pointing out local gems. Many of the two- to three-hour guided visits are in areas outside the main tourist spots, such as Charonne, Belleville or Canal St-Martin, while intimacy is guaranteed thanks to the policy of limiting groups to six people.

If you're fed up with crowds, Paris Privé (www.parisprive.com) organises private tours of monuments such as the Louvre and the Château de Versailles outside public hours. Other exclusive visits include tours around famous artists' studios or a behind-the-scenes look at a top Paris restaurant.

Foodies can also opt for an English-language gourmand's tour of the city with www.meetingthe french.com. Choices include an exploration of family cooking in the Latin Quarter or an introduction to some of Paris's finest *pâtisseries* and *chocolatiers*. All walks include a generous amount of tasting. Paris Sweet Paris (www.parissweetparis.com) also offers a range of gourmet tours that take in local markets and their produce.

Other companies offer traditional tours by unconventional means. Fitness fans may like to jog around the sights. Get in Shape (www.getinshape.fr) has a number of runner's tours, from the 3km (1 mile) circuit of the Hôtel de Ville and Bastille to the 20km (12.5 mile) run that takes in everything from the Champs-Elysées and Montmartre to Notre-Dame and the Eiffel Tower.

A gentler way to combine sport and tourism is a city bike tour, which come in all shapes and sizes. For a traditional two-wheeled experience, Fat Tire Bike (www.fattirebiketoursparis.com) and Bike About Tours (www.bikeabouttours.com) offer English-language guides, while the less athletic can be chauffeured around the sights on the back of a tricycle (www.cyclobulle.com). Alternatively, City Segway Tours (www.citysegwaytours.com) offers guided excursions around the city on a contraption called an i2, a self-balancing, personal transportation device. How's that for alternative?

trench on the western front and, most sobering of all, white plastercasts of the hideously mutilated faces of two soldiers. The World War II wing takes in not just the Resistance, but also the Battle of Britain and the war in the Pacific (there's a replica of Little Boy, the bomb dropped on Hiroshima). Also included in the entry price is the Historial Charles de Gaulle.
Event highlights La Description de L'Egypte (until 21 Sept 2009)

Maison de la Culture du Japon

101bis quai Branly, 15th (01.44.37. 95.00/www.mcjp.asso.fr). M° Bir-Hakeim/RER Champ de Mars Tour Eiffel. **Open** noon-7pm Tue, Wed, Fri, Sat; noon-8pm Thur. Closed Aug. **Admission** free. **Map** p123 A2 ❹
Constructed in 1996, this opalescent glass-fronted Japanese cultural centre screens films and puts on exhibitions and plays. It also contains a library, an authentic Japanese tea pavilion on the roof, where you can watch the tea ceremony, and a well-stocked shop.

Musée National Rodin

Hôtel Biron, 79 rue de Varenne, 7th (01.44.18.61.10/www.musee-rodin.fr). M° Varenne. **Open** *Apr-Sept* 9.30am-5.45pm Tue-Sun (gardens until 6.45pm). *Oct-Mar* 9.30am-4.45pm Tue-Sun (gardens until 5pm). **Admission** €6; free-€4 reductions. *Exhibitions* €7; €5 reductions. *Gardens* €1. **Map** p123 D2 ❺
The Rodin museum occupies the *hôtel particulier* where the sculptor lived in the final years of his life. The *Kiss*, the *Cathedral*, the *Walking Man*, portrait busts and early terracottas are exhibited indoors. Rodin's works are accompanied by pieces by his mistress and pupil, Camille Claudel. The walls are hung with paintings by Van Gogh, Monet, Renoir, Carrière and Rodin himself. Most visitors have greatest affection for the gardens: look out for the *Burghers of Calais*, the elaborate *Gates of Hell*, and the *Thinker*.

Musée du Quai Branly

37-55 quai Branly, 7th (01.56.61.70. 00/www.quaibranly.fr). RER Pont de l'Alma. **Open** 11am-7pm Tue, Wed, Sun; 11am-9pm Thur-Sat. **Admission** €8.50; free-€6 reductions. **Map** p123 B1 ❻
Surrounded by trees on the banks of the Seine, this museum, housed in an extraordinary building by Jean Nouvel, is a showcase for non-European cultures. Dedicated to the ethnic art of Africa, Oceania, Asia and the Americas, it joins together the collections of the Musée des Arts d'Afrique et d'Océanie and the Laboratoire d'Ethnologie du Musée de l'Homme, as well as indigenous art. Treasures include a tenth-century anthropomorphic Dogon statue from Mali, Vietnamese costumes, Gabonese masks, Aztec statues, Peruvian feather tunics, and rare frescoes from Ethiopia.

Eating & drinking

Le 144 Petrossian

18 bd de La Tour-Maubourg, 7th (01.44.11.32.32/www.petrossian.fr). M° La Tour Maubourg. **Open** noon-2.30pm, 7.30-10.30pm Tue-Sat. **€€€**. **Russian**. **Map** p123 C1 ❼
Young Senegalese-French chef Rougui Dia directs the kitchen of this famed caviar house. You'll find Russian specialities such as blinis, salmon and caviar (at €39 an ounce) from the Petrossian boutique downstairs, but Dia has added preparations and spices from all over the world. You might start with a divine risotto made with carnaroli rice, codfish caviar and crisp parmesan. In a similar Med-meets-Russia vein are main courses of lamb 'cooked for eleven hours' on a raisin-filled blini, and roast sea bream with a terrific lemon-vodka sauce. At dinner bottles of wine start at €40.

L'Ami Jean

27 rue Malar, 7th (01.47.05.86.89). M° Ecole Militaire. **Open** noon-2pm, 7pm-midnight Tue-Sat. Closed Aug. **€**. **Bistro**. **Map** p123 C1 ❽

PARIS BY AREA

This long-running Basque address is an ongoing hit thanks to chef Stéphane Jégo. Excellent bread from baker Jean-Luc Poujauran is a perfect nibble when slathered with a tangy, herby *fromage blanc* – as are starters of sautéed baby squid on a bed of ratatouille. Tender veal shank comes de-boned with a side of baby onions and broad beans with tiny cubes of ham, and house-salted cod is soaked, sautéed and doused with an elegant vinaigrette.

L'Arpège

84 rue de Varenne, 7th (01.47.05.09.06/www.alain-passard.com). M° Varenne. **Open** noon-2.30pm, 8-10.30pm Mon-Fri. **€€€€. Haute cuisine. Map** p123 E2 ⑨

Assuming that you can swallow an exceptionally high bill – we're talking €42 for a potato starter – chances are you'll have a spectacular time at chef Alain Passard's Left Bank establishment. His attempt to plane down and simplify the haute cuisine experience – the chrome-armed chairs look like something from the former DDR – seems a misstep at first; but then something edible comes to the table, such as a platter of tiny smoked potatoes served with a horseradish *mousseline*. A main course of sautéed free-range chicken with a roasted shallot, an onion, potato *mousseline* and pan juices is the apotheosis of comfort food.

Le Bardélo

NEW *64 av Bosquet, 7th (01.44.18.01.25/www.lebardelo.com). M° Ecole Militaire.* **Open** 6pm-2am Tue-Sat. **Bar. Map** p123 C2 ⑩

This former cigar bar has swapped its outlawed tobacco for jazz, whisky, cocktails and fine wines. Leather sofas, exposed stone walls and plenty of dark wood create a smart setting for the moneyed clientele: a mix of young professionals and middle-aged bourgeois folk, all with one thing in common – a love of the performing and gustative arts. Wine-tasting sessions occur throughout the year; check the website for details. Live jazz and *café-théâtre* take place most Saturday evenings.

Fromagerie Quatrehomme p128

Le Café du Marché

38 rue Cler, 7th (01.47.05.51.27). M° Ecole Militaire. **Open** 7am-midnight Mon-Sat; 7am-5pm Sun. **€. Café. Map** p123 C2 ⑪

This well-loved address is frequented by trendy locals, shoppers hunting down a particular type of cheese and tourists who've managed to make it this far from the Eiffel Tower. Le Café du Marché really is a hub of neighbourhood activity. Its *pichets* of decent house plonk go down a treat, and mention must be made of the food – such as the huge house salad featuring lashings of foie gras and Parma ham.

Jules Verne

Pilier Sud, Eiffel Tower, 7th (01.45.55.61.44/www.lejulesverne-paris.com). M° Bir Hakeim or RER Tour Eiffel. **Open** 12.15-1.30pm, 7-9.30pm daily. **€€€€. Haute cuisine. Map** p123 A2 ⑫

You have to have courage to take on an icon like the Eiffel Tower, but Alain Ducasse has done just that in taking over the Jules Verne, perched in its spectacular eyrie 123 metres above the city. He has transformed the cuisine and brought in his favourite designer, Patrick Jouin. But it's the food that counts, in the hands of Ducasse protégé Pascal Féraud, who updates French classics with light, modern textures and sauces. Try dishes like lamb with artichokes, turbot with champagne zabaglione, and a fabulously airy ruby grapefruit soufflé. Reserve well ahead.

Les Ombres

27 quai Branly, 7th (01.47.53.68.00). M° Alma-Marceau. **Open** noon-2.30pm, 7-10.30pm daily. **€€. Bistro. Map** p123 B1 ⑬

The full-on view of the Eiffel Tower at night would be reason enough to come to this glass-and-iron restaurant on the top floor of the Musée du Quai Branly, but young chef Arnaud Busquet's food also demands that you sit up and take notice. His talent shows in dishes such as thin green asparagus curved into a nest with tiny *lardons* and topped with a breaded poached egg, ribbons of parmesan and meat *jus*.

Il Vino

13 bd de La Tour-Maubourg, 7th (01.44.11.72.00/www.ilvinobyenricobernardo.com). M° La Tour-Maubourg. **Open** noon-2pm, 7-10pm Tue-Sat. **€€€€. Italian. Map** p123 D1 ⑭

Enrico Bernardo, youngest-ever winner of the World's Best Sommelier award, runs this restaurant where, for once, food plays second fiddle to wine. You are presented with nothing more than a wine list. Each of 15 wines by the glass is matched with a surprise dish, or the chef can build a meal around the bottle of your choice. Best for a first visit is one of the blind tasting menus for €75, €100 or (why not?) €1,000. The impeccably prepared food shows a strong Italian influence.

Shopping

Fromagerie Quatrehomme

62 rue de Sèvres, 7th (01.47.34.33.45). M° Duroc or Vaneau. **Open** 8.45am-1pm, 4-7.45pm Tue-Thur; 8.45am-7.45pm Fri, Sat. **Map** p123 E3 ⑮

Marie Quatrehomme runs this *fromagerie*. Justly famous for her comté fruité, beaufort and st-marcellin, she also sells specialities such as goat's cheese with pesto.

Marie-Anne Cantin

12 rue du Champ-de-Mars, 7th (01.45.50.43.94/www.cantin.fr). M° Ecole Militaire or Latour Maubourg. **Open** 2-7.30pm Mon; 8.30am-7.30pm Tue-Sat; 8.30am-1pm Sun. **Map** p123 B3 ⑯

Cantin, a defender of unpasteurised cheese and supplier to posh Paris restaurants, offers aged *chèvres* and amazing morbier, mont d'or and comté.

Village Suisse

38-78 av de Suffren or 54 av de La Motte-Picquet, 15th (www.villagesuisseparis.com). M° La Motte Picquet Grenelle. **Open** 10.30am-7pm Mon, Thur-Sun. **Map** p123 B3 ⑰

The mountains and waterfalls created for the Swiss Village at the 1900 Exposition Universelle are long gone, but the village lives on. Rebuilt as blocks of flats, the street level has been colonised by some 150 boutiques offering pricey antiques and collectibles.

Arts & leisure

La Pagode

57bis rue de Babylone, 7th (01.45.55.48.48). M° St-François-Xavier. **Admission** €8; €6.50 Mon, Wed, students, under-21s. No credit cards. **Map** p123 D3 ⑱

This glorious edifice is not, as local legend might have it, a block-by-block import, but a 19th-century replica of a pagoda. Renovated in the 1990s, this is one of the loveliest cinemas in the world.

Jardin du Luxembourg p132

St-Germain-des-Prés & Odéon

In the first half of the 20th century, St-Germain-des-Prés was prime arts and literature territory. Writers and painters swapped concepts and girlfriends on its café terraces before World War II, and former GIs jammed in its cellars when the fighting was over. The heart of the Paris jazz boom and haunt of Camus, Prévert, Picasso and Giacometti epitomised a very Parisian amalgam of carefree living and audacious thinking.

Some of that intellectual and hedonistic lore still clings to this small part of the Left Bank, but for decades the main concern here has been more sartorial than Sartrian. St-Germain-des-Prés is now serious fashion territory, and has some of the most expensive property – and cafés – in the city.

St-Germain-des-Prés grew up around the medieval abbey, the oldest church in Paris and site of an annual fair that drew merchants from across Europe. There are traces of its cloister and part of the abbot's palace behind the church on rue de l'Abbaye. Constructed in 1586 in red brick with stone facing, the palace prefigured the architecture of place des Vosges. Charming place de Furstemberg (once the palace stables) is home to the house and studio where the elderly Delacroix lived when painting the murals in St-Sulpice; it now houses the **Musée National Delacroix**. Wagner, Ingres and Colette all lived on nearby rue Jacob; its elegant 17th-century *hôtels particuliers* now contain specialist book, design and antiques shops and a few pleasant hotels.

Further east, rue de Buci hosts a street market and upmarket food shops. In the 18th century, Dr Joseph-Ignace Guillotin first tested out his notorious device – designed,

Eglise St-Germain-des-Prés

believe it or not, to make executions more humane – in the cellars of what is today the Pub St-Germain; the first victim was, reputedly, a sheep. Jacobin regicide Billaud-Varenne was among those who felt the steel of Guillotin's gadget.

Sights & museums

Ecole Nationale Supérieure des Beaux-Arts (Ensb-a)

14 rue Bonaparte, 6th (01.47.03.50.00/ www.ensba.fr). M° St-Germain-des-Prés. **Open** *Courtyard* 9am-5pm Mon-Fri. *Exhibitions* 1-5pm Tue-Sun. **Admission** €4; €2 reductions. *Exhibitions* prices vary. **Map** p131 C1 ❶

The city's most prestigious fine arts school resides in what remains of the 17th-century Couvent des Petits-Augustins, the 18th-century Hôtel de Chimay, some 19th-century additions and chunks of various French châteaux moved here after the Revolution (when the buildings briefly served as a museum of French monuments). The entrance is on quai Malaquais.

Eglise St-Germain-des-Prés

3 pl St-Germain-des-Prés, 6th (01.55.42.81.33/www.eglise-sgp.org). M° St-Germain-des-Prés. **Open** 8am-7.45pm Mon-Sat; 9am-8pm Sun. **Map** p131 C2 ❷

The oldest church in Paris. On the advice of Germain (later Bishop of Paris), Childebert, son of Clovis, had a basilica and monastery built here around 543. It was first dedicated to St Vincent, and came to be known as St-Germain-le-Doré because of its copper roof, then later as St-Germain-des-Prés ('of the fields'). During the Revolution the abbey was burned and a saltpetre refinery installed; the spire was added in a clumsy 19th-century restoration. Still, most of the present structure is 12th-century, and ornate carved capitals and the tower remain from the 11th. Tombs include those of Jean-Casimir, deposed King of Poland who became Abbot of St-Germain in 1669, and of Scots nobleman William Douglas. Under the window in the second chapel is the funeral stone of philosopher-mathematician Descartes.

Eglise St-Sulpice

Pl St-Sulpice, 6th (01.42.34.59.98/ www.paroisse-saint-sulpice.org). M° St-Sulpice. **Open** 7.30am-7.30pm daily. **Map** p131 C3 ❸

It took 120 years (starting in 1646) and six architects to finish St-Sulpice. The grandiose Italianate façade, with its two-tier colonnade, was designed by Jean-Baptiste Servandoni. He died in 1766 before the second tower was finished, leaving one tower five metres shorter than the other. The trio of murals by Delacroix in the first chapel – *Jacob's Fight with the Angel, Heliodorus Chased from the Temple* and *St Michael Killing the Dragon* – create a suitably sombre atmosphere.

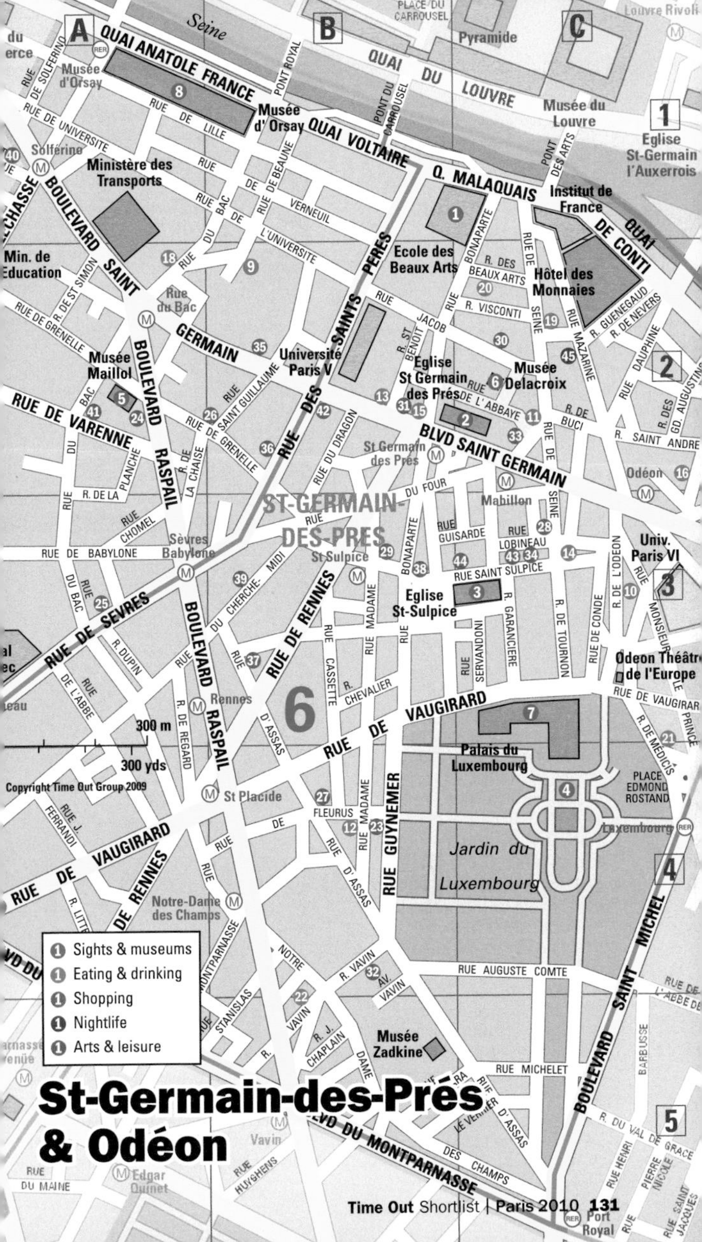
St-Germain-des-Prés
& Odéon
Seine
A
B
C
1
2
3
4
5
6
Place du Carrousel
Louvre Rivoli
Pyramide
Quai Anatole France
Quai du Louvre
Musée du Louvre
Eglise St-Germain l'Auxerrois
Musée d'Orsay
Quai Voltaire
Q. Malaquais
Institut de France
Quai de Conti
Pont Royal
Pont du Carrousel
Pont des Arts
Rue de Lille
Rue de Beaune
Rue de Verneuil
Rue de l'Université
Rue du Bac
Rue de Solferino
Solférino
Ministère des Transports
Boulevard Saint Germain
Min. de Education
R. de St Simon
Rue de Grenelle
Rue du Bac
Musée Maillol
Rue de Varenne
Boulevard Raspail
Ecole des Beaux Arts
R. des Beaux Arts
Rue Bonaparte
R. Visconti
Rue de Seine
Hôtel des Monnaies
Rue Guénégaud
R. de Nevers
Rue Dauphine
Rue Mazarine
Rue Jacob
Université Paris V
Rue des Saints Pères
Eglise St Germain des Prés
Rue de l'Abbaye
Musée Delacroix
R. de Buci
R. Saint André des Arts
R. des Gd. Augustins
Blvd Saint Germain
St Germain des Prés
Rue Saint Guillaume
Rue du Dragon
Rue du Four
Mabillon
Odéon
St-Germain-des-Prés
Rue Guisarde
Rue Lobineau
Univ. Paris VI
Rue de l'Odéon
Rue Monsieur le Prince
Rue de la Chaise
R. de la Planche
Rue Chomel
Sèvres Babylone
Rue de Babylone
St Sulpice
Rue Saint Sulpice
Eglise St-Sulpice
R. Garancière
R. de Tournon
Rue de Condé
Rue Servandoni
Rue du Cherche-Midi
Rue de Rennes
Rue Madame
Rue Cassette
R. Chevalier
Rue de Sèvres
R. Dupin
Rue de l'Abbé
Boulevard Raspail
Rennes
R. de Regard
Rue d'Assas
Rue de Vaugirard
Odéon Théâtre de l'Europe
Palais du Luxembourg
R. de Médicis
Place Edmond Rostand
Luxembourg
Jardin du Luxembourg
300 m
300 yds
Copyright Time Out Group 2009
St Placide
Rue de Fleurus
Rue Guynemer
Rue J. Ferrandi
Rue de Vaugirard
Rue de Rennes
Notre-Dame des Champs
Rue Notre Dame des Champs
Rue Montparnasse
Rue Stanislas
R. Vavin
Av. Vavin
R. J. Chaplain
Musée Zadkine
Rue Auguste Comte
Rue Michelet
Boulevard Saint Michel
Rue de l'Abbé de l'Epée
Rue Barbusse
R. du Val de Grace
Rue Henri Barbusse
Pierre Nicole
Rue Saint Jacques
Rue Le Verrier
Rue d'Assas
Blvd du Montparnasse
Vavin
Edgar Quinet
Rue du Maine
Rue Huyghens
Port Royal
Sights & museums
Eating & drinking
Shopping
Nightlife
Arts & leisure

Bouq club

The *bouquinistes*, who operate out of the famous dark green boxes fixed to the stone walls along the Seine, are a cultural amenity shared by no other city in the world. But today, the 240 or so hardy booksellers, who have to cope with the inclemencies of the northern European climate and the pollution from passing cars as well as the more familiar book trade challenges (stock control, display, and customers who can't remember the title of the book they're looking for), fear they're being squeezed out of business. Internet book dealers have taken a large slice of the rare and second-hand book market, and more and more of the green boxes are resorting to selling postcards and tourist souvenirs to survive.

In any other city, the law of the marketplace might be given free rein. But this is Paris, and there's a reputation to maintain. The Mairie worries that the increasing number of displays of postcards, replica street signs and models of the Eiffel Tower will damage what it calls the city's 'cultural landscape', and has held talks with the booksellers to encourage them to stock more improving merchandise; there are also plans to stimulate the trade with book festivals, organised tours of the stalls and the reinstatement of the annual literary prize awarded by the booksellers themselves. The *bouquinistes* may be up against the wall, but there's still life in those old boxes yet.

Musée d'Orsay p134

Jardin & Palais du Luxembourg

Pl Auguste-Comte, pl Edmond-Rostand or rue de Vaugirard, 6th (01.44.54.19.49/www.senat.fr/visite). M° Odéon/RER Luxembourg.
Open *Jardin* summer 7.30am-dusk daily; winter 8am-dusk daily.
Map p131 C4 ❹

The palace itself was built in the 1620s for Marie de Médicis, widow of Henri IV, by Salomon de Brosse on the site of the former mansion of the Duke of Luxembourg. Its Italianate style was intended to remind her of the Pitti Palace in her native Florence. The palace now houses the French parliament's upper house, the Sénat.

The mansion next door (Le Petit Luxembourg) is the residence of the Sénat's president. The gardens, though, are the real draw: part formal (terraces and gravel paths), part 'English garden' (lawns and mature trees), they are the quintessential Paris park. The garden is crowded with sculptures: a looming Cyclops (on the 1624 Fontaine de Médicis), queens of France, a miniature Statue of Liberty, wild animals, busts of

Flaubert and Baudelaire, and a monument to Delacroix. There are orchards (300 varieties of apples and pears) and an apiary. The Musée National du Luxembourg hosts prestigious exhibitions. Most interesting, though, are the people: an international mixture of *flâneurs* and *dragueurs*, chess players and martial-arts practitioners, as well as children on ponies, in sandpits, on roundabouts and playing with the sailing boats on the pond.

Musée Maillol

59-61 rue de Grenelle, 7th (01.42.22.59.58/www.museemaillol.com). M° Rue du Bac. **Open** 11am-6pm (last admission 5.15pm) Mon, Wed-Sun. **Admission** €8; free-€6 reductions. **Map** p131 A2 ❺

Dina Vierny was 15 when she met Aristide Maillol (1861-1944) and became his principal model for the next decade, idealised in such sculptures as *Spring*, *Air* and *Harmony*. In 1995 she opened this delightful museum, exhibiting Maillol's drawings, engravings, pastels, tapestry panels, ceramics and early Nabis-related paintings, as well as the sculptures and terracottas that epitomise his calm, modern classicism. Vierny also set up a Maillol Museum in the Pyrenean village of Banyuls-sur-Mer. This Paris venue has works by Picasso, Rodin, Gauguin, Degas and Cézanne, a room of Matisse drawings, rare Surrealist documents and works by naïve artists. Vierny has also championed Kandinsky and Ilya Kabakov, whose *Communal Kitchen* installation recreates the atmosphere of Soviet domesticity. Monographic exhibitions are devoted to contemporary artists.

Musée National Delacroix

6 pl de Furstemberg, 6th (01.44.41.86.50/www.musee-delacroix.fr). M° St-Germain-des-Prés. **Open** *Sept-May* 9.30am-5pm Mon, Wed-Sun. *June-Aug* 9.30am-5.30pm Mon, Wed-Sun. **Admission** €5; free reductions. **Map** p131 C2 ❻

Eugène Delacroix moved to this apartment and studio in 1857 to be near the Eglise St-Sulpice, where he was painting murals. This collection includes small oil paintings, free pastel studies of skies, sketches and lithographs.

La Palette p136

The building was originally a train station, designed by Victor Laloux to coincide with the Exposition Universelle in 1900. Now it's a huge museum spanning the fertile art period between 1848 and 1914. It follows a chronological route, from the ground floor to the upper level and then to the mezzanine, showing links between Impressionist painters and their forerunners: here you'll find a profusion of paintings by Delacroix, Corot, Manet, Renoir, Pissarro, Gauguin, Monet, Caillebotte, Cézanne, Van Gogh, Toulouse-Lautrec and others. A central sculpture aisle takes in monuments and maidens by Rude, Barrye and Carrier-Belleuse, but the outstanding pieces are by Carpeaux. The sculpture terraces include busts by Rodin, heads by Rosso and bronzes by Bourdelle and Maillol.

Musée National du Luxembourg

19 rue de Vaugirard, 6th (01.42.34. 25.95/www.museeduluxembourg.fr). M° Cluny La Sorbonne or Odéon/RER Luxembourg. **Open** 10.30am-10pm Mon, Fri, Sat; 10.30am-7pm Tue-Thur; 9.30am-7pm Sun. **Admission** €11; free-€9 reductions. **Map** p131 C3 ⑦

When it opened in 1750, this small museum was the first public gallery in France. Its current stewardship by the national museums and French Senate has brought imaginative touches and some impressive coups. Book ahead to avoid queues.

Musée d'Orsay

1 rue de la Légion-d'Honneur, 7th (01.40.49.48.14/recorded information 01.45.49.11.11/www.musee-orsay.fr). M° Solférino/RER Musée d'Orsay. **Open** 9.30am-6pm Tue, Wed, Fri-Sun; 9.30am-9.45pm Thur. **Admission** €9.50; free-€7 reductions. **Map** p131 A1 ⑧

Eating & drinking

L'Atelier de Joël Robuchon

5 rue de Montalembert, 7th (01.42.22. 56.56/www.joel-robuchon.com). M° Rue du Bac. **Open** 11.30am-3.30pm, 6.30pm-midnight daily. **€€. International. Map** p131 B2 ⑨

This is star chef Joël Robuchon's Paris take on a New York coffee-shop-cum-sushi-and-tapas-bar. The lacquer interior and two U-shaped bars are the epitome of sassy Left Bank chic. The menu is split into three different *formules*: start with caviar, Spanish ham, a large seasonal salad or maybe an assortment of little tasting plates. Then go classic (a steak), fanciful (*vitello tonnato*, veal in tuna and anchovy sauce) or lush (sublime cannelloni of roast Bresse chicken, stuffed with foie gras and served with wild mushrooms).

Le Bar Dix

10 rue de l'Odéon, 6th (01.43.26. 66.83). M° Odéon. **Open** 6pm-2am daily. No credit cards. **Bar. Map** p131 C3 ⑩

Generations of students have glugged back jugs of the celebrated home-made sangría (€3 a glass in happy hour) while squeezed into the cramped upper bar, tattily authentic with its Jacques Brel record sleeves, Yves Montand handbills and pre-war light fittings. Spelunkers and hopeless romantics negotiate the hazardous stone staircase to drink in the cellar bar, with its candlelight and old advertising murals. Can someone please come and slap a preservation order on the place?

Le Bar du Marché

75 rue de Seine, 6th (01.43.26.55.15). M° Mabillon or Odéon. **Open** 8am-2am daily. **Bar**. **Map** p131 C2 ⑪

The market in question is the Cours des Halles, the bar a convivial corner café opening on to the pleasing bustle of St-Germain-des-Prés. Simple dishes like a ham omelette or a plate of herring in the €7 range, and Brouilly or muscadet at €4-€5 a glass, are proffered by beret-topped waiters. Locals easily outnumber tourists, confirming Rod Stewart's astute observation that Paris gives the impression that no one is ever working.

Bread & Roses

7 rue de Fleurus, 6th (01.42.22.06.06). M° St-Placide. **Open** 8am-8pm Mon-Sat. Closed Aug & 1wk Dec. **€€**. **Café**. **Map** p131 B4 ⑫

Giant wedges of cheesecake sit alongside French pastries, and huge savoury puff-pastry tarts are perched on the counter. Attention to detail shows even in the taramasalata, which is matched with buckwheat-and-seaweed bread. Prices reflect the quality of the often organic ingredients, but that doesn't seem to deter the moneyed locals, who order towering birthday cakes here for their snappily dressed offspring.

Café de Flore

172 bd St-Germain, 6th (01.45.48.55.26/www.cafe-de-flore.com). M° St-Germain-des-Prés. **Open** 7.30am-1.30am daily. **€€**. **Café**. **Map** p131 B2 ⑬

Bourgeois locals crowd the terrace tables at lunch, eating club sandwiches with knives and forks as anxious waiters frown at couples with pushchairs or single diners occupying tables for four. This historic café, former HQ of the Lost Generation intelligentsia, attracts tourists, and celebrities from time to time. But a *café crème* is €4.60, a Perrier €5 and the omelettes and *croques* are best eschewed in favour of the better dishes on the menu (€15-€25). There are play readings on Mondays and philosophy debates on the first Wednesday of the month, both at 8pm, in English.

Le Comptoir

Hôtel Le Relais Saint-Germain, 9 carrefour de l'Odéon, 6th (01.43.29.12.05). M° Odéon. **Open** noon-6pm, 8.30-midnight (last orders 9pm) Mon-Fri; noon-11pm Sat, Sun. Closed 3wks Aug. **€**. **Brasserie**. **Map** p131 C3 ⑭

Yves Camdeborde runs the bijou 17th-century Hôtel Le Relais Saint-Germain, whose art deco dining room, modestly dubbed Le Comptoir, serves brasserie fare from noon to 6pm and on weekend nights, and a five-course prix fixe feast on weekday evenings. The single dinner sitting lets the chef take real pleasure in his work. On the daily menu, you might find dishes like rolled saddle of lamb with vegetable-stuffed 'Basque ravioli'. The catch? The prix fixe dinner is booked up as much as six months in advance.

Les Deux Magots

6 pl St-Germain-des-Prés, 6th (01.45.48.55.25/www.lesdeuxmagots.com). M° St-Germain-des-Prés. **Open** 7.30am-1am daily. **€€**. **Café**. **Map** p131 B2 ⑮

If you stand outside Les Deux Magots, you have to be prepared to photograph tourists wanting proof of their encounter with French philosophy. The former haunt of Sartre and de Beauvoir now draws a less pensive crowd that can be all too *m'as-tu vu*, particularly at weekends. The hot chocolate is still good (and the only item served in generous portions) – but, like everything else, it's pricey. Visit on a weekday afternoon when the editors return, manuscripts in hand, to the inside tables, leaving enough elbow room to engage in some serious discussion.

L'Epigramme

NEW *9 rue de l'Eperon, 6th (01.44.41.00.09). M° Odéon.* **Open** noon-2.30pm, 7-11.30pm Tue-Sat; noon-2pm Sun. **€**. **Bistro**. **Map** p131 C2 16

The recently opened L'Epigramme is a pleasantly bourgeois dining room with terracotta floor tiles, wood beams, a glassed-in kitchen and comfortable chairs. Like the decor, the food doesn't aim to innovate but sticks to tried and true classics with the occasional twist. Marinated mackerel in a mustardy dressing on toasted country bread gets things off to a promising start, but the chef's skill really comes through in main courses such as perfectly seared lamb with glazed root vegetables and intense *jus*. It's rare to find such a high standard of cooking at this price.

La Ferrandaise

8 rue de Vaugirard, 6th (01.43.26.36.36/www.laferrandaise.com). M° Odéon/RER Luxembourg. **Open** noon-2.30pm, 7-10.30pm Tue-Thur; noon-2.30pm, 7pm-midnight Fri; 7pm-midnight Sat. **€€**. **Bistro**. **Map** p131 A4 17

This bistro has quickly established a faithful following. In the modern bistro tradition, the northern French chef serves solid, classic food with a twist. A platter of excellent ham, sausage and terrine arrives as you study the blackboard menu, and the bread is crisp-crusted, thickly sliced sourdough. Two specialities are the potato stuffed with escargots in a camembert sauce, and a wonderfully flavoured, slightly rosé slice of veal. Desserts might include intense chocolate with rum-soaked bananas. Wines start at €14.

Gaya Rive Gauche

44 rue du Bac, 7th (01.45.44.73.73/www.pierre-gagnaire.com). M° Rue du Bac. **Open** noon-2.30pm, 7.30-10.45pm Mon-Fri. **€€€**. **Seafood**. **Map** p131 A2 18

Pierre Gagnaire runs this relatively affordable fish restaurant. The menu enumerates ingredients without much clue as to how they are put together, though the helpful waiters will explain if you don't like a surprise. But then surprises are what Gagnaire is famous for. The Fats Waller, for instance, turns out to be a soup of grilled red peppers with a bloody mary sorbet in the centre and daubs of quinoa, basmati rice and Chinese spinach. For the mains, diners are treated like sophisticated children – everything has been detached from the bone or carapace. Light desserts complete the successful formula.

La Palette

43 rue de Seine, 6th (01.43.26.68.15). M° Odéon. **Open** 9am-2am Mon-Sat. Closed Aug. **€**. **Café**. **Map** p131 C2 19

La Palette is the café-bar of choice for the Beaux-Arts students who study at the venerable institution around the corner, and young couples who steal kisses in the wonderfully preserved art-deco back room decorated with illustrations. Grab a spot on the leafy terrace if you can – there's formidable competition for seats.

Le Restaurant

L'Hôtel, 13 rue des Beaux-Arts, 6th (01.44.41.99.01/www.l-hotel.com). M° St-Germain-des-Prés. **Open** 12.30-2pm, 7.30-10pm Tue-Sat. **€€€**. **Haute cuisine**. **Map** p131 C2 20

Since being taken over by Oxford-based Cowley Manor, L'Hôtel has rechristened its restaurant (formerly Le Belier) and put the talented Philippe Bélisse in charge of the kitchen. You can choose from a short seasonal menu with dishes such as pan-fried tuna, John Dory or suckling pig. But for the same price you could also enjoy the marvellous

PARIS BY AREA

four-course *menu dégustation* (€74) or, even better, the *menu surprise* at €125. Highlights of the autumn menu were the wild Breton crab stuffed with fennel, avocado and *huile d'Argan*, and a main course of pigeon on a bed of beetroot.

Le Rostand

6 pl Edmond-Rostand, 6th (01.43.54. 61.58). RER Luxembourg. **Open** 8am-2am daily. **Bar**. **Map** p131 C3 ㉑

Le Rostand has a truly wonderful view of the Jardin du Luxembourg from its classy interior, decked out with oriental paintings, a long mahogany bar and wall-length mirrors. It's a terribly well-behaved place; consider arriving draped in furs or sporting the latest designer eyewear if you want to fit in with the well-heeled clientele. Whiskies and cocktails are pricey, as is the brasserie menu, but the snack menu serves delicious omelettes and *croques* for around €8 (salad €4 extra). Perfect for a civilised drink after a stroll round the gardens.

Le Timbre

3 rue Ste-Beuve, 6th (01.45.49.10.40). M° Vavin. **Open** noon-1.30pm, 7.30-10.30pm Tue-Sat. Closed Aug & 1wk Dec. **€**. **Bistro**. **Map** p131 B4 ㉒

Chris Wright's restaurant, open kitchen included, might be the size of the average student garret, but this Mancunian aims high. Typical of his cooking is a plate of fresh asparagus elegantly cut in half lengthwise and served with dabs of anise-spiked sauce and balsamic vinegar, and a little crumbled parmesan. Main courses are also pure in presentation and flavour – a thick slab of pork, pan-fried but not the least bit dry, comes with petals of red onion that retain a light crunch.

Shopping

APC

38 rue Madame, 6th (01.42.22.12.77/ www.apc.fr). M° St-Placide. **Open** 11am-7.30pm Mon-Sat. **Map** p131 B4 ㉓

The art of amour

They invented the French kiss, speak the language of love and are renowned the world over for their powers of seduction. So you'd be forgiven for thinking that the French would know a thing or two about romance. Think again. According to Véronique J Corniola, founder of **L'Ecole de la Séduction** (01.42.61.84.45, www.ecoledeseduction.com), France's first school in the art of wooing, the French have forgotten how to make contact with each other.

So how does the school work? Véronique works closely with life coaches, a psychologist and an image consultant. Over eight months, they delve deeply into their students' personal history, dusting out whatever may be lurking in their innermost closets, boosting self-esteem and, where necessary, offering haircuts, a new wardrobe and even singles holidays. Students are then encouraged to hit the town over an eight-day module, during which the teachers give training in body language, self-image, and breathing and voice techniques, before following them into bars, restaurants and nightclubs to watch them in action. It's a pricey business (€6,000 minimum), but it seems to work – Véronique boasts a 90 per cent success rate.

So what is the secret to nabbing a partner in France today? According to Véronique, it's pretty much the same across the world: you have to be generous, empathetic and warm.

Poilâne p140

The look is simple but stylish: think perfectly cut basics in muted tones. Hip without trying too hard, its jeans are a big hit – the skinny version caused a stampede when they came out.

L'Artisan Parfumeur

24 bd Raspail, 7th (01.42.22.23.32/ www.artisanparfumeur.com). M° Rue du Bac. **Open** 10.30am-7.30pm Mon-Sat. **Map** p131 A2 24

Among the scented candles, potpourri and charms, you'll find the best vanilla perfume that Paris can offer – Mûres et Musc, a bestseller for two decades.

Le Bon Marché

24 rue de Sèvres, 7th (01.44.39. 80.00/www.bonmarche.fr). M° Sèvres Babylone. **Open** 10am-7.30pm Mon-Wed; 10am-9pm Thur; 10am-8pm Fri; 9.30am-8pm Sat. **Map** p131 A3 25

Luxury boutiques, Dior and Chanel among them, take pride of place on the ground floor; escalators designed by Andrée Putman take you up to the fashion floor, which has an excellent selection of designer labels. Designer names also abound in Balthazar, the men's section. For top-notch nibbles, try the Grande Epicerie (01.44.39.81.00, www.lagrandeepicerie.fr).

Bruno Frisoni

34 rue de Grenelle, 6th (01.42.84. 12.30/www.brunofrisoni.fr). M° Rue du Bac. **Open** 10.30am-7pm Tue-Sat. **Map** p131 B2 26

Innovative Frisoni's shoes have a cinematic, pop edge: modern theatrics for the unconventional.

Christian Constant

37 rue d'Assas, 6th (01.53.63.15.15). M° Rennes or St-Placide. **Open** 8.30am-9pm Mon-Fri; 8.30am-8pm Sat, Sun. **Map** p131 B4 27

A master chocolate-maker and *traiteur*, Constant scours the globe for ideas. His *ganaches* are subtly flavoured with verbena, jasmine or cardamom.

Gérard Mulot

76 rue de Seine, 6th (01.43.26.85.77/ http://gerard-mulot.com). M° Odéon. **Open** 6.45am-8pm Mon, Tue, Thur-Sun. Closed Easter & Aug. **Map** p131 C3 28

Gérard Mulot rustles up stunning pastries. Try the *mabillon*: caramel mousse with apricot marmalade.

Hervé Chapelier

1bis rue du Vieux-Colombier, 6th (01.44.07.06.50/www.hervechapelier.fr). M° St-Germain-des-Prés or St-Sulpice. **Open** 10.15am-7pm Mon-Sat. **Map** p131 B3 29

Pick up a classic bicoloured bag. Prices range from a dinky purse at €22 to a weekend bag at €130.

Huilerie Artisanale Leblanc

6 rue Jacob, 6th (01.46.34.61.55/ www.huile-leblanc.com). M° St-Germain-des-Prés. **Open** noon-7pm Tue-Fri; 10am-7pm Sat. Closed 2wks Aug. No credit cards. **Map** p131 C2 30

The Leblanc family started making walnut oil before branching out to press pure oils from hazelnuts, almonds, pine nuts, grilled peanuts and olives.

La Hune

170 bd St-Germain, 6th (01.45.48. 35.85). M° St-Germain-des-Prés. **Open** 10am-11.45pm Mon-Sat; 11am-7.45pm Sun. **Map** p131 B2 31

This Left Bank institution boasts a global selection of art and design books, and a truly magnificent collection of French literature and theory.

Jean-Paul Hévin

3 rue Vavin, 6th (01.43.54.09.85/ www.jphevin.com). M° Notre-Dame-des-Champs or Vavin. **Open** 10am-7pm Tue-Sat. Closed Aug. **Map** p131 B4 32

Hévin specialises in the beguiling combination of chocolate with potent cheese fillings, which loyal customers serve with wine as an aperitif.

Lefranc.ferrant

NEW *22 rue de l'Echaudé, 6th (01.44.07.37.96/www.lefranc-ferrant.fr). M° St-Germain-des-Prés.* **Open** 11am-7pm Tue-Sat and by appointment. **Map** p131 C2 33

The opening of this boutique has been eagerly awaited by keen followers of the talented Paris duo Béatrice Ferrant and Mario Lefranc. Their trademark is a surreal approach to tailoring, as in a strapless yellow evening gown made like a pair of men's trousers – complete with flies. Prices are in the €1,000 range and they love to do commissions.

Marie Mercié

23 rue St-Sulpice, 6th (01.43.26.45.83). M° Odéon. **Open** 11am-7pm Mon-Sat. **Map** p131 C3 34

Mercié's creations make you wish you lived in an era when hats were de rigueur. Step out in one shaped like curved fingers (with shocking-pink nail varnish and pink diamond ring) or a beret like a face with red lips and turquoise eyes. Ready-to-wear starts at €30; *sur mesure* takes ten days.

Patrick Roger

108 bd St-Germain, 6th (01.43.29. 38.42/www.patrickroger.com). M° Odéon. **Open** 10.30am-7.30pm Mon-Sat. **Map** p131 B2 35

Roger is shaking up the art of chocolate-making. Whereas other *chocolatiers* aim for gloss, Roger may create a brushed effect on hens so realistic you almost expect them to lay (chocolate) eggs.

Paul & Joe

64 rue des Sts-Pères, 7th (01.42.22. 47.01/www.paulandjoe.com). M° Rue du Bac or St-Germain-des-Prés. **Open** 10am-7pm Mon-Sat. **Map** p131 B2 36

Fashionistas have taken a shine to Sophie Albou's retro-styled creations. The latest collection dresses leggy young things in a range of winter shorts, colourful mini dresses and voluminous trousers, with their intellectual paramours in slouchy woollens, tailored jackets and chunky boots.

Peggy Huyn Kinh

9-11 rue Coëtlogon, 6th (01.42.84. 83.82/www.phk.fr). M° St-Sulpice. **Open** 11am-7pm Mon-Sat. **Map** p131 B3 37

Once creative director at Cartier, Peggy Huyn Kinh now makes bags of boar skin and python, plus silver jewellery.

Pierre Hermé

72 rue Bonaparte, 6th (01.43.54.47.77). M° Mabillon, St-Germain-des-Prés or St-Sulpice. **Open** 10am-7pm Tue-Fri, Sun; 10am-7.30pm Sat. Closed 1st 3wks Aug. **Map** p131 B3 ㊳

Pastry superstar Hermé attracts connoisseurs from near and far with his seasonal collections.

Poilâne

8 rue du Cherche-Midi, 6th (01.45.48.42.59/www.poilane.com). M° Sèvres Babylone or St-Sulpice. **Open** 7.15am-8.15pm Mon-Sat. **Map** p131 B3 ㊴

Apollonia Poilâne runs the family shop, where locals queue for fresh country *miches*, flaky-crusted apple tarts and shortbread biscuits.

Richart

258 bd St-Germain, 7th (01.45.55.66.00/www.richart.com). M° Solférino. **Open** 10am-7pm Mon-Sat. **Map** p131 A1 ㊵

Each chocolate *ganache* has an intricate design, packages look like jewel boxes, and each purchase comes with a tract on how best to savour the stuff.

Ryst Dupeyron

79 rue du Bac, 7th (01.45.48.80.93/www.dupeyron.com). M° Rue du Bac. **Open** 12.30-7.30pm Mon; 10.30am-7.30pm Tue-Sat. Closed 2wks Aug. **Map** p131 A2 ㊶

The Dupeyrons have been selling armagnac for four generations, and still have bottles from 1868. Treasures here include 200 fine Bordeaux wines and an extensive range of vintage port.

Sonia Rykiel

175 bd St-Germain, 6th (01.49.54.60.60/www.soniarykiel.com). M° St-Germain-des-Prés or Sèvres Babylone. **Open** 10.30am-7pm Mon-Sat. **Map** p131 B2 ㊷

The queen of St-Germain celebrated the 40th birthday of her flagship store with a glamorous black and smoked glass refit perfect for narcissists. Menswear is located across the street, and two newer boutiques stock the younger, more affordable Sonia by Sonia Rykiel range (59 rue des Sts-Pères, 6th, 01.49.54.61.00) and kids' togs (4 rue de Grenelle, 6th, 01.49.54.61.10). For something a bit on the wild side, Rykiel Woman (6 rue de Grenelle, 6th, 01.49.54.66.21) stocks a range of designer sex toys.

Vanessa Bruno

25 rue St-Sulpice, 6th (01.43.54.41.04/www.vanessabruno.com). M° Odéon. **Open** 10.30am-7.30pm Mon-Sat. **Map** p131 C3 ㊸

Mercerised cotton tanks, flattering trousers and feminine tops have a Zen-like quality that stems from Bruno's stay in Japan, and they somehow manage to flatter every figure type. She also makes great bags; the ample Lune was created to mark ten years in the business.

Yves Saint Laurent

6 pl St-Sulpice, 6th (01.43.29.43.00/www.ysl.com). M° St-Sulpice. **Open** 11am-7pm Mon; 10.30am-7pm Tue-Sat. **Map** p131 C3 ㊹

The memory of the founding designer, who died in 2008, lives on in this wonderfully elegant boutique, which was splendidly refitted in red in the same year. You'll find the menswear collection at no.12 (01.43.26.84.40).

Nightlife

Wagg

62 rue Mazarine, 6th (01.55.42.22.01/www.wagg.fr). M° Odéon. **Open** 11.30pm-6am Fri, Sat; 3pm-midnight Sun. **Admission** €12 Fri, Sat; €12 Sun (incl 1 drink). **Map** p131 C2 ㊺

Wagg went through a period of attracting big name DJs, but has settled down as home to a well-to-do Left Bank crowd. Expect funk, house and disco, plus salsa lessons on Sundays.

Jardin Tino Rossi

The Latin Quarter & the 13th

The Latin Quarter

The Latin Quarter holds a considerable mystique for many foreign visitors, thanks to the historical presence of Hemingway, Orwell and Miller and the seedbed of the 1968 revolt. However, traces of those fabled eras are becoming harder to find: property in the Latin Quarter is now among the dearest in Paris, and every year another relic is renovated out of existence. To cite just one example, the removal of the ancient wooden 'Vieux Chêne' sign from a building in rue Mouffetard in 2005 went almost wholly unnoticed and unlamented.

The 'Latin' in the area's name probably derives from the fact that it has been the university quarter since medieval times, when Latin was the language of instruction.

Sights & museums

Arènes de Lutèce

Rue Monge, rue de Navarre or rue des Arènes, 5th. M° Cardinal Lemoine or Place Monge. **Open** *Summer* 8am-10pm daily. *Winter* 8am-5.30pm daily. **Admission** free. **Map** p143 B4 ❶

This Roman arena, where wild beasts and gladiators fought, could seat 10,000 people. It was still visible during the reign of Philippe-Auguste in the 12th century, then disappeared under rubble. The site now attracts skateboarders, footballers and boules players.

Eglise St-Etienne-du-Mont

Pl Ste-Geneviève, 5th (01.43.54.11.79). M° Cardinal Lemoine/RER Luxembourg. **Open** 10am-7pm Tue-Sun. **Map** p143 B4 ❷

Geneviève, patron saint of Paris, is credited with having miraculously saved the city from the ravages of Attila the

Hun in 451, and her shrine has been a site of pilgrimage ever since. The present church was built in an amalgam of Gothic and Renaissance styles between 1492 and 1626, and the interior is wonderfully tall and light, with soaring columns and a classical balustrade. The stunning Renaissance rood screen, with its double spiral staircase and ornate stone strapwork, is the only surviving one in Paris. At the back of the church (reached through the sacristy), the catechism chapel constructed by Baltard in the 1860s has a cycle of paintings relating the saint's life story.

Eglise St-Séverin

3 rue des Prêtres-St-Séverin, 5th (01.42.34.93.50). M° Cluny La Sorbonne or St-Michel. **Open** 11am-7.30pm daily. **Map** p143 A3 ❸

Built on the site of the chapel of the hermit Séverin, itself set on a much earlier Merovingian burial ground, this lovely Flamboyant Gothic edifice was long the parish church of the Left Bank. The church dates from the 15th century, though the doorway, carved with foliage, was added in 1837 from the demolished Eglise St-Pierre-aux-Boeufs on Ile de la Cité. The double ambulatory is famed for its forest of 'palm tree' vaulting, which meets at the end in a unique spiral column that inspired a series of paintings by Robert Delaunay. The bell tower, a survivor from one of the earlier churches on the site, has the oldest bell in Paris (1412).

Eglise du Val-de-Grâce

Pl Alphonse-Laveran, 5th (01.40.51.47.28). RER Luxembourg or Port-Royal. **Open** noon-6pm Tue, Wed, Sat, Sun. **Admission** €5; free-€2.50 reductions. No credit cards. **Map** p143 A5 ❹

Anne of Austria, the wife of Louis XIII, vowed to erect 'a magnificent temple' if God blessed her with a son. She got two. The resulting church and surrounding Benedictine monastery – these days a military hospital and the Musée du Service de Santé des Armées – were built by François Mansart and Jacques Lemercier. This is the most luxuriously baroque of the city's 17th-century domed churches. In contrast, the surrounding monastery offers the perfect example of François Mansart's classical restraint. Phone in advance if you're after a guided visit.

Grande Galerie de l'Evolution

36 rue Geoffroy-St-Hilaire, 2 rue Bouffon or pl Valhubert, 5th (01.40.79.56.01). M° Gare d'Austerlitz or Jussieu. **Open** *Grande Galerie* 10am-6pm Mon, Wed-Sun. *Other galleries* 10am-5pm Mon, Wed-Fri; 10am-6pm Sat, Sun. **Admission** *Grande Galerie* €8; free-€6 reductions. *Other galleries* (each) €7; free-€5 reductions. No credit cards. **Map** p143 C5 ❺

One of the city's most child-friendly attractions, this is guaranteed to bowl adults over too. Located within the Jardin des Plantes, this 19th-century iron-framed, glass-roofed structure has been modernised with lifts, galleries and false floors, and filled with life-size models of tentacle-waving squids, open-mawed sharks, tigers hanging off elephants and monkeys swarming down from the ceiling. The centrepiece is a procession of African wildlife across the first floor that resembles the procession into Noah's Ark. Glass-sided lifts take you up through suspended birds to the second floor, which deals with man's impact on nature (crocodile into handbag). The third floor focuses on endangered species.

Institut du Monde Arabe

1 rue des Fossés-St-Bernard, 5th (01.40.51.38.38/www.imarabe.org). M° Jussieu. **Open** *Museum* 10am-6pm Tue-Sun. *Library* 1-8pm Tue-Sat. *Café* noon-6pm Tue-Sun. *Tours* 3pm Tue-Fri; 3pm & 4.30pm Sat, Sun. **Admission** *Roof terrace, library* free. *Museum* €5; free-€4 reductions. *Exhibitions* varies. *Tours* €8. **Map** p143 C3 ❻

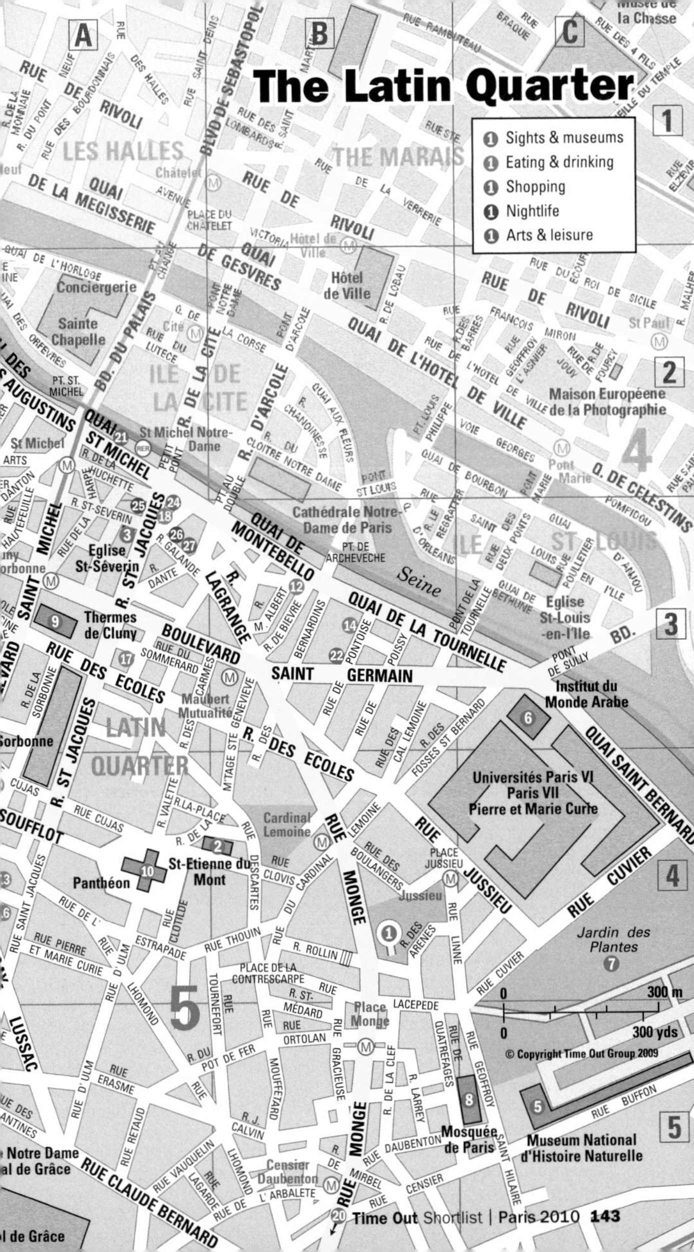

The Latin Quarter
Sights & museums
Eating & drinking
Shopping
Nightlife
Arts & leisure
A
B
C
1
2
3
4
5
LES HALLES
THE MARAIS
ILE DE LA CITE
ILE ST LOUIS
LATIN QUARTER
Seine
Châtelet
Hôtel de Ville
Cité
St Michel
St Michel Notre-Dame
Maubert Mutualité
Cardinal Lemoine
Jussieu
Place Monge
Censier Daubenton
Pont Marie
St Paul
Conciergerie
Sainte Chapelle
Cathédrale Notre-Dame de Paris
Eglise St-Séverin
Thermes de Cluny
Sorbonne
Panthéon
St-Etienne du Mont
Institut du Monde Arabe
Universités Paris VI Paris VII Pierre et Marie Curie
Maison Européene de la Photographie
Eglise St-Louis-en-l'Ile
Jardin des Plantes
Mosquée de Paris
Museum National d'Histoire Naturelle
Musée de la Chasse
RUE DE RIVOLI
QUAI DE LA MEGISSERIE
QUAI DE GESVRES
QUAI DE L'HOTEL DE VILLE
BD. DU PALAIS
BLVD DE SEBASTOPOL
BD. SAINT MICHEL
QUAI DES GRANDS AUGUSTINS
QUAI ST MICHEL
QUAI DE MONTEBELLO
QUAI DE LA TOURNELLE
QUAI SAINT BERNARD
Q. DE CELESTINS
BOULEVARD SAINT GERMAIN
RUE DES ECOLES
R. DES ECOLES
RUE MONGE
RUE JUSSIEU
RUE CUVIER
RUE SOUFFLOT
R. ST JACQUES
RUE CLAUDE BERNARD
RUE RAMBUTEAU
RUE SAINT DENIS
RUE DES HALLES
PLACE DU CHÂTELET
AVENUE VICTORIA
PONT NOTRE DAME
PONT D'ARCOLE
R. D'ARCOLE
R. DE LA CITE
PONT ST LOUIS
PONT DE SULLY
BD. HENRI IV
PLACE DE LA CONTRESCARPE
PLACE JUSSIEU
RUE MOUFFETARD
RUE DESCARTES
RUE DU CARDINAL LEMOINE
RUE THOUIN
RUE CLOVIS
RUE CUJAS
RUE DE L'ESTRAPADE
RUE D'ULM
RUE LHOMOND
RUE TOURNEFORT
RUE POT DE FER
RUE LACEPEDE
RUE GEOFFROY SAINT HILAIRE
RUE BUFFON
RUE CENSIER
RUE DAUBENTON
RUE DE L'ARBALETE
RUE GAY LUSSAC
RUE PIERRE ET MARIE CURIE
RUE ERASME
RUE VAUQUELIN
0
300 m
300 yds
© Copyright Time Out Group 2009

Musée National du Moyen Age – Thermes de Cluny

A clever blend of high-tech and Arab influences, this Seine-side *grand projet* was constructed between 1980 and 1987 to a design by Jean Nouvel. Shuttered windows, inspired by the screens of Moorish palaces, act as camera apertures, contracting or expanding according to the amount of sunlight. A museum covering the history and archaeology of the Islamic Arab world occupies the upper floors: start at the seventh with Classical-era finds and work down via early Islamic dynasties to the present day. The Institut hosts several major, crowd-pleasing exhibitions throughout the year. What's more, there's an excellent Middle East bookshop on the ground floor and the views from the roof terrace (access is free) are fabulous.

Jardin des Plantes

36 rue Geoffroy-St-Hilaire, 2 rue Bouffon, pl Valhubert or 57 rue Cuvier, 5th. M° Gare d'Austerlitz, Jussieu or Place Monge. **Open** *Main garden* Winter 8am-dusk daily. Summer 7.30am-8pm daily. *Alpine garden* Apr-Sept 8am-4.30pm Mon-Fri; 1-5pm Sat, Sun. Closed Oct-Mar. *Ménagerie* Apr-Sept 9am-5pm daily. **Admission** *Alpine Garden* free Mon-Fri; €1 Sat, Sun. *Jardin des Plantes* free. *Ménagerie* €7; free-€5 reductions. **Map** p143 C4 ❼

The Paris botanical garden – which contains more than 10,000 species and includes tropical greenhouses and rose, winter and Alpine gardens – is an enchanting place. Begun by Louis XIII's doctor as the royal medicinal plant garden in 1626, it opened to the public in 1640. The formal garden, which runs between two avenues of trees, is like something out of *Alice in Wonderland*. There's also a small zoo and the terrific Grande Galerie de l'Evolution. Ancient trees on view include a false acacia planted in 1636. A plaque on the old laboratory declares that this is where Henri Becquerel discovered radioactivity in 1896.

La Mosquée de Paris

2 pl du Puits-de-l'Ermite, 5th (01.45.35.97.33/tearoom 01.43.31.38.20/baths 01.43.31.18.14/www.mosquee-de-paris.net). M° Monge. **Open** *Tours* 9am-noon, 2-6pm Mon-Thur, Sat, Sun (closed Muslim hols). *Tearoom* 10am-11.30pm daily. *Restaurant* noon-2.30pm, 7.30-10.30pm daily. *Baths* (women) 10am-9pm Mon, Wed, Sat; 2-9pm Fri; (men) 2-9pm Tue, Sun. **Admission** €3; free-€2 reductions. *Tearoom* free. *Baths* €15-€35. **Map** p143 C5 ❽

This vast Hispano-Moorish construct is the spiritual heart of France's Algerian-dominated Muslim population. In plan and function it divides into three sections: religious (grand patio, prayer room and minaret, all for worshippers and not curious tourists); scholarly (Islamic school and library); and, via rue Geoffroy-St-Hilaire, commercial (café and domed hammam). La Mosquée café is delightful – a courtyard shaded beneath green foliage and scented with the sweet smell of sheesha smoke.

Musée National du Moyen Age – Thermes de Cluny

6 pl Paul-Painlevé, 5th (01.53.73.78.00/ www.musee-moyenage.fr). M° Cluny La Sorbonne. **Open** 9.15am-5.45pm Mon, Wed-Sun. **Admission** €7.50; free-€5.50 reductions. **Map** p143 A3 ❾

The national museum of medieval art is best known for the beautiful, allegorical *Lady and the Unicorn* tapestry cycle, but it also has important collections of medieval sculpture and enamels. The building itself, commonly known as Cluny, is also a rare example of 15th-century secular Gothic architecture, with its foliate Gothic doorways, hexagonal staircase jutting out of the façade and vaulted chapel. It was built from 1485 to 1498 – on top of a Gallo-Roman baths complex. The baths, built in characteristic Roman bands of stone and brick masonry, are the finest Roman remains in Paris. The vaulted frigidarium (cold bath), tepidarium (warm bath), caldarium (hot bath) and part of the hypocaust heating system are all still visible. A themed garden fronts the whole complex.

Le Panthéon

Pl du Panthéon, 5th (01.44.32.18.00). M° Cardinal Lemoine/RER Luxembourg. **Open** 10am-6pm (until 6.30pm summer) daily. **Admission** €7.50; free-€4.80 reductions. **Map** p143 A4 ❿

Soufflot's neo-classical megastructure was the architectural *grand projet* of its day, commissioned by a grateful Louis XV to thank Sainte Geneviève for his recovery from illness. But by the time it was ready in 1790, a lot had changed; during the Revolution, the Panthéon was rededicated as a 'temple of reason' and the resting place of the nation's great men. The austere barrel-vaulted crypt now houses Voltaire, Rousseau, Hugo and Zola. New heroes are installed but rarely: Pierre and Marie Curie's remains were transferred here in 1995; Alexandre Dumas in 2002. Mount the steep spiral stairs to the colonnade encircling the dome for superb views.

Eating & drinking

Allard

41 rue St-André-des-Arts, 6th (01.43.26.48.23). M° Odéon. **Open** noon-2.30pm, 7-11.30pm Mon-Sat. Closed 3wks Aug. **€€**. **Bistro**. **Map** p143 A2 ⓫

This traditional bistro has a pre-war feel, an impression confirmed by the kitchen, which sends out the sort of Gallic grub you come to Paris for. Start with sliced Lyonnaise sausage studded with pistachios and served with potato salad in delicious vinaigrette, or a sauté of wild mushrooms; then try roast Bresse chicken with sautéed ceps or roast duck with olives. Finish up with *tarte fine de pommes*.

Atelier Maître Albert

1 rue Maître-Albert, 5th (01.56.81. 30.01/www.ateliermaitrealbert.com). M° Maubert Mutualité or St-Michel. **Open** noon-2.30pm, 6.30-11.30pm Mon-Wed; noon-2.30pm, 6.30pm-1am Thur, Fri; 6.30pm-1am Sat; 6.30-11.30pm Sun. **€€**. **Bistro**. **Map** p143 B3 ⓬

This Guy Savoy outpost in the fifth has slick decor by Jean-Michel Wilmotte. The indigo-painted, grey marble-floored dining room with open kitchen and rôtisseries on view is attractive but very noisy at night. The short menu lets you have a Savoy classic or two to start with, including oysters in seawater *gelée* or more inventive dishes such as the ballotine of chicken, foie gras and celery root in a chicken-liver sauce. Next up, perhaps, tuna served with tiny iron casseroles of dauphinois potatoes, and cauliflower in béchamel sauce.

Le Crocodile

6 rue Royer-Collard, 5th (01.43.54. 32.37/www.lecrocodile.fr). RER Luxembourg. **Open** 10pm-late Mon-Sat. Closed Aug. **Bar**. **Map** p143 A4 ⓭

Ignore the apparently boarded-up windows at Le Crocodile; if you're here late, then it's open. Friendly young regulars line the sides of this small, narrow bar

PARIS BY AREA

and try to decide what to drink – not easy, given the length of the cocktail list: at last count there were 312 varieties. The generous €6-per-cocktail happy hour (Monday to Thursday before midnight) will allow you to start with a champagne *accroche-coeur*, followed up with a Goldschläger (served with gold leaf) before moving on to one of the other 310.

Itinéraires

NEW *5 rue de Pontoise, 5th (01.46.33.60.11). M° Maubert Mutualité.* **Open** noon-2pm, 8-11pm Tue-Sat. **€€. Bistro. Map** p143 B3 14

Chef Sylvain Sendra played to a full house every night at his little bistro Le Temps au Temps near the Bastille before moving to this larger space near Notre Dame. The sleek space brings together all the elements that make for a successful bistro today: a long *table d'hôte*, a bar for solo meals or quick bites, and a reasonably priced, market-inspired menu. Not everything is a wild success, but it's hard to fault a chef who so often hits the mark, in dishes such as squid-ink risotto with clams, *botargo* (dried mullet roe) and tomato.

Lapérouse

51 quai des Grands-Augustins, 6th (01.43.26.68.04/www.laperouse.fr). M° St-Michel. **Open** noon-2.30pm, 7.30-10pm Mon-Fri; 7.30-10pm Sat. Closed 1wk Jan & Aug. **€€€. Brasserie. Map** p143 A2 15

Lapérouse was formerly a clandestine rendezvous for French politicians and their mistresses; the tiny private dining rooms upstairs used to lock from the inside. Chef Alain Hacquard does a reasonable take on classic French cooking: his beef fillet is smoked for a more complex flavour; a tender saddle of rabbit is cooked in a clay crust, flavoured with lavender and rosemary and served with ravioli of onions. The only snag is the cost, especially of the wine – a half-bottle of Pouilly-Fuissé is nearly €35.

Le Pantalon

7 rue Royer-Collard, 5th (no phone). RER Luxembourg. **Open** 5.30pm-2am Mon-Sat. No credit cards. **€. Café. Map** p143 A4 16

Le Pantalon is a local café that seems familiar yet is utterly surreal. It has the standard fixtures, including the old soaks at the bar – but the regulars and staff are enough to tip the balance into eccentricity. Friendly and funny French grown-ups and foreign students chat in a mishmash of languages; drinks are cheap enough to make you tipsy without the worry of a cash hangover.

Le Pré Verre

8 rue Thénard, 5th (01.43.54.59.47/www.lepreverre.com). M° Maubert Mutualité. **Open** noon-2pm, 7.30-10.30pm Tue-Sat. Closed 3wks Aug & 2wks Dec. **€€. Bistro. Map** p143 A3 17

Philippe Delacourcelle knows how to handle spices like few other French chefs. Salt cod with cassia bark and smoked potato purée is a classic: what the fish lacks in size it makes up for in rich, cinnamon-like flavour and crunchy texture, and smooth potato cooked in a smoker makes a startling accompaniment. Spices have a way of making desserts seem esoteric rather than decadent, but the roast figs with olives are an exception to the rule.

Ribouldingue

10 rue St-Julien-le-Pauvre, 5th (01.46.33.98.80). M° St-Michel. **Open** noon-2pm, 7-11pm Mon-Sat. **€. Bistro. Map** p143 A3 18

This bistro facing St-Julien-le-Pauvre church is the creation of Nadège Varigny, who spent ten years working with Yves Camdeborde before opening a restaurant inspired by the food of her childhood in Grenoble. It's full of people, including critics and chefs, who love simple, honest bistro fare, such as *daube de boeuf* or seared tuna on a bed of melting aubergine. If you have an appetite for offal, go for the gently sautéed brains with new potatoes or

Diptyque

veal kidneys with a perfectly prepared potato gratin. For dessert, try the fresh ewe's cheese with bitter honey.

Le Salon

Cinéma du Panthéon, 13 rue Victor-Cousin, 5th (01.56.24.88.80/ www.cinemadupantheon.fr). RER Luxembourg. **Open** noon-7pm Mon-Fri. **€€. Café. Map** p143 A4 ⑲

This address in the Latin Quarter has quickly been colonised by film people, PR types and ladies who tea, which is hardly surprising when you discover that the array of old sofas, pouffes, tables and ceramic lamps were picked up at Les Puces by Catherine Deneuve herself. The setting for Deneuve's foray into interior decoration is a loft-like space hidden above Paris's oldest art-house cinema. Food is ideal for a light lunch: soup, smoked salmon, salads.

Shopping

Le Boulanger de Monge

123 rue Monge, 5th (01.43.37.54.20/ www.leboulangerdemonge.com). M° Censier Daubenton. **Open** 7am-8.30pm Tue-Sun. **Map** p143 B5 ⑳

Dominique Saibron uses spices to give inimitable flavour to his organic sourdough *boule*. Every day about 2,000 bread-lovers visit this boutique, which also produces one of the city's best baguettes.

Bouquinistes

Along the quais, especially quai de Montebello & quai St-Michel, 5th. M° St-Michel. **Open** times vary from stall to stall, generally Tue-Sun. No credit cards. **Map** p143 A2 ㉑

The green, open-air boxes along the *quais* are one of the city's institutions. As well as the inevitable postcards and tourist tat, most sell a good selection of second-hand books – rummage through boxes packed with ancient paperbacks for something Existential.

Diptyque

34 bd St-Germain, 5th (01.43.26.45.27/ www.diptyqueparis.com). M° Maubert Mutualité. **Open** 10am-7pm Mon-Sat. **Map** p143 B3 ㉒

Diptyque's divinely scented candles are the quintessential gift from Paris. They come in 48 varieties and are probably the best you'll ever find.

Shakespeare & Company

Princesse Tam-Tam
52 bd St-Michel, 6th (01.42.34.99.31/ www.princessetam-tam.com). M° Cluny La Sorbonne. **Open** 1.30-7pm Mon; 10am-7pm Tue-Sat. **Map** p143 A4 ㉓
This fun, inexpensive underwear and swimwear brand features lots of bright colours and sexily transparent gear.

Shakespeare & Company
37 rue de la Bûcherie, 5th (01.43.25.40.93/www.shakespeare andcompany.com). M° St-Michel. **Open** 10am-11pm Mon-Sat; 11am-11pm Sun. **Map** p143 A3 ㉔
Unequivocably the best bookshop in Paris, the historic and ramshackle Shakespeare & Co is always packed with ex-pat and tourist book lovers. There is a large second-hand section, antiquarian books next door, and just about anything you could ask for new.

Nightlife

Caveau de la Huchette
5 rue de la Huchette, 5th (01.43.26. 65.05/www.caveaudelahuchette.fr). M° St-Michel. **Open** *Concerts* 9.30pm-2.30am Mon-Wed, Sun; 9.30pm-6am Thur-Sat. **Admission** €11 Mon-Thur, Sun; €13 Fri, Sat; €9 reductions. **Map** p143 A2 ㉕
This medieval cellar has been a mainstay for 60 years. The jazz shows are followed by early-hours performances in a swing, rock, soul or disco vein.

Caveau des Oubliettes
52 rue Galande, 5th (01.46.34.23.09/ www.caveaudesoubliettes.com). M° St-Michel. **Open** 5pm daily. *Concerts* 10pm daily. **Admission** free. **Map** p143 A3 ㉖
A foot-tapping frenzy echoes in this medieval dungeon, complete with instruments of torture and underground passages. There are various jam sessions in the week, and on Sundays.

Arts & leisure

Studio Galande
42 rue Galande, 5th (01.43.54.72.71/ www.studiogalande.fr). M° Cluny La Sorbonne or St-Michel. **Admission** €7.80; €6 Wed, students. No credit cards. **Map** p143 A3 ㉗

Some 20 different films are screened in subtitled versions at this venerable Latin Quarter venue every week: international arthouse fare, combined with the occasional instalment from the *Matrix* series. On Friday and Saturday nights, dedicated fans of *The Rocky Horror Picture Show* turn up in drag, equipped with rice and water pistols.

The 13th

The construction in the mid-1990s of the **Bibliothèque Nationale de France** breathed life into the desolate area, now known as the ZAC Rive Gauche, between Gare d'Austerlitz and the Périphérique. The ambitious, long-term ZAC project includes a new university quarter, new housing projects and a tramway providing links to the suburbs. Paris's latest big cultural venue, the **Cité de la Mode et du Design**, opened in 2009.

Sights & museums

Bibliothèque Nationale de France François Mitterrand

10 quai François-Mauriac, 13th (01.53.79.59.59/www.bnf.fr). M° Bibliothèque François Mitterrand. **Open** 2-7pm Mon; 9am-7pm Tue-Sat; 1-7pm Sun. **Admission** *1 day* €3.30. *2 weeks* €20. *1 year* €35; €18 reductions. **Map** p151 E2 ㉘

Opened in 1996, the new national library was the last and costliest of Mitterrand's *grands projets*. Its architect, Dominique Perrault, was criticised for his curiously dated design. He also forgot to specify blinds to protect books from sunlight; they had to be added afterwards. The library houses over ten million volumes. Much of the library is open to the public: books, newspapers and periodicals are accessible to anyone over 18, and you can browse through photographic, film and sound archives in the audiovisual section.

Chapelle St-Louis-de-la-Salpêtrière

47 bd de l'Hôpital, 13th (01.42.16.04.24). M° Gare d'Austerlitz. **Open** 8.30am-6pm Mon-Fri, Sun; 11am-6pm Sat. **Admission** free. **Map** p151 C2 ㉙

This austerely beautiful chapel, designed by Bruand and completed in 1677, features an octagonal dome in the centre and eight naves in which the sick were separated from the insane, the destitute from the debauched. Around the chapel sprawls the vast Hôpital de la Pitié-Salpêtrière, which became a centre for research into insanity in the 1790s, when renowned doctor Philippe Pinel began to treat some of the inmates as sick rather than criminal; Charcot later pioneered neuropsychology here. Salpêtrière is one of the city's main teaching hospitals.

Manufacture Nationale des Gobelins

42 av des Gobelins, 13th (tours 01.44.08.53.49). M° Les Gobelins. **Open** *Tours* 2pm, 3pm Tue-Thur. **Admission** €10; free-€6 reductions. No credit cards. **Map** p151 B2 ㉚

The royal tapestry factory, founded by Colbert, is named after Jean Gobelin, a dyer who owned the site. Tapestries are still made here (mainly for French embassies), and visitors can watch weavers at work. The tour (in French) through the 1912 factory takes in the 18th-century chapel and the Beauvais workshops. Arrive 30 minutes before the tour starts.

Eating & drinking

L'Avant-Goût

26 rue Bobillot, 13th (01.53.80.24.00). M° Place d'Italie. **Open** noon-2pm, 7.45-10.45pm Tue-Sat. Closed 3wks Aug. **€**. **Bistro**. **Map** p151 B3 ㉛

Self-taught chef Christophe Beaufront has turned this nondescript street on the edge of the villagey Butte-aux-Cailles into a foodie destination. Typical of Beaufront's cooking is his

Sport for all

After years without a home, the **Musée National du Sport** (p152) has finally found a space for its permanent collection. Located in the heart of the up-and-coming area around Bibliothèque François Mitterrand, the new museum traces the history of sport via a small selection of the 100,000 artefacts in its collection.

Formerly tucked away inside the Parc des Princes stadium, the museum was uprooted prior to the 1998 FIFA World Cup. The collection has since been used sporadically in temporary exhibitions, but not until now has it been given a permanent home. While the new space is only big enough to accommodate some 300 works and objects, it offers a snapshot of some of the defining moments in French sporting history.

The museum is loosely organised into three sections: a general introduction, featuring samples of equipment and sportswear from the entire sporting universe (even cricket gets a look in); sporting history, which traces the evolution of competitive sport in France; and contemporary sports issues, which takes a look at recent political and social developments such as doping and marketing.

Explanatory panels are in both French and English and, even if the thrust of the collection is French sports and heroes, many of the exhibits will be familiar to an international audience: a clutch of Olympic medals from the 1992 Winter Games in Albertville; an autographed ball used in France's triumphant 1998 World Cup victory; the *ballon d'or* won by Zinedine Zidane; and Alain Prost's protective bodysuit (which contrasts radically with a feather-covered driver's coat from the 1930s). Cycling fans will enjoy the display of early bicycles such as the penny farthing and hobby horse, and will no doubt stare with amazement at the boneshaking single-gear machine that Lucien Petit-Breton pedalled to victory in one of the earliest editions of the Tour de France.

Note that the museum is closed on Saturday mornings and all day Sunday.

The 13th
Sights & museums
Eating & drinking
Shopping
Nightlife
Arts & leisure
Museum National d'Histoire Naturelle
Gare d'Austerlitz
Hôpital La Pitié Salpêtrière
Mosquée de Paris
Eglise Notre Dame de Val de Grâce
Val de Grâce
Hôpital Cochin
Maison d'Arrêt de la Santé
Ministère des Finances
Palais Omnisports de Paris Bercy
Gare de Paris Bercy
Bibliothèque Nationale de France
Seine
QUAI D'AUSTERLITZ
QUAI DE LA RAPÉE
QUAI DE LA GARE
QUAI FRANÇOIS MAURIAC
QUAI DE BERCY
BOULEVARD DE BERCY
PT. DE BERCY
PONT DE TOLBIAC
PONT CHARLES DE GAULLE
PASSERELLE SIMONE-DE-BEAUVOIR
BOULEVARD DE L'HOPITAL
BOULEVARD SAINT MARCEL
BOULEVARD DE PORT ROYAL
BOULEVARD ARAGO
AVENUE DES GOBELINS
BOULEVARD VINCENT AURIOL
BD. VINCENT AURIOL
BOULEVARD AUGUSTE BLANQUI
AVENUE D'ITALIE
AVENUE DE CHOISY
RUE NATIONALE
RUE JEANNE D'ARC
RUE CLAUDE BERNARD
RUE MONGE
PLACE D'ITALIE
PLACE JEANNE D'ARC
RUE DE TOLBIAC
RUE DU CHAYEAU DES RENTIERS
RUE DU CHEVALERET
RUE DE LA SANTÉ
RUE DE LA GLACIÈRE
RUE DU MOULIN DES PRES
RUE DE LA BUTTE AUX CAILLES
Place d'Italie
Les Gobelins
Campo Formio
Nationale
Chevaleret
St Marcel
Quai de la Gare
Bibliotheque F. Mitterrand
Tolbiac
Glacière
Censier Daubenton
Place Monge
Bercy
5
13
1
2
3
A
B
C
D
E
0
500 m
500 yds
© Copyright Time Out Group 2009

pot-au-feu de cochon aux épices, a much-written-about dish that has been on his menu for years. It's good, if not earth-shaking; however, a starter of piquillo pepper stuffed with smoked haddock rillettes does illustrate his talent. Beaufront's food is available to take away at the *épicerie* across the street.

L'Ourcine

92 rue Broca, 13th (01.47.07.13.65). Mº Glacière or Les Gobelins. **Open** noon-2pm, 7-10.30pm Tue-Thur; noon-2.30pm, 7-11pm Fri, Sat. Closed 4wks July-Aug. €. **Bistro**. **Map** p151 B2 ㉜

This restaurant near Gobelins is a wonderful bistro stop. Start with *pipérade*, succulent chorizo or a spread of sliced beef tongue with piquillo peppers; then try the sautéed baby squid with parsley, garlic and Espelette peppers, or the *piquillos* stuffed with puréed cod and potato. An appealing atmosphere is generated by a growing band of regulars.

Nightlife

Batofar

Opposite 11 quai François-Mauriac, 13th (recorded information 01.53.60.17.30/www.batofar.org). Mº Quai de la Gare. **Open** 11pm-6am Mon-Sat; 6am-noon 1st Sun of mth. **Admission** €5-€12. **Map** p151 E2 ㉝

In recent years the Batofar has gone through a rapid succession of management teams, with varying levels of success. The current managers have helped revive the venue's tradition of playing cutting-edge music, including electro, dub step, techno and dancehall nights featuring international acts. It's also a destination for early morning clubbers determined to shun their beds.

Arts & leisure

Cité de la Mode et du Design (Docks en Seine)

NEW *28-36 quai d'Austerlitz, 13th. Mº Chevaleret or Gare d'Austerlitz.* **Map** p151 D1 ㉞

The striking bright green Cité de la Mode et du Design, designed by Jakob + MacFarlane, contains restaurants and cafés, a concert and club venue, shops, the Institut Français de la Mode fashion and management school, and a riverside promenade. The most radical element is the 'plug over' system – a framework of green steel tubing and screenprinted glass that clips on to the 1907 reinforced concrete warehouse complex beneath to create a new fluid public space.

MK2 Bibliothèque

128-162 av de France, 13th (08.92.69.84.84/www.mk2.com). Mº Bibliothèque François Mitterrand or Quai de la Gare. **Admission** €9.80; €6.80 students and over-60s (except weekends); €5.90 under-18s; €19.80 monthly pass. **Map** p151 E2 ㉟

The MK2 chain's flagship offers 14 screens, three restaurants, a bar open until 5am at weekends and two-person 'love seats'. A paragon of imaginative programming, MK2 is growing all the time; it has added ten more venues in town, including two situated along the Bassin de la Villette.

Musée National du Sport

NEW *93 av de France, 13th (01.45.83.15.80/www.museedusport.fr). Mº Bibliothèque François Mitterrand.* **Open** 10am-6pm Tue-Fri; 2-6pm Sat. **Map** p151 E3 ㊱

See box p150.

Piscine Josephine-Baker

Quai François-Mauriac, 13th (01.56.61.96.50). Mº Quai de la Gare. **Open** 7-8.30am, 1-9pm Mon; 1pm-midnight Tue; 7-8.30am, 1-9pm Wed; noon-11pm Thur; 7-8.30am, 11am-8pm Sat; 10am-8pm Sun. **Admission** €2.60; €1.50 reductions. **Map** p151 E2 ㊲

Moored on the Seine, the Piscine Josephine-Baker complex boasts a 25m main pool (with sliding glass roof), a paddling pool and café, and a busy schedule of exercise classes.

View from Tour Montparnasse p156

Montparnasse

Artists Picasso, Léger and Soutine fled to 'Mount Parnassus' in the early 1900s to escape the rising rents of Montmartre. They were soon joined by Chagall, Zadkine and other refugees from the Russian Revolution, along with Americans such as Man Ray, Henry Miller, Ezra Pound and Gertrude Stein. Between the wars the neighbourhood was the epitome of modernity: studios with large windows were built by avant-garde architects; artists, writers and intellectuals drank and debated in the quarter's showy bars; and naughty pastimes – including the then risqué tango – flourished.

Sadly, the Montparnasse of today has lost much of its former soul, dominated as it is by the lofty **Tour Montparnasse** – the first skyscraper to be built in central Paris. The dismay with which its construction was greeted prompted a change in building regulations in the city. At its foot are a shopping centre, the **Red Light** and **Mix Club** nightclubs, and, in winter, an ice rink. There are fabulous views from the café on the 56th floor.

Sights & museums

Les Catacombes

1 av Colonel Henri-Rol-Tanguy, 14th (01.43.22.47.63/www.catacombes-de-paris.fr). M°/RER Denfert Rochereau. **Open** 10am-5pm Tue-Sun. **Admission** €7; free-€5.50 reductions. **Map** p155 C3 ❶

This is the official entrance to the 3,000km (1,864-mile) tunnel network that runs under much of the city. With public burial pits overflowing in the era of the Revolutionary Terror, the bones of six million people were transferred to the *catacombes*. The bones of Marat, Robespierre and their cronies are packed in with wall upon wall of their fellow citizens. A damp, cramped tunnel takes you through a series of galleries before you reach the ossuary, the entrance to which is announced by a sign engraved in the stone: 'Stop! This is the empire of death.'

Cimetière du Montparnasse

3 bd Edgar-Quinet, 14th (01.44.10.86.50). M° Edgar Quinet or Raspail. **Open** *16 Mar-5 Nov* 8am-6pm Mon-Fri; 8.30am-6pm Sat; 9am-6pm Sun. *6 Nov-15 Mar* 8am-5.30pm Mon-Fri; 8.30am-5.30pm Sat; 9.30am-5.30pm Sun. **Admission** free. **Map** p155 B2 ❷

This huge cemetery was formed by commandeering three farms (you can still see the ruins of a windmill by rue Froidevaux) in 1824. As with much of the Left Bank, the boneyard has literary clout: Beckett, Baudelaire, Sartre, de Beauvoir, Maupassant, Ionesco and Tristan Tzara all rest here. There are also artists, including Brancusi, Henri Laurens, Frédéric Bartholdi (sculptor of the Statue of Liberty) and Man Ray. The celebrity roll-call continues with Serge Gainsbourg, André Citroën, Coluche and Jean Seberg.

Fondation Cartier pour l'Art Contemporain

261 bd Raspail, 14th (01.42.18.56.50/ recorded information 01.42.18.56.51/ www.fondation.cartier.fr). M° Denfert-Rochereau or Raspail. **Open** 11am-10pm Tue; 11am-8pm Wed-Sun. **Admission** €6.50; free-€4.50 reductions. **Map** p155 C2 ❸

Jean Nouvel's glass and steel building, an exhibition centre with Cartier's offices above, is as much a work of art as the installations inside. Shows by artists and photographers have wide-ranging themes. Live events around the shows are called Nuits Nomades.

Fondation Henri Cartier-Bresson

2 impasse Lebouis, 14th (01.56.80.27.00/www.henricartierbresson.org). M° Gaîté. **Open** 1-6.30pm Tue-Fri,

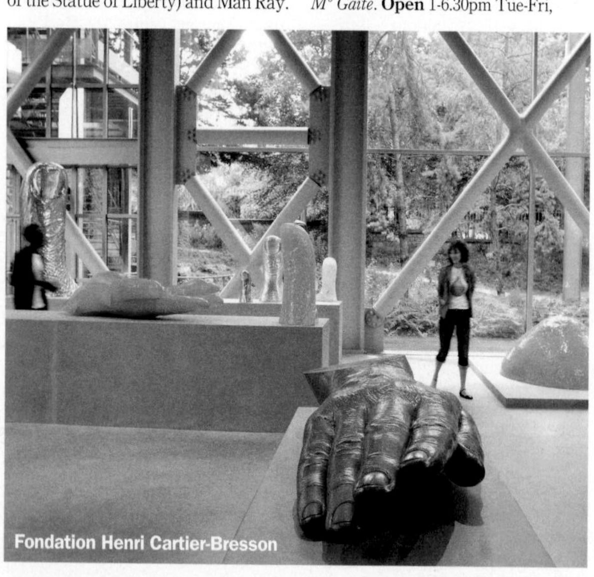

Fondation Henri Cartier-Bresson

Sun; 1-8.30pm Wed; 11am-6.45pm Sat. Closed Aug & between exhibitions. **Admission** €6; €3 reductions. No credit cards. **Map** p155 A2 ❹

This two-floor gallery is dedicated to the work of acclaimed photographer Henri Cartier-Bresson. It consists of a tall, narrow *atelier* in a 1913 building, with a minutely catalogued archive, open to researchers, and a lounge on the fourth floor screening films. In the spirit of Cartier-Bresson, who assisted on three Jean Renoir films and drew and painted all his life (some drawings are also found on the fourth floor), the Fondation opens its doors to other disciplines with three annual shows.

Musée Bourdelle

16-18 rue Antoine-Bourdelle, 15th (01.49.54.73.73/www.bourdelle.paris.fr). M° Falguière or Montparnasse Bienvenüe. **Open** 10am-6pm Tue-Sun. **Admission** free. *Exhibitions* prices vary. **Map** p155 A1 ❺

Les Catacombes p153

The sculptor Antoine Bourdelle (1861-1929), a pupil of Rodin, produced a number of monumental works, including the modernist relief friezes at the Théâtre des Champs-Elysées, inspired

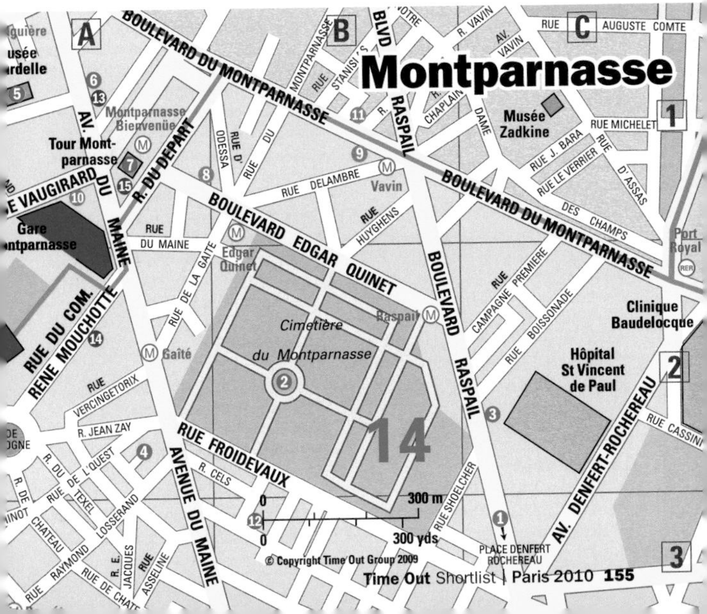

by Isadora Duncan and Nijinsky. Set around a small garden, the museum includes the artist's apartment and studios. A 1950s extension tracks the evolution of Bourdelle's equestrian monument to General Alvear in Buenos Aires, and his masterful *Hercules the Archer*. A new wing houses bronzes.
Event highlights Isadora Duncan (1877-1927): Une Sculpture Vivante (20 Nov 2009-15 Mar 2010)

Musée du Montparnasse

21 av du Maine, 15th (01.42.22.91.96/ www.museedumontparnasse.net). M° Montparnasse Bienvenüe. **Open** 12.30-7pm Tue-Sun. **Admission** €6; free-€5 reductions. No credit cards. **Map** p155 A1 ❻

Set in one of the last surviving alleys of studios, this was home to Marie Vassilieff, whose own academy and cheap canteen welcomed poor artists Picasso, Cocteau and Matisse. Trotsky and Lenin were also guests. Shows focus on present-day artists and the area's creative past.

Tour Montparnasse

33 av du Maine, 15th (01.45.38.52.56/ www.tourmontparnasse56.com). M° Montparnasse Bienvenüe. **Open** *1 Oct-31 Mar* 9.30am-10.30pm daily. *1 Apr-30 Sept* 9.30am-11.30pm daily. **Admission** €10; free-€7 reductions. **Map** p155 A1 ❼

Built in 1974 on the site of the old station, this 209m (686ft) steel-and-glass monolith is shorter than the Eiffel Tower, but better placed for fabulous views of the city. A lift whisks you up in 38 seconds to the 56th floor, where you'll find a display of aerial scenes of Paris, an upgraded café-lounge, a souvenir shop – and plenty of sky.

Eating & drinking

La Cerisaie

70 bd Edgar Quinet, 14th (01.43.20.98.98). M° Edgar Quinet or Montparnasse. **Open** noon-2pm, 7-10pm Mon-Fri. Closed Aug & 1wk Dec. **€€. Bistro. Map** p155 A1 ❽

Nothing about La Cerisaie's unprepossessing red façade hints at the talent that lurks inside. With a simple starter of white asparagus served with preserved lemon and drizzled with bright green parsley oil, chef Cyril Lalanne proves his ability to select and prepare the finest produce. On the daily changing blackboard menu you might find *bourride de maquereau*, a thrifty take on the garlicky southern French fish stew, or *cochon noir de Bigorre*, an ancient breed of pig that puts ordinary pork to shame. *Baba à l'armagnac*, a variation on the usual rum cake, comes with great chantilly.

La Coupole

102 bd du Montparnasse, 14th (01.43.20.14.20/www.flobrasseries.com/ coupoleparis). M° Vavin. **Open** 8am-1am Mon-Fri; 8.30am-1am Sat, Sun. **€€. Brasserie. Map** p155 B1 ❾

La Coupole still glows with some of the old glamour. The people-watching remains superb, inside and out, and the long ranks of linen-covered tables, professional waiters, 32 art deco columns painted by different artists of the epoch, mosaic floor and sheer scale of the operation still make coming here an event. The set menu offers unremarkable steaks, foie gras, fish and autumn game stews, but the real treat is the shellfish, which is displayed along a massive counter. Take your pick from the *claires*, *spéciales* and *belons*, or go for a platter with crabs, oysters, prawns, periwinkles and clams.

L'Ostréade

11 bd de Vaugirard, 15th (01.43.21.87.41/www.ostreade.com). M° Montparnasse-Bienvenüe. **Open** noon-3pm, 7-10pm daily. **€€. Seafood. Map** p155 A1 ❿

From the outside, L'Ostréade (sandwiched between Gare Montparnasse and a Quick fast-food joint), might look like a tourist trap, but is in fact a chic

PARIS BY AREA

La Coupole

address, dressed up like a luxury yacht, coveted by seafood aficionados hooked on big 'n' juicy oysters and perfect fish. If they're in season, try the Part-Ar-Cum oysters, fresh from the Finistère in Brittany, renowned for their hazelnut-like flavour; then the sea bass served with saffron sauerkraut; and finish with a crackly-topped passion fruit crème brûlée.

Le Select

99 bd du Montparnasse, 6th (01.45.48.38.24). M° Vavin. **Open** 7am-2am Mon-Thur, Sun; 7am-4am Fri, Sat. **€. Café. Map** p155 B1 ⓫

For a decade between the wars, the junction of boulevards Raspail and du Montparnasse was where Man Ray, Cocteau and Lost Generation Americans hung out in the vast, glass-fronted cafés. Eight decades on, Le Select is the best of these inevitable tourist haunts. Sure, its pricey menu is big on historical detail and short on authenticity, but by and large it manages to hold on to its heyday with dignity.

Shopping

Paris Accordéon

80 rue Daguerre, 14th (01.43.22.13.48/www.parisaccordeon.com). M° Denfert Rochereau or Gaîté. **Open** 9am-noon, 1-7pm Tue-Fri; 9am-noon, 1-6pm Sat. **Map** p155 B3 ⓬

Accordions galore, from squeezeboxes to beautiful tortoiseshell models, both second-hand and new.

Nightlife

Mix Club

24 rue de l'Arrivée, 15th (01.56.80.37.37/www.mixclub.fr). M° Montparnasse Bienvenüe. **Open** 11pm-6am Wed-Sat; 5pm-1am Sun. **Admission** €12-€20. **Map** p155 A1 ⓭

The Mix Club has one of the city's biggest dancefloors. Regular visitors include Erick Morillo's Subliminal and Ministry of Sound parties, and in-house events include David Guetta's 'Fuck Me I'm Famous' and 'Hipnotic', plus just about everyone else who's big in France – or anywhere else in the world.

Le Petit Journal Montparnasse

13 rue du Commandant-René-Mouchotte, 14th (01.43.21.56.70/www.petitjournal-montparnasse.com). M° Gaîté or Montparnasse-Bienvenüe. **Open** *Concerts* 10pm Mon-Sat. **Admission** (incl 1 drink) €25; €15 reductions. **Map** p155 A2 ⓮

Two-level jazz brasserie in the shadow of the Tour Montparnasse with Latin sounds, R&B and soul-gospel.

Red Light

34 rue du Départ, 15th (01.42.79.94.53/www.enfer.fr). M° Edgar Quinet or Montparnasse Bienvenüe. **Open** midnight-11am Fri, Sat. **Admission** (incl 1 drink) €20-€25. **Map** p155 A1 ⓯

The former Enfer ('Hell') remains a trance, techno and house dynamo with local and global DJs spinning to a young, up-for-it, often gay crowd.

Worth the Trip

North

Basilique St-Denis

1 rue de la Légion-d'Honneur, 93200 St-Denis (01.48.09.83.54). M° St-Denis Basilique/tram 1. **Open** *Apr-Sept* 10am-6.15pm Mon-Sat; noon-6.15pm Sun. *Oct-Mar* 10am-5.15pm Mon-Sat; noon-5.15pm Sun. **Tours** 10.30am, 3pm Mon-Sat; 12.15pm, 3pm Sun. **Admission** €6.50; free-€4.50 reductions.

Legend has it that when St Denis was beheaded, he picked up his noggin and walked with it to Vicus Catulliacus (now St-Denis) to be buried. The first church, parts of which can be seen in the crypt, was built over his tomb in around 475. The present edifice was begun in the 1130s. It is considered the first example of Gothic architecture. In the 13th century, master mason Pierre de Montreuil erected the spire and rebuilt the choir nave and transept. St-Denis was the burial place for all but three French monarchs between 996 and the end of the *ancien régime*, so the ambulatory is a museum of French funerary sculpture. It includes a fanciful Gothic tomb for Dagobert, the austere effigy of Charles V, and the Renaissance tomb of Louis XII and his wife Anne de Bretagne. In 1792 these tombs were desecrated, and the royal remains thrown into a pit.

Musée de l'Air et de l'Espace

Aéroport de Paris-Le Bourget, 93352 Le Bourget Cedex (01.49.92.71.99/ recorded information 01.49.92.70.62/ www.mae.org). M° Gare du Nord, then bus 350/RER Le Bourget, then bus 152. **Open** *Apr-Sept* 10am-6pm Tue-Sun. *Oct-Mar* 10am-5pm Tue-Sun. **Admission** €7; free-€5 reductions. *With Concorde & Boeing 747* €9.50; free-€8 reductions.

The impressive air and space museum is set in the former passenger terminal at Le Bourget airport. The collection begins with the pioneers, including fragile-looking biplanes and the command cabin of a Zeppelin airship. On the runway are Mirage fighters, a US Thunderchief, and Ariane launchers 1 and 5. A hangar houses the prototype Concorde 001 and wartime survivors. A scale models gallery opened in 2008.

East

104

104 rue d'Aubervilliers, 19th (01.53.35. 50.00/www.104.fr). M° Riquet. **Open** 11am-8pm Mon, Sun; 11am-11pm Tue-Sat. **Admission** free. *Exhibitions* €5; €3 reductions.

It's more than a century since tourist-choked Montmartre was the centre of artistic activity in Paris. But now the north of Paris is again where the action is, in a previously neglected area of bleak railway goods yards and dilapidated social housing. 104, described as a 'space for artistic creation', occupies a vast 19th-century building on the rue d'Aubervilliers that used to house Paris's municipal undertakers. There aren't any constraints on the kind of work the resident artists do – 104 is open to 'all the arts' – but they're expected to show finished pieces in one of four annual 'festivals'. And they're also required to get involved in projects with the public.

La Cité des Sciences et de l'Industrie

La Villette, 30 av Corentin-Cariou, 19th (01.40.05.70.00/www.cite-sciences.fr). M° Porte de la Villette. **Open** 10am-6pm Tue-Sat; 10am-7pm Sun. **Admission** €8; free-€6 reductions.

This ultra-modern science museum pulls in five million visitors a year. Explora, the permanent show, occupies the upper two floors, whisking visitors through 30,000sq m (320,000sq ft) of space, life, matter and communication: scale models of satellites including the Ariane space shuttle, planes and robots, plus the chance to experience weightlessness, make for an exciting trip. In the Espace Images, try the delayed camera and other optical illusions, draw 3D images on a computer or lend your voice to the *Mona Lisa*. The hothouse garden investigates developments in agriculture and bio-technology. The Cité des Enfants runs workshops for younger children.

Disneyland Paris/ Walt Disney Studios Park

Marne-la-Vallée (08.25.30.60.30/from UK 0870 503 0303/www.disneyland paris.com). 32km E of Paris. RER A or TGV Marne-la-Vallée-Chessy. By car, A4 exit 14. **Open** *Disneyland Paris* Sept-mid July 10am-8pm Mon-Fri; 9am-8pm Sat, Sun. Mid July-Aug 9am-11pm daily. *Studios Park* Winter 10am-6pm Mon-Fri; 9am-6pm Sat, Sun. Summer 9am-7pm daily. **Admission** *1 park* €47; free-€39 reductions. *1-day hopper* (both parks) €57; free-€49 reductions.

Young ones will get a real kick out of Fantasyland, with its Alice maze, Sleeping Beauty's castle and teacup rides. Walt Disney Studios focuses on special effects and the tricks of the animation trade. Disney's newest adrenalin ride, the Twilight Zone Tower of Terror, sends daredevils plummeting down a 13-storey lift shaft.

South

Musée Fragonard

7 av du Général de Gaulle, 94704 Maisons-Alfort (01.43.96.71.72/ http://musee.vet-alfort.fr). M° Ecole Vétérinaire de Maisons-Alfort. **Open** 2-6pm Wed, Thur; 1-6pm Sat, Sun. Closed Aug. **Admission** €7; free under-18s.

See box p161.

Parc André Citroën

Rue Balard, rue St-Charles or quai Citroën, 15th. M° Balard or Javel. **Open** 8am-dusk Mon-Fri; 9am-dusk Sat, Sun, public hols.

This park is a fun, postmodern version of a French formal garden, designed by Gilles Clément and Alain Prévost. It comprises glasshouses, computerised fountains, waterfalls, a wilderness and themed gardens with different coloured plants and even sounds. Stepping stones and water jets make it a garden for pleasure as well as philosophy. The tethered Eutelsat helium balloon takes visitors up for panoramic views. Call 01.44.26.20.00 to check the programme.

West

Bois de Boulogne

16th. M° Les Sablons or Porte Dauphine. **Admission** free.

Covering 865 hectares, the Bois was once the Forêt de Rouvray hunting grounds. It was landscaped in the 1860s, when artificial grottoes and waterfalls were created around the Lac Inférieur. The Jardin de Bagatelle is famous for its roses, daffodils and water lilies. The Jardin d'Acclimatation is a children's amusement park, complete with miniature train, farm, rollercoaster and boat rides. The Bois also boasts two racecourses (Longchamp and Auteuil), sports clubs and stables, and restaurants.

Musée Marmottan – Claude Monet

2 rue Louis-Boilly, 16th (01.44.96.50.33/ www.marmottan.com). M° La Muette. **Open** 10am-6pm Mon, Wed-Sun (last entry 5.30pm); 11am-9pm Tue (last entry 8.30pm). **Admission** €9; free-€5 reductions.

This old hunting pavilion has become a famed holder of Impressionist art thanks to two bequests: the first by the daughter of the doctor of Manet, Monet, Pissarro, Sisley and Renoir; the second by Monet's son Michel. Its Monet collection, the largest in the world, numbers 165 works, plus sketchbooks, palette and photos. A special circular room was created for the stunning late water lily canvases; upstairs are works by Renoir, Manet, Gauguin, Caillebotte and Berthe Morisot, 15th-century primitives, a Sèvres clock and a collection of First Empire furniture.

Versailles

Centuries of makeovers have made Versailles the most sumptuously clad château in the world. Architect Louis Le Vau first embellished the original building – a hunting lodge built during Louis XIII's reign – after Louis XIV saw Vaux-le-Vicomte, the impressive residence of his finance minister, Nicolas Fouquet. The Sun King had the unlucky minister jailed, and stole not only his architect but also his painter, Charles Le Brun, and his landscaper, André Le Nôtre, who turned the boggy marshland into terraces, parterres, fountains and lush groves.

After Le Vau's death in 1670, Jules Hardouin-Mansart took over as principal architect, transforming Versailles into the château we know today. He dedicated the last 30 years of his life to adding the two main wings, the Cour des Ministres and the Chapelle Royale. In 1682, Louis moved in, accompanied by his court; thereafter, he rarely set foot in Paris. In the 1770s, Louis XV commissioned Jacques-Ange Gabriel to add the sumptuous Opéra Royal. The expense of building and running Versailles cost France dear. With the fall of the monarchy in 1792, most of the furniture was lost – but the château was saved from demolition after 1830 by Louis-Philippe.

Versailles has hosted the official signings of many historic treaties and it is still used by the French government for summits. In the gardens, the Grand Trianon accommodates heads of state.

The gardens are works of art in themselves, their ponds and statues once again embellished by a fully working fountain system. On summer weekends, the spectacular jets of water are set to music, a prelude to the occasional fireworks displays of the Fêtes de Nuit.

Human interest

Macabre masterpieces at the Musée Fragonard.

In 18th-century French medical schools, study aids were produced in one of two ways. They were either painstakingly sculpted in coloured wax or made from the real things – organs, limbs, tangled vascular systems – dried or preserved in formaldehyde.

Veterinary surgeon Honoré Fragonard (cousin of the famous rococo painter) was a master of the second method, and when Louis XV established a veterinary school in 1766 in Maisons-Alfort, Fragonard – its first director and professor of anatomy – set to work preparing thousands of anatomical samples.

Some of his most striking works are now on display at the **Musée Fragonard** (p159). *Homme à la mandibule* is a flayed, grimacing man holding a jawbone in his right hand – an allusion to the story of Samson slaying the Philistines. *Tête humaine injectée* is a rather more sober human head whose blood vessels were injected with coloured wax, red for arteries and blue for veins. *Groupe de foetus humains dansant la gigue* is a nightmarish chorus line of three human foetuses, a scene that might have been imagined by Goya. And, most grandiose of all, *Cavalier de l'apocalypse* is a flayed man on the back of a flayed galloping horse, inspired, according to the museum's notes, by a painting by Dürer.

The museum reopened late in 2008 after a 20-month renovation programme, and although the aforementioned *écorchés* (flayed specimens) are the most dramatic items, the rest of its 4,200 exhibits – largely from the animal kingdom, as you'd expect – are unusual, well presented and of considerable interest. The *écorchés* will inevitably remind visitors of the controversial human anatomy exhibitions put on by Günther von Hagens – proof, if any were needed, that there's nothing new under the scalpel.

Château de Versailles

78000 Versailles (01.30.83.78.00/ advance tickets 08.92.68.46.94/www. chateauversailles.fr). **Open** *Apr-Oct* 9am-6.30pm Tue-Sun. *Nov-Mar* 9am-5.30pm Tue-Sun. **Admission** €13.50; free-€10 reductions.

Versailles is a masterpiece – and it's almost always packed with visitors. Allow yourself a whole day to appreciate the sumptuous State Apartments and the Hall of Mirrors, the highlights of any visit – and mainly accessible with just a day ticket. The Grand Appartement, where Louis XIV held court, consists of six gilded salons (Venus, Mercury, Apollo and so on), all opulent examples of Baroque craftsmanship. No less luxurious, the Queen's Apartment includes her bedroom, where royal births took place in full view of the court. Hardouin-Mansart's showpiece, the Hall of Mirrors, where a united Germany was proclaimed in 1871 and the Treaty of Versailles was signed in 1919, is flooded with natural light from its 17 vast windows.

PARIS BY AREA

Domaine de Versailles

Gardens **Open** *Apr-Oct* 7am-dusk daily. *Nov-Mar* 8am-dusk daily. **Admission** *Winter* free (statues covered over). *Summer* €3; free-€1.50 reductions. *Grandes Eaux Musicales* (01.30.83.78.88). **Open** *Apr-Sept* Sat, Sun. **Admission** €7; free-€5.50 reductions. *Park* **Open** dawn-dusk daily. **Admission** free.

Sprawling across 8sq km (3sq miles), the carefully planned gardens consist of formal parterres, ponds, elaborate statues – many commissioned by Colbert in 1674 – and a spectacular series of fountains, served by an ingenious hydraulic system only recently restored to working order. On weekend afternoons in the spring and autumn, the fountains are set in action to music for the Grandes Eaux Musicales – and also serve as a backdrop, seven times a year, for the extravagant Fêtes de Nuit celebrations.

Grand Trianon/Petit Trianon/Domaine de Marie-Antionette

Open *Apr-Oct* noon-7pm daily. *Nov-Mar* noon-5.30pm daily. **Admission** *Summer* €9; €5 after 5pm; free under-18s. *Winter* €5; free under-18s.

In 1687, Hardouin-Mansart built the pink marble Grand Trianon in the north of the park, away from the protocol of the court. Here Louis XIV and his children's governess and secret second wife, Madame de Maintenon, could admire the intimate gardens from the colonnaded portico. It retains the Empire decor of Napoleon, who stayed here with his second Empress, Marie-Louise. The Petit Trianon, built for Louis XV's mistress Madame de Pompadour, is a wonderful example of neo-classicism. It later became part of the Domaine de Marie-Antoinette, an exclusive hideaway located beyond the canal in the wooded parkland. Given to Marie-Antoinette as a wedding gift by her husband Louis XVI in 1774, the domain also includes the chapel adjoining the Petit Trianon, plus a theatre, a neo-classical 'Temple d'Amour', and Marie-Antoinette's fairy-tale farm and dairy. Here, the queen escaped from the discontent of her subjects by pretending to be a humble milkmaid.

Getting there

By car

20km (12.5 miles) from Paris by the A13 or D10.

By train

For the station nearest the château, take the RER C5 (VICK or VERO trains) to Versailles-Rive Gauche.

Tourist information

Office de Tourisme

2bis av de Paris, 78000 Versailles (01.39.24.88.88/www.versailles-tourisme.com). **Open** 11am-5pm Mon, Sun; 9am-6pm Tue-Sat.

Essentials

Je dis merde à l'amour, à ses baisers de velours...
Richard loves Tom
J'aime la C.G.T.
J'ai reçu l'amour en héritage

Hôtel Ritz p169

Hotels

Paris remains one of the most visited cities in the world: 28 million tourists came here in 2007, a record figure for the city. But as the euro strengthens and people around the world tighten their belts, good-quality, affordable accommodation is increasingly of the essence. The longstanding luxury palaces remain popular, of course, at least with travellers on above-average budgets. But the good news is that the city's lower-end hoteliers have considerably bucked up their ideas, and there are now more decent bargain beds in Paris than ever before.

The local scene

At the top end of the scale, places such as the **Crillon**, the **George V** and the **Bristol** are as much a part of Paris's scenery as the Eiffel Tower, and have rates to match. But if your idea of luxury has more to do with intimacy and exclusivity, old-timers like **L'Hôtel** and newcomers **Hôtel Particulier Montmartre** and **Jays Paris** offer guests the same attention and comfort levels as the top-end hotels in rather cosier surroundings.

These grand old spots have been joined by a new breed of hotel in recent years, offering style on a shoestring. Take Franck Altruie's chain of boutique hotels, including **Quartier Bercy Square**; and **Hôtel Amour** in the ninth, where beautiful people bed up on a budget amid artsy photos and cutting-edge decor. And if your wallet won't stretch to a hotel, check out the city's youth hostels, in particular newcomer **St Christopher's Inn**.

Classification

We've divided the hotels by area, then listed them in four categories, according to the standard prices (not including seasonal offers or discounts) for one night in a double room with en suite shower/bath. For deluxe hotels (**€€€€**), you can expect to pay more than €350; for properties in the expensive bracket (**€€€**), €220-€350; for moderate properties (**€€**), allow €130-€219; while budget rooms (**€**) go for less than €130.

In the know

Note that all hotels in France charge a room tax (*taxe de séjour*) of around €1 per person per night, although this is sometimes included in the rate. Hotels are often booked solid and cost more during the major trade fairs (January, May, September), and it's hard to find a good room during Fashion Weeks (January, March, July and October). At quieter times, hotels can often offer special deals at short notice; phone ahead or check websites.

Several websites offer discount booking: **www.parishotels.com** guarantees the lowest prices online (up to 70 per cent off), and **www.ratestogo.com** offers big discounts on last-minute reservations. And remember that reserving via a hotel's website can be 50 per cent cheaper, even at the trendiest places.

SHORTLIST

Best newcomers
- Hôtel Villa Madame (p180)
- Mama Shelter (p172)

Best spa splurge
- Four Seasons George V (p165)
- Hôtel Fouquet's Barrière (p167)
- Le Meurice (p171)

Best alfresco breakfast
- Hôtel de l'Abbaye Saint Germain (p179)
- Mama Shelter (p172)
- Paris Yacht (p177)

Best bars
- Hôtel Plaza Athénée (p167)
- Hôtel Westminster (p171)
- Kube Rooms & Bar (p172)

Best for fashion week
- Le Bellechasse (p177)
- L'Hôtel (p179)

Best bathrooms
- Hôtel le A (p167)
- Hôtel de Vigny (p168)

Best bargain beds
- Grand Hôtel Jeanne d'Arc (p173)
- Hôtel Chopin (p168)
- Mama Shelter (p172)
- St Christopher's Inn (p172)

Chic sleeps
- L'Hôtel (p179)
- Hôtel Amour (p171)
- Kube Rooms & Bar (p172)
- Le Sezz (p168)

Lap of luxury
- Four Seasons George V (p165)
- Hôtel de Crillon (p169)
- Hôtel Ritz (p169)
- Le Meurice (p171)

Champs-Elysées & Western Paris

Deluxe

Four Seasons George V

31 av George V, 8th (01.49.52.70.00/ fax 01.49.52.70.10/www.fourseasons.com/paris). M° Alma Marceau or George V. **€€€€**.

There's no denying that the George V is serious about luxury: chandeliers, marble and tapestries, over-attentive staff, glorious flower arrangements,

divine bathrooms, and ludicrously comfortable beds in some of the largest rooms in Paris. The Versailles-inspired spa area includes whirlpools, saunas and treatments for an unabashedly metrosexual clientele; non-guests can now reserve appointments. It's worth every euro.

Hôtel le A

4 rue d'Artois, 8th (01.42.56.99.99/fax 01.42.56.99.90/www.paris-hotel-a.com). M° Franklin D. Roosevelt or St-Philippe-du-Roule. €€€€.

The black-and-white decor of this designer boutique hotel provides a fine backdrop for the models, artists and media types hanging out in the lounge bar area; the only splashes of colour come from the graffiti-like artworks by conceptual artist Fabrice Hybert. The 26 rooms all have granite bathrooms, and the starched white furniture slip covers, changed after each guest, make the smallish spaces seem larger than they are. The dimmer switches are a nice touch – as are the lift lights changing colour at each floor.

Hôtel Daniel

8 rue Frédéric-Bastiat, 8th (01.42.56.17.00/fax 01.42.56.17.01/ www.hoteldanielparis.com). M° Franklin D. Roosevelt or St-Philippe-du-Roule. €€€€.

A romantic hideaway close to the monoliths of the Champs-Elysées, the city's new Relais & Châteaux is decorated in chinoiserie and a palette of rich colours, with 26 rooms (free Wi-Fi) cosily appointed in *toile de Jouy* and an intricately hand-painted restaurant that feels like a courtyard. At about €50 a head, the gastronomic restaurant Le Lounge, run by chef Denis Fetisson, is a good deal for this neighbourhood; the bar menu is served at all hours.

Hôtel Fouquet's Barrière

46 av George V, 8th (01.40.69.60.00/ fax 01.40.69.60.05/www.fouquets barriere.com). M° George V. €€€€.

This grandiose five-star is built around the fin-de-siècle brasserie Le Fouquet's. Five buildings form the hotel complex, with 107 rooms (including 40 suites), upmarket restaurant Le Diane, the Sparis spa, indoor pool and a rooftop terrace for hire. Jacques Garcia, of Hôtel Costes and Westin fame, was responsible for the interior design, which retains the Empire style of the exterior while incorporating luxurious touches inside – flat-screen TVs and mist-free mirrors in the marble bathrooms. And, of course, it's unbeatable for location – right at the junction of avenue George V and the Champs-Elysées.

Hôtel Plaza Athénée

25 av Montaigne, 8th (01.53.67.66.67/ fax 01.53.67.66.66/www.plaza-athenee-paris.com). M° Alma Marceau. €€€€.

This palace is ideally placed for power shopping at Chanel, Louis Vuitton, Dior and other avenue Montaigne boutiques. Material girls and boys will enjoy the high-tech room amenities such as remote-controlled air con, internet and video-game access on the TV via infrared keyboard, and mini hi-fi. Make time for a drink in the Bar du Plaza, a cocktail bunny's most *outré* fantasy.

Hôtel Regent's Garden

6 rue Pierre-Demours, 17th (01.45.74. 07.30/fax 01.40.55.01.42/www.hotel-paris-garden.com). M° Charles de Gaulle Etoile or Ternes. €€€.

This elegant hotel – built for Napoleon III's physician – features Second Empire high ceilings and plush upholstery, and a lounge overlooking a walled patio. There are 39 large bedrooms, some with gilt mirrors and fireplaces. It's an oasis of calm ten minutes from the Champs-Elysées, and the first hotel in Paris to receive an Ecolabel.

Hôtel de Sers

41 av Pierre-1er-de-Serbie, 8th (01.53.23.75.75/fax 01.53.23.75.76/ www.hoteldesers.com). M° Alma Marceau or George V. €€€€.

Behind its stately 19th-century façade, the Hôtel de Sers calls itself a baby palace, displaying an ambitious mix of minimalist contemporary furnishings, with a few pop art touches. Original architectural details, such as the grand staircase and reception, complete the picture. The large top floor apartment affords dreamy views over Paris's rooftops. Free Wi-Fi.

Hôtel Square

3 rue de Boulainvilliers, 16th (01.44.14.91.90/fax 01.44.14.91.99/ www.hotelsquare.com). M° Passy/ RER Avenue du Pdt Kennedy. **€€€**.

Located in the upmarket 16th, this courageously modern hotel has a dramatic yet welcoming interior, and attentive service that comes from having to look after only 22 rooms. They're decorated in amber, brick or slate colours, with exotic woods, quality fabrics and bathrooms seemingly cut from one huge chunk of Carrara marble. View exhibitions in the atrium gallery or mingle with media types at the hip Zebra Square restaurant and DJ bar.

Hôtel de Vigny

9-11 rue Balzac, 8th (01.42.99.80.80/ fax 01.42.99.80.40/www.hoteldevigny. com). M° George V. **€€€€**.

One of only two Relais & Châteaux in the city, this hotel has the feel of a private, plush town-house. Although it's just off the Champs-Elysées, the Vigny pulls in a discerning, low-key clientele. Its 37 rooms and suites are decorated in tasteful stripes or florals, with marble bathrooms. Enjoy dinner in the art deco Baretto restaurant, or a cup of tea in the library.

Jays Paris

6 rue Copernic, 16th (01.47.04.16.16/ fax 01.47.04.16.17/www.jays-paris.com). M° Kléber or Victor Hugo. **€€€€**.

Introducing a new concept on the Paris hotel scene, Jays is a luxurious *boutique-apart* hotel that trades on a clever blend of antique furniture, modern design and high-tech equipment. The marble staircase, lit entirely by natural light filtered through the glass atrium overhead, gives an instant feeling of grandeur, and leads to five suites, each with a fully equipped kitchenette and free Wi-Fi. A cosy salon is available to welcome in-house guests and their visitors.

Le Sezz

6 av Frémiet, 16th (01.56.75.26.26/ fax 01.56.75.26.16/www.hotelsezz. com). M° Passy. **€€€**.

Le Sezz opened its doors in 2005 with 27 sleek, luxurious rooms and suites – the work of acclaimed French furniture designer Christophe Pillet. The understated decor represents a refreshingly modern take on luxury, with black parquet flooring, rough-hewn stone walls and bathrooms partitioned off with sweeping glass façades. The bar and public areas are equally sleek and chic. Free Wi-Fi.

Opéra to Les Halles

Hôtel Brighton

218 rue de Rivoli, 1st (01.47.03.61.61/ fax 01.42.60.41.78/www.esprit-de-france.com). M° Tuileries. **€€**.

With several of the bedrooms looking out over the Tuileries gardens, the Brighton is great value, so ask for a room with a view. Recently restored, it has a classical atmosphere, from the high ceilings in the rooms to the faux-marble and mosaic decor downstairs.

Hôtel Chopin

10 bd Montmartre or 46 passage Jouffroy, 9th (01.47.70.58.10/fax 01.42.47.00.70/www.hotel-chopin.com). M° Grands Boulevards. **€**.

Handsomely set in a historic, glass-roofed arcade next door to the Grévin musuem, the Chopin's original 1846 façade adds to its old-fashioned appeal. The 36 rooms are quiet and functional, done out in salmon and green or blue.

Le Meurice p171

Hôtel Concorde St-Lazare

108 rue St-Lazare, 8th (01.40.08.44.44/ fax 01.42.93.01.20/www.concorde stlazare-paris.com). M° St-Lazare. **€€€**.

Guests here are cocooned in soundproofed luxury. The 19th-century Eiffel-inspired lobby with jewel-encrusted pink granite columns is a historic landmark: the high ceilings, walls and sculptures look much as they have for over a century. Rooms are spacious, with double entrance doors and exclusive Annick Goutal toiletries; the belle époque brasserie, Café Terminus, and sexy Golden Black Bar were designed by Sonia Rykiel. Guests have access to a nearby fitness centre and there's free Wi-Fi.

Hôtel de Crillon

10 pl de la Concorde, 8th (01.44.71.15.00/fax 01.44.71.15.02/ www.crillon.com). M° Concorde. **€€€€**.

The Crillon lives up to its palais reputation with decor strong on marble, mirrors and gold leaf. If you have €10,500 to spare, opt for the Presidential Suite (the only one with a view over the American Embassy). The Winter Garden tearoom is a must. Free Wi-Fi and parking available.

Hôtel Langlois

63 rue St-Lazare, 9th (01.48.74.78.24/ fax 01.49.95.04.43/www.hotel-langlois.com). M° Trinité. **€€**.

Built as a bank in 1870, this belle époque building became the Hôtel des Croisés in 1896. In 2001, after featuring in the Jonathan Demme film *Charade*, it changed its name to Hôtel Langlois in honour of the founder of the Cinémathèque Française. Its 27 spacious, air-conditioned bedrooms (with free Wi-Fi) are decorated in art nouveau style; the larger ones have delightful hidden bathrooms.

Hôtel Madeleine Opéra

12 rue Greffulhe, 8th (01.47.42.26.26/ fax 01.47.42.89.76/www.hotel-madeleine-opera.com). M° Havre-Caumartin or Madeleine. **€**.

This bargain hotel is located just north of the Eglise de la Madeleine, in the heart of the city's theatre and *grands magasins* districts. Its sunny lobby sits behind a 200-year-old façade that was once a shopfront. The 23 rooms are perhaps a touch basic, but still nice enough, and breakfast is brought to your room every morning.

Hôtel Ritz

15 pl Vendôme, 1st (01.43.16.30.30/ fax 01.43.16.31.78/www.ritzparis.com). M° Concorde or Opéra. **€€€€**.

Chic hasn't lost its cool at the grande dame of Paris hotels, where each of the 162 bedrooms, from the romantic Frédéric Chopin to the glitzy Impérial, ooze sumptuousness. But then what else can one expect from a hotel that has proffered hospitality to the likes of Coco Chanel, the Duke of Windsor, Proust, and Dodi and Di? There are plenty of corners to strike a pose or quench a thirst, from Hemingway's cigar bar to the poolside hangout.

Hôtel Westminster

13 rue de la Paix, 2nd (01.42.61.57.46/ fax 01.42.60.30.66/www.warwick westminsteropera.com). M° Opéra/ RER Auber. **€€€€**.

This luxury hotel near place Vendôme has more than a touch of British warmth about it, no doubt owing to the influence of its favourite 19th-century guest, the Duke of Westminster (after whom the hotel was named; the current Duke reportedly still stays here). The hotel fitness centre has an enviable top-floor location, with a beautiful tiled steam room and views over the city, and the cosy bar features deep leather chairs, a fireplace and live jazz at weekends.

InterContinental Paris Le Grand

2 rue Scribe, 9th (01.40.07.32.32/ fax 01.42.66.12.51/www.paris. intercontinental.com). M° Opéra. **€€€€**.

This 1862 hotel is the chain's European flagship – but, given its sheer size, perhaps 'mother ship' would be more appropriate: this landmark establishment occupies the entire block (three wings, almost 500 rooms) next to the opera house; some 80 of the honey-coloured rooms overlook the Palais Garnier. The space under the vast *verrière* is one of the best oases in town, and the hotel's restaurant and elegant coffeehouse, the Café de la Paix, poached its chef, Laurent Delarbre, from the Ritz. For a truly relaxing daytime break, head to the I-Spa for one of its seawater treatments.

Le Meurice

228 rue de Rivoli, 1st (01.44.58.10.10/ fax 01.44.58.10.15/www.lemeurice. com). M° Tuileries. **€€€€**.

With its extravagant Louis XVI decor, intricate mosaic tiled floors and clever, modish restyling by Philippe Starck, Le Meurice is looking grander than ever. All 160 rooms (kitted out with iPod-ready radio alarms) are done up in distinct historical styles; the Belle Etoile suite on the seventh floor provides 360-degree panoramic views of Paris from its terrace. You can relax in the Winter Garden to the strains of jazz performances; for more intensive intervention, head over to the lavishly appointed spa with treatments by Valmont. The hotel's three Michelin-starred restaurant has chef Yannick Alléno at the helm.

Hôtel Amour

Montmartre & Pigalle

Hôtel Amour

8 rue Navarin, 9th (01.48.78.31.80/fax 01.48.74.14.09/www.hotelamour.com). M° St-Georges. **€€**.

Opened back in 2006, this boutique hotel is a real hit with the in crowd. Each of the 20 rooms (with free Wi-Fi) is unique, decorated on the theme of love or eroticism by a coterie of contemporary artists and designers such as Marc Newson, M&M, Stak, Pierre Le Tan and Sophie Calle. Seven of the rooms contain artists' installations, and two others have their own private bar and a large terrace on which to hold your own party. The late-night brasserie has a coveted outdoor garden, and the crowd is young, beautiful and loves to entertain.

Hôtel Particulier Montmartre

23 av Junot, 18th (01.42.58.00.87/fax 01.42.58.00.87/www.hotel-particulier-montmartre.com). M° Lamarck Caulaincourt. **€€€€**.

Visitors lucky (and wealthy) enough to manage to book a suite at the Hôtel Particulier Montmartre will find themselves in one of the city's hidden gems. Nestled in a quiet passage off rue Lepic, this sumptuous *Directoire*-style house is dedicated to art, with each of the five luxurious suites personalised by an avant-garde artist. Free Wi-Fi.

Hôtel Royal Fromentin

11 rue Fromentin, 9th (01.48.74.85.93/fax 01.42.81.02.33/www.hotelroyalfromentin.com). M° Blanche or Pigalle. **€€**.

Wood panelling, art deco windows and a vintage glass lift echo the hotel's origins as a 1930s cabaret hall; its theatrical feel attracted Blondie and Nirvana. Many of its 47 rooms overlook Sacré-Coeur. Rooms have been renovated in French style, with bright fabrics and an old-fashioned feel, and offer free Wi-Fi.

Kube Rooms & Bar

1-5 passage Ruelle, 18th (01.42.05.20.00/fax 01.42.05.21.01/www.kubehotel.com). M° La Chapelle. **€€€**.

The younger sister of the Murano Urban Resort, Kube is a more hip and affordable design hotel. Like the Murano, it sits behind an unremarkable façade in an unlikely neighbourhood, the ethnically diverse Goutte d'Or. The Ice Kube bar serves vodka in glasses that, like the bar itself, are carved from ice. Also on the menu are 'apérifood' and 'snackubes' by Pierre Auge. Access to the 41 rooms is by fingerprint identification technology and there's free Wi-Fi access.

Timhotel Montmartre

11 rue Ravignan, 18th (01.42.55.74.79/fax 01.42.55.71.01/www.timhotel.fr). M° Abbesses or Pigalle. **€€**.

The location adjacent to picturesque place Emile-Goudeau makes this one of the most popular hotels in the Timhotel chain. It has 59 rooms, comfortable without being plush; try to bag one on the fourth or fifth floor for stunning views over Montmartre. Special offers are often available.

North-east Paris

Mama Shelter

109 rue de Bagnolet, 20th (01.43.48.48.48/fax 01.44.54.38.66/www.mamashelter.com). M° Alexandre Dumas, Maraîchers or Porte de Bagnolet. **€**.

Philippe Starck's latest design commission is set a stone's throw east of Père Lachaise, and its decor appeals to the young-at-heart with Batman and Incredible Hulk light fittings, dark walls, polished wood and splashes of bright fabrics. Every room comes with an iMac computer, TV, free internet access and a CD and DVD player; and when hunger strikes, there's a brasserie with a romantic terrace. If you're sure of your dates, book online and take advantage of the saver's rate.

St Christopher's Inn

NEW *159 rue de Crimée, 19th (01.40.34.34.40/www.st-christophers.co.uk/paris-hostels). M° Crimée, Jaurès, Laumière or Stanlingrad.* **€**.

If you don't mind bunking up with others, you could try this Paris branch of the English youth hostel chain housed in a former boat hangar on the ever-gentrifying Canal de l'Ourcq. The decor in the bedrooms has a sailor's cabin feel, with round, colourful mirrors, bubble-pattern wallpaper and 1950s-inspired cabin furniture. The hostel really comes into its own in its bar Belushi's, where the usual backpack brigade are joined by Parisians

Hôtel Particulier Montmartre

bent on taking advantage of the canal-side setting, satellite sports, lunchtime brasserie and some of the cheapest drinks in the capital.

The Marais & Eastern Paris

Grand Hôtel Jeanne d'Arc

3 rue de Jarente, 4th (01.48.87.62.11/fax 01.48.87.37.31/www.hoteljeannedarc.com). M° Chemin Vert. **€**.

The Jeanne d'Arc's strong point is its lovely location on a quiet road close to pretty place du Marché-Ste-Catherine. Recent refurbishment has made the reception area striking. Rooms are simple but comfortable.

Hôtel Bourg Tibourg

19 rue du Bourg-Tibourg, 4th (01.42.78.47.39/fax 01.40.29.07.00/www.hotelbourgtibourg.com). M° Hôtel de Ville. **€€€**.

The Bourg Tibourg has the same owners as Hôtel Costes and the same interior decorator – but don't expect this jewel box of a boutique hotel to look like a miniature replica. Aside from its enviable location in the heart of the Marais and its fashion-pack fans, here it's all about Jacques Garcia's neo-Gothic-cum-Byzantine decor – impressive and imaginative. Exotic, scented candles, mosaic-tiled bathrooms and luxurious fabrics in rich colours create the perfect escape from the outside world. There's no restaurant or lounge – posing is done in the neighbourhood bars. Free Wi-Fi.

Hôtel de la Bretonnerie

22 rue Ste-Croix-de-la-Bretonnerie, 4th (01.48.87.77.63/fax 01.42.77.26.78/www.bretonnerie.com). M° Hôtel de Ville. **€€**.

With its combination of wrought ironwork, exposed stone and wooden beams, the labyrinth of corridors and

passages in this 17th-century *hôtel particulier* are full of atmosphere. Tapestries, rich colours and the occasional four-poster bed give the 29 suites and bedrooms individuality. Location is convenient too. Free Wi-Fi.

Hôtel Duo

11 rue du Temple, 4th (01.42.72.72.22/ fax 01.42.72.03.53/www.duoparis.com). M° Hôtel de Ville. **€€.**

Formerly the Axial Beauborg, this stylish boutique hotel, decorated with white marble floors, mud-coloured walls, crushed velvet sofas and exposed beams, is close to the Centre Pompidou. Rooms are not large, but exude refinement and comfort. Free Wi-Fi.

Hôtel du Petit Moulin

29-31 rue de Poitou, 3rd (01.42.74. 10.10/fax 01.42.74.10.97/www. hoteldupetitmoulin.com). M° St-Sébastien Froissart. **€€.**

Within striking distance of the Musée Picasso and the hip shops situated on and around rue Charlot, this listed, turn-of-the-century façade masks what was once the oldest *boulangerie* in Paris, lovingly restored as a boutique hotel by Nadia Murano and Denis Nourry. The couple recruited no lesser figure than fashion designer Christian Lacroix for the decor, and the result is a riot of colour, trompe l'oeil effects and a savvy mix of old and new. Each of its 17 exquisitely appointed rooms is unique, and the walls in rooms 202, 204 and 205 feature swirling, extravagant drawings and scribbles taken from Lacroix's sketchbook. Free parking.

Hôtel St-Merry

78 rue de la Verrerie, 4th (01.42.78. 14.15/fax 01.40.29.06.82/www.hotel marais.com). M° Châtelet or Hôtel de Ville. **€€.**

The Gothic decor of this former presbytery attached to the Eglise St-Merry is ideal for a Dracula set, with wooden beams, stone walls and plenty of iron; behind the door of room nine, an imposing flying buttress straddles the carved antique bed. There are 11 rooms in all, spread over five floors. On the downside, the historic building has no lift, and only the suite has a TV.

Mama Shelter p172

Murano Urban Resort

13 bd du Temple, 3rd (01.42.71.20.00/ fax 01.42.71.21.01/www.muranoresort. com). M° Filles du Calvaire or Oberkampf. **€€€€.**

Behind this unremarkable façade is a super cool and supremely luxurious hotel, popular with the fashion set for its slick lounge-style design, excellent restaurant and high-tech flourishes – including coloured light co-ordinators that enable you to change the mood of your room at the touch of a button. The handsome bar has a mind-boggling 140 varieties of vodka to sample, which can bring the op art fabrics in the lift to life and make the fingerprint access to the hotel's 43 rooms and nine suites (two of which feature private pools) a late-night godsend. Free Wi-Fi.

Stylish B&Bs

Think of bed and breakfast and you probably conjure up images of a cosy retreat in the countryside or by the coast. Few visitors consider B&B for a city break, but it's a growing trend in Paris with a wealth of choices available.

In 2005, the Mairie created the Charte Hôtes Qualité Paris, an initiative to encourage locals to offer B&B, and you can now search and book rooms all over the city via its website (www.hotesqualiteparis.fr).

Also worth a look is *Chambres d'hôtes à Paris* (€16, Hachette), a new guide to B&B options in the city. Written by Pascale Desclos, the book picks out 100 of the best B&Bs, covering a vast range of styles, locations and prices. Prices begin at €55 for two people, and almost a third of the featured rooms come in at under €80. Among the more opulent entries are an elegant suite in a Montmartre mansion house (€430 per night), and a spacious third-floor room with garden and balcony view of the Eiffel Tower (€380).

The city boasts plenty of quirky B&Bs too, none more so than Le Loft (www.chezbertrand.com). This eccentric apartment, on the ground floor of an old fireplace shop, features a circular double bed, kitchenette and, the pièce de résistance, a shiny red, open-topped Citroën 2CV sleeping 'two lovers', ideal for a bit of back-seat action. And if Bertrand's B&B gives you any design inspiration, the world's biggest flea market is just around the corner.

Le Quartier Bastille, Le Faubourg

9 rue de Reuilly, 12th (01.43.70.04.04/ fax 01.43.70.96.53/www.lequartier hotelbf.com). M° Faidherbe Chaligny or Reuilly-Diderot. €€€.

Within walking distance of Bastille and the hip 11th arrondissement, the Quartier Bastille (a branch of Franck Altruie's chain of budget design hotels) flashes funky, neo-1970s furniture and just the right amount of colour. Rooms are minimalist but very comfortable.

The Seine & Islands

Hôtel des Deux-Iles

59 rue St-Louis-en-l'Ile, 4th (01.43.26.13.35/fax 01.43.29.60.25/ www.deuxiles-paris-hotel.com). M° Pont Marie. €€.

This peaceful 17th-century townhouse offers 17 soundproofed, air-conditioned rooms kitted out in toned down stripes, *toile de Jouy* fabrics and neo colonial-style furniture. Its star feature is a tiny courtyard off the lobby and a vaulted stone breakfast area. All the rooms and bathrooms were freshened up in 2007 (fortunately saving the lovely blue earthenware tiles on the bathroom walls). There's free Wi-Fi too.

Hôtel du Jeu de Paume

54 rue St-Louis-en-l'Ile, 4th (01.43.26.14.18/fax 01.40.46.02.76/ www.jeudepaumehotel.com). M° Pont Marie. €€€.

With a discreet courtyard entrance, 17th-century beams, private garden and a unique timbered breakfast room that was once a real tennis court built under Louis XIII, this is a charming and romantic hotel. These days it is filled with an attractive array of modern and classical art, and has a coveted billiards table. A dramatic glass lift and catwalks lead to the rooms and two self-catering apartments, which are simple and tasteful, the walls hung with Pierre Frey fabric.

Paris Yacht

Quai de la Tournelle, 5th (06.88.70. 26.36/www.paris-yacht.com). M° Maubert Mutualité. No credit cards. **€€€**.

Paris Yacht has to be the city's quirkiest place to sleep – as long as you don't get seasick. Bobbing peacefully on the Left Bank opposite the Ile St-Louis and five minutes' walk from Notre-Dame, this two-cabin houseboat was built in 1933, and has been in service everywhere from Bastia to the Canal de Bourgogne. Now converted to accommodate up to four guests (welcomed with a bottle of champagne from the owners), the boat is equipped with everything from central heating to high-speed internet. During the summer, the terrace on the upper deck provides the perfect Seine-side setting for dinner.

The 7th & Western Paris

Le Bellechasse

8 rue de Bellechasse, 7th (01.45.50.22.31/fax 01.45.51.52.36/ www.lebellechasse.com). M° Assemblée Nationale or Solférino/RER Musée d'Orsay. **€€€€**.

A former *hôtel particulier*, the Bellechasse fell into the hands of Christian Lacroix, already responsible for the makeover of the Hôtel du Petit Moulin. It reopened in 2007, duly transformed into a trendy boutique hotel. Only a few steps away from the Musée d'Orsay, it offers 34 splendid – though small – rooms, in seven decorative styles. Book early, as the Bellechasse remains *the* hotel of the moment.

Hôtel Duc de Saint-Simon

14 rue de St-Simon, 7th (01.44.39. 20.20/fax 01.45.48.68.25/www.hotel ducdesaintsimon.com). M° Rue du Bac. **€€€**.

A lovely courtyard leads the way into this popular hotel on the edge of St-Germain-des-Prés. Of the 34 bedrooms, four have terraces over a closed-off, leafy garden. It's perfect for lovers, though if you can do without a four-poster bed there are more spacious rooms than the Honeymoon Suite.

Hôtel Eiffel Rive Gauche

6 rue du Gros-Caillou, 7th (01.45.51.24.56/fax 01.45.51.11.77/ www.hotel-eiffel.com). M° Ecole Militaire. **€**.

The Provençal decor and warm welcome make this a nice retreat. All 29 rooms feature Empire-style bedheads and modern bathrooms. Outside, there's a tiny, tiled courtyard with a bridge. If this is fully booked, try sister hotel Eiffel Villa Garibaldi (48 bd Garibaldi, 15th, 01.56.58.56.58), which has equally reasonable rates.

Hôtel Lenox

9 rue de l'Université, 7th (01.42.96. 10.95/fax 01.42.61.52.83/www.lenox saintgermain.com). M° St-Germain-des-Prés. **€€**.

Its location may be in the seventh arrondissement, but this venerable literary and artistic haunt is unmistakeably part of St-Germain-des-Prés. The art deco-style Lenox Club Bar, open to the public, features comfortable leather club chairs and jazz instruments on the walls. Bedrooms, which are reached by an astonishing glass lift, have traditional decor and city views.

Le Montalembert

3 rue Montalembert, 7th (01.45.49.68.68/fax 01.45.49.69.49/ www.montalembert.com). M° Rue du Bac. **€€€€**.

Grace Leo-Andrieu's impeccable boutique hotel is a benchmark of quality and service. It has everything that *mode* maniacs (who flock here for Fashion Week) could want: bathrooms stuffed with Molton Brown toiletries, a set of digital scales and plenty of mirrors with which to keep an eye on their figure. Decorated in pale lilac, cinnamon and olive tones, the entire hotel

has Wi-Fi access, and each room is equipped with a flat-screen TV. Clattery two-person stairwell lifts are a nice nod to old-fashioned ways in a hotel that is otherwise *tout moderne*.

St-Germain-des-Prés & Odéon

Le Clos Médicis

56 rue Monsieur-le-Prince, 6th (01.43.29.10.80/fax 01.43.54.26.90/ www.closmedicis.com). M° Odéon/RER Luxembourg. **€€**.

Designed more like a stylish, private townhouse than a hotel, Le Clos Médicis is located by the Luxembourg gardens. The hotel's decor is refreshingly modern, with rooms done out with taffeta curtains and chenille bedcovers, and antique floor tiles in the bathrooms. The cosy lounge has a working fireplace.

Grand Hôtel de l'Univers

6 rue Grégoire-de-Tours, 6th (01.43.29.37.00/fax 01.40.51.06.45/ www.hotel-paris-univers.com). M° Odéon. **€€**

Making the most of its 15th-century origins, this hotel features exposed wooden beams, high ceilings, antique furnishings and toile-covered walls. Manuel Canovas fabrics lend a posh touch, but there are also useful services such as a laptop for hire. The same team runs the Hôtel St-Germain-des-Prés (36 rue Bonaparte, 6th, 01.43.26.00.19), which has a medieval-themed room and the sweetest attic in Paris.

L'Hôtel

13 rue des Beaux-Arts, 6th (01.44.41.99.00/fax 01.43.25.64.81/ www.l-hotel.com). M° Mabillon or St-Germain-des-Prés. **€€€**.

Guests at the sumptuously decorated L'Hôtel are more likely to be models and film stars than the starving writers who frequented it during Oscar Wilde's last days (the playwright died in a room on the ground floor in November 1900). Under Jacques Garcia's careful restoration, each room has its own theme: Mistinguett's *chambre* retains its art deco mirror bed, and Oscar's tribute room is appropriately clad in green peacock murals. In the basement is a small pool, which is wonderfully private – only two people are allowed down here at a time and staff will surround it with candles if you want. Don't miss out on lunch or dinner in the decadent one-star restaurant, run by talented chef Philippe Bélisse.

Hôtel de l'Abbaye Saint Germain

10 rue Cassette, 6th (01.45.44.38.11/ fax 01.45.48.07.86/www.hotelabbaye paris.com). M° Rennes or St-Sulpice. **€€€**.

A monumental entrance opens the way through a courtyard into this tranquil hotel, originally part of a convent. Wood panelling, well-stuffed sofas and an open fireplace in the drawing room make for a relaxed atmosphere, but, best of all, there's a surprisingly large garden where breakfast is served in the warmer months. The 43 rooms and duplex apartment are tasteful and luxurious.

Hôtel du Globe

15 rue des Quatre-Vents, 6th (01.43.26.35.50/fax 01.46.33.62.69/ www.hotel-du-globe.fr). M° Odéon. **€€**.

The Hôtel du Globe has managed to retain much of its 17th-century character – and very pleasant it is too. Gothic wrought-iron doors open into the florid corridors, and an unexplained suit of armour supervises guests from the tiny salon. The rooms with baths are somewhat larger than those with showers, and if you're an early booker you might even get the room with the four-poster bed.

Hôtel Lutetia

45 bd Raspail, 6th (01.49.54.46.46/fax 01.49.54.46.00/www.lutetia-paris.com). M° Sèvres Babylone. **€€€€**.

This historic Left Bank hotel is a masterpiece of art nouveau and early art deco architecture that dates from 1910. It has a plush jazz bar and lively brasserie. Its 250 rooms, revamped in purple, gold and pearl grey, maintain a 1930s feel. Big-name guests in years past have included Picasso, Josephine Baker and de Gaulle. It was also Abwehr HQ during the Nazi occupation.

Hôtel des Saints-Pères

65 rue des Sts-Pères, 6th (01.45.44.50.00/fax 01.45.44.90.83/www.espritfrance.com). M° St-Germain-des-Prés. €€.

Built in 1658 by one of Louis XIV's architects, this hotel has an enviable location near St-Germain-des-Prés' boutiques. It boasts a charming garden and a sophisticated, if small, bar. The most coveted room is no.100, with its fine 17th-century ceiling by painters from the Versailles School; it also has an open bathroom, so you can gaze at scenes from the myth of Leda and the Swan while you scrub.

Hôtel Villa Madame

NEW *44 rue Madame, 6th (01.45.48.02.81/fax 01.45.44.85.73). M° St-Sulpice.* €€€.

This newly revamped hotel (formerly the Regents) located in a quiet street is a lovely surprise, its courtyard garden used for breakfast during the summer months. The honey- and chocolate-coloured woods mix with warm-toned velvets to make the rooms (all with plasma screens) feel cosy and inviting; some even have small balconies with loungers.

Relais Saint-Germain

9 carrefour de l'Odéon, 6th (01.43.29.12.05/fax 01.46.33.45.30/www.hotel-paris-relais-saint-germain.com). M° Odéon. €€€.

The rustic, wood-beamed ceilings remain intact at the Relais Saint-Germain, a 17th-century hotel bought and renovated by acclaimed chef Yves Camdeborde (originator of the *bistronomique* dining trend) and his wife Claudine. Each of the 22 rooms has a different take on eclectic Provençal charm, and the marble bathrooms are huge by Paris standards. Guests get first dibs on a highly sought-after seat in the 15-table Le Comptoir restaurant next door.

The Latin Quarter & the 13th

Familia Hôtel

11 rue des Ecoles, 5th (01.43.54.55.27/fax 01.43.29.61.77/www.hotel-paris-familia.com). M° Cardinal Lemoine or Jussieu. €.

This old-fashioned Latin Quarter hotel has balconies hung with tumbling plants and walls draped with replica French tapestries. Owner Eric Gaucheron extends a warm welcome, and the 30 rooms have personalised touches such as sepia murals, cherry-wood furniture and stone walls. The Gaucherons also own the Minerve next door – book in advance for both.

Five Hôtel

3 rue Flatters, 5th (01.43.31.74.21/fax 01.43.31.61.96/www.thefivehotel.com). M° Les Gobelins or Port Royal. €€.

The rooms in this stunning boutique hotel may be small, but they're all exquisitely designed, with Chinese lacquer and velvety fabrics. Fibre optics built into the walls create the illusion of sleeping under a starry sky, and you can choose from four different fragrances to subtly perfume your room (the hotel is non-smoking). Guests staying in the suite have access to a private garden with a jacuzzi.

Hôtel les Degrés de Notre-Dame

10 rue des Grands-Degrés, 5th (01.55.42.88.88/fax 01.40.46.95.34/www.lesdegreshotel.com). M° Maubert-Mutualité or St-Michel. €€.

On a tiny street across the river from Notre-Dame, this vintage hotel is an absolute gem. Its ten rooms are full of character, with original paintings, antique furniture and exposed wooden beams (nos.47 and 501 have views of the cathedral). It has an adorable restaurant and, a few streets away, two studio apartments that the owner rents to preferred customers only.

Hôtel la Demeure

51 bd St-Marcel, 13th (01.43.37.81.25/ fax 01.45.87.05.03/www.hotel-paris-lademeure.com). M° Les Gobelins. **€€**.

This comfortable, modern hotel on the edge of the Latin Quarter has 43 air-conditioned rooms with internet access, plus suites with sliding doors to separate sleeping and living space. The wrap-around balconies of the corner rooms offer lovely views of the city, and bathrooms feature luxurious tubs or shower heads with elaborate massage possibilities.

Hôtel du Panthéon

19 pl du Panthéon, 5th (01.43.54. 32.95/fax 01.43.26.64.65/www.hoteldupantheon.com). M° Cluny La Sorbonne or Maubert Mutualité/ RER Luxembourg. **€€**.

The 36 rooms of this elegant hotel are beautifully decorated with classic French *toile de Jouy* fabrics, antique furniture and painted woodwork. Some enjoy impressive views of the Panthéon; others squint out on to a hardly less romantic courtyard, complete with chestnut tree.

Hôtel Résidence Henri IV

50 rue des Bernardins, 5th (01.44.41.31.81/fax 01.46.33.93.22/ www.residencehenri4.com). M° Cardinal Lemoine. **€€**.

This belle époque style hotel has a mere eight rooms and five apartments, so guests are assured of the staff's full attention. Peacefully situated next to leafy square Paul-Langevin, it's just minutes away from Notre-Dame. The four-person apartments come with a mini-kitchen featuring a hob, fridge and microwave. Free Wi-Fi available.

Hôtel de la Sorbonne

6 rue Victor-Cousin, 5th (01.43.54.58.08/fax 01.40.51.05.18/ www.hotelsorbonne.com). M° Cluny La Sorbonne/RER Luxembourg. **€**.

It's out with the old at this charming, freshly renovated hotel, whose new look is very much a modern take on art nouveau, with bold wallpapers, floral prints, lush fabrics and quotes from French literature woven into the carpets. Rooms are all equipped with iMac computers.

Montparnasse

Hôtel Aviatic

105 rue de Vaugirard, 6th (01.53.63. 25.50/fax 01.53.63.25.55/www. aviatic.fr). M° Duroc, Montparnasse Bienvenüe or St-Placide. **€€**.

This historic hotel has masses of character, from the Empire-style lounge and garden atrium to the bistro-style breakfast room and marble floor in the lobby. New decoration throughout, in beautiful steely greys, warm reds, elegant, striped velvets and *toile de Jouy* fabrics, lends an impressive touch of glamour, and the service is excellent.

Hôtel Istria Saint-Germain

29 rue Campagne-Première, 14th (01.43.20.91.82/fax 01.43.22.48.45/ www.istria-paris-hotel.com). M° Raspail. **€€**.

Behind this unassuming façade is the place where the artistic royalty of Montparnasse's heyday – the likes of Man Ray, Marcel Duchamp and Louis Aragon – once lived. The Istria Saint-Germain has been modernised since then, but it still has plenty of charm, with 26 bright, simply furnished rooms, a cosy breakfast room and a comfortable communal area. Film fans take note: the artists' studios next door featured in Godard's *A Bout de Souffle*.

Getting Around

Airports

Roissy-Charles-de-Gaulle

01.70.36.39.50/www.adp.fr. 30km (19 miles) north-east of Paris.
For most international flights. The two main terminals are some way apart; check which one you need for your flight back. The **RER B** line (08.92.69.32.46, www.transilien.com) is the quickest way to central Paris (40mins to Gare du Nord; 45mins to RER Châtelet-Les Halles; €8.40 single). A new station gives direct access from Terminal 2; from Terminal 1 take the free shuttle. RER trains run every 10-15mins, 4.56am-11.56pm daily.

Air France buses (08.92.35.08.20, www.cars-airfrance.com; €14 single, €22 return) leave every 15mins, 5.45am-11pm daily, from both terminals, and stop at Porte Maillot and place Charles-de-Gaulle (35-50min trip). Buses also run to Gare Montparnasse and Gare de Lyon (€15 single, €24 return) every 30mins (45-60min trip), 7am-9pm daily; a bus between Roissy and Orly (€18) runs every 30mins, 5.55am-10.25pm Mon-Fri, 7am-10.30pm Sat, Sun.

RATP Roissybus (08.92.69.32.46, www.ratp.fr; €8.90) runs every 15-20mins, 5.45am-11pm daily, between the airport and the corner of rue Scribe/rue Auber (at least 45mins); buy your tickets on the bus.

Paris Airports Service is a 24-hour door-to-door minibus service between airports and hotels, seven days a week. Roissy prices go from €26 for one to €12.40 each person for eight people, 6am-8pm (minimum €41, 4-6am, 8-10pm); you can reserve a place on 01.55.98.10.80, www.parisairportservice.com. A **taxi** into central Paris from Roissy-Charles-de-Gaulle airport should take 30-60mins and cost €30-€50, plus €1 per luggage item.

Orly

01.70.36.39.50/www.adp.fr. About 18km (11 miles) south of Paris.
Orly-Sud terminal is mainly international and Orly-Ouest is mainly domestic.

Air France buses (08.92.35.08.20, www.cars-airfrance.com; €10 single, €16 return) leave both terminals every 30mins, 6.15am-11.15pm daily, and stop at Invalides and Montparnasse (30-45mins).

The **RATP Orlybus** (08.92.69.32.46, www.ratp.fr) runs to Denfert-Rochereau every 15mins, 5.35am-11.05pm Mon-Fri, 5.35am-12.05am Sat-Sun (30mins trip); buy tickets (€6.30) on the bus. High-speed **Orlyval** shuttle trains (www.orlyval.fr) run every 4-7mins (6am-11pm daily) to RER B station Antony (€13.50 to Châtelet-les-Halles); allow about 35mins for central Paris.

Orly prices for the Paris Airports Service (*see left*) are €25 for one and €5-€12 per passenger depending on the number. A **taxi** takes 20-40mins and costs €16-€26.

Paris Beauvais

08.92.68.20.66/www.aeroportbeauvais.com. 70km (43 miles) north of Paris.
Budget hub. **Buses** (€13) to Porte Maillot leave 15-30mins after each arrival and 3hrs 15mins before each departure. Tickets from Arrivals or buy tickets on the bus.

Arriving by car

Options for crossing the Channel with a car include: **Eurotunnel** (08.10.63.03.04, www.eurotunnel.com); **Brittany Ferries**

(08.25.82.88.28, www.brittany ferries.com), **P&O Ferries** (08.25.12.01.56, www.poferries.com) and **SeaFrance** (UK: 08705 711 711, www.seafrance.com).

Arriving by coach

International coaches arrive at **Gare Routière Internationale Paris-Galliéni** at Porte de Bagnolet, 20th. For tickets (in English) call Eurolines on 08.92.89.90.91 or (UK) 01582 404 511, or visit www.eurolines.fr.

Arriving by rail

Eurostar from London St Pancras International (01233 617575, www.eurostar.com) to Paris Gare du Nord (08.92.35.35.39) takes 2hrs 15mins direct. You must check in at least 30mins before departure.

Maps

Free maps of the métro, bus and RER systems are available at airports and métro stations.

Public transport

RATP (08.92.69.32.46, www.ratp.fr) runs the bus, métro and suburban tram routes, as well as lines A and B of the RER express railway, which connects with the métro inside Paris. State rail **SNCF** (08.92.35.35.35, www.sncf.com) runs RER lines C, D and E for the suburbs.

Fares & tickets

Paris and its suburbs are divided into six travel zones, with 1 and 2 covering the city centre. RATP tickets and passes are valid on the métro, bus and RER. Tickets and *carnets* can be bought at métro stations, tourist offices and tobacconists; single tickets can be bought on buses. Retain your ticket in case of spot checks; you'll also need it to exit from RER stations.

A ticket is €1.60, a carnet of ten €11.40. A Mobilis day pass is €5.80 for zones 1 and 2 and €16.40 for zones 1-6 (not including airports).

Métro & RER

The Paris **métro** is the fastest way of getting around. Trains run daily 5.30am-12.40am Mon-Thur, 5.30am-1.30am Fri-Sun. Numbered lines have their direction named after the last stop. Follow the orange *Correspondance* signs to change lines. The five **RER** lines run 5.30am-1am daily across Paris and into commuterland. Métro tickets are valid for RER zone 1.

Buses

Buses run 6.30am-8.30pm, with some routes continuing until 12.30am, Mon-Sat; limited services operate on selected lines Sun and public holidays. You can use a métro ticket, a ticket bought from the driver (€1.60) or a travel pass. Tickets should be punched in the machine next to the driver; passes should be shown to the driver.

Night buses

The 42 **Noctilien** lines run from place du Châtelet to the suburbs (hourly 12.30am-5.30am Mon-Thur; half-hourly 1am-5.35am Fri, Sat); look out for the Noctilien logo or the N in front of the route number. A ticket costs €1.60; travel passes are valid.

River transport

Batobus

08.25.05.01.01/www.batobus.com. Nov-Mar 10.30am-4.30pm*; Mar-May & Sept-Nov* 10am-7pm*; June-Aug* 10am-

9.30pm. *One-day pass* €12 (€6, €8). River buses stop every 15-25mins at the Eiffel Tower, Musée d'Orsay, St-Germain-des-Prés (quai Malaquais), Notre-Dame, Jardin des Plantes, Hôtel de Ville, the Louvre, Champs-Elysées (Pont Alexandre III). Tickets are available from Batobus stops, RATP and tourist offices.

Rail travel

Versailles and Disneyland Paris are served by the RER. Most locations out of the city are served by the SNCF railway; the TGV high-speed train has slashed journey times and is steadily being extended to all the main regions. Tickets can be bought at any SNCF station (not only the one from which you'll travel), SNCF shops and travel agents. If you reserve online or by phone, you can pay and pick up your tickets from the station or have them sent to your home. SNCF automatic machines (*billeterie automatique*) only work with French credit/debit cards. Buy tickets in advance to secure the cheaper fare. Before you board any train, stamp your ticket in the orange *composteur* machines on the platforms, or you might have to pay a hefty fine.

SNCF
08.92.35.35.35/www.sncf.com.
Open 7am-10pm daily.
The line can also be reached (inside France) by dialling 3635 and saying '*billet*' at the prompt.

Taxis

Taxis are hard to find at rush hour or early in the morning. Ranks are indicated with a blue sign. A white light on a taxi's roof means it's free; an orange one means it's busy. You also pay for the time it takes your radioed taxi to arrive. Payment by credit card – mention this when you order – is €15 minimum.

Airportaxis
01.41.50.42.50/www.taxiparisien.fr.
Alpha
01.45.85.85.85/www.alphataxis.fr.
G7
01.47.39.47.39/www.taxis-g7.fr.
Taxis Bleus
08.91.70.10.10/www.taxis-bleus.com.

Driving

If you bring your car to France, you must bring its registration and insurance documents. An insurance green card, available from insurance companies and the AA and RAC in the UK, is not compulsory but is useful. Traffic information for Ile-de-France is given at 08.26.02.20.22, www.securiteroutiere.gouv.fr.

Breakdown services

The AA or RAC do not have reciprocal arrangements with an equivalent organisation in France, so it's advisable to take out additional breakdown insurance cover, for example with Europ Assistance (0870 737 5720, www.europ-assistance.co.uk). If you don't have insurance, you can use its service (08.10.00.50.50), but it will charge you the full cost. Other 24-hour breakdown services in Paris include: Action Auto Assistance (01.45.58.49.58); Dan Dépann Auto (01.40.06.06.53).

Parking

There are still a few free on-street parking areas in Paris, but they're often full. If you park illegally, your car may be clamped or towed away. Don't park in zones marked for deliveries (*livraisons*) or taxis. *Horodateurs*, pay-and-display machines, which take a special card (*carte de stationnement* at €10 or €30, from tobacconists). Parking is often free at weekends, after 7pm and in August. Underground car parks cost around €2.50 per hour. Some have lower rates after 6pm. See www.parkingsdeparis.com.

Vehicle removal

If your car is impounded, contact the nearest police station. There are eight car pounds (*préfourrières*) in Paris; to find out where your car might be, contact 01.53.73.53.73, 08.91.01.22.22 or www.prefecture-police-paris.interieur.gouv.fr.

Car hire

To hire a car you must be 25 or over and have held a licence for at least a year. Some agencies accept drivers aged 21-24, but a day fee of €20-€25 is usual. Take your licence and passport. There are often good weekend offers. Weekly deals are better at bigger companies: around €300 a week for a small car with insurance and 1,750km included. Costlier hire companies allow the return of a car in other French cities and abroad. Cheaper ones may have a high charge for damage: read the small print before signing.

Ada
08.25.16.91.69/www.ada.fr.

Avis
08.20.05.05.05/www.avis.fr.

Budget
08.25.00.35.64/www.budget.fr.

EasyCar
01.70.61.85.52/www.easycar.com.

Europcar
08.25.35.83.58/www.europcar.fr.

Hertz
01.39.38.38.38/www.hertz.fr.

Rent-a-Car
08.91.70.02.00/www.rentacar.fr.

Cycling

In 2007, the mayor launched a municipal bike hire scheme – Vélib (www.velib.paris.fr). There are now over 20,000 bicycles available 24 hours a day, at nearly 1,500 'stations' across the city. Just swipe your travel card to release the bikes from their stands. The *mairie* actively promotes cycling in the city and the Vélib scheme is complemented by the 372km (231 miles) of bike lanes snaking their way around Paris.

A free *Paris à Vélo* map can be picked up at any *mairie* or from bike shops. Cycle lanes (*pistes cyclables*) run mostly N–S and E–W. N–S routes include rue de Rennes, av d'Italie, bd Sébastopol and av Marceau. E–W routes take in the rue de Rivoli, bd St-Germain, bd St-Jacques and av Daumesnil. You could be fined (€22) if you don't use them, which is a bit rich considering the lanes are often blocked by delivery vans and the €135 fine for obstructing a cycle lane is barely enforced. Cyclists are also entitled to use certain bus lanes (especially the new ones, which are set off by a strip of kerb stones); look out for traffic signs with a bike symbol.

Don't let the locals' blasé attitude to helmets and lights convince you it's not worth using them.

Cycle hire

Note that bike insurance may not cover theft: check before you sign.

Maison Roue Libre

1 passage Mondétour, 1st (01.44.76.86.43/08.10.44.15.34). M° Châtelet. **Open** 10am-6pm daily. Bike hire. Helmets free. Passport and €200 deposit required. *Other locations: 37 bd Bourdon, 4th (01.42.71.54.54).*

Resources A-Z

Accident & emergency

Most of the following services operate 24 hours a day. In a medical emergency, you should call the Sapeurs-Pompiers, who have trained paramedics.

Ambulance (SAMU)	**15**
Police	**17**
Fire (Sapeurs-Pompiers)	**18**
Emergency (from a mobile phone)	**112**

Credit card loss

In case of credit card loss or theft, call one of the following 24hr services that have English-speaking staff.

American Express
01.47.77.70.00
Diners Club
01.49.06.17.50
MasterCard
01.45.16.65.65
Visa
08.92.70.57.05

Customs

Non-EU residents can claim a tax refund or *détaxe* (around 12%) on VAT if you spend over €175 in any one purchase and if you live outside the EU for more than six months in the year. At the shop ask for a *bordereau de vente à l'exportation.*

Dental emergencies

Look in the *Pages Jaunes* (www.pagesjaunes.fr) under *Dentistes.* For emergencies contact:

Hôpital de la Pitié-Salpêtrière
47-83 bd de l'Hôpital, 13th (01.42.16.00.00). M° Gare d'Austerlitz. **Open** 24hrs.
SOS Dentaire
87 bd Port-Royal, 13th (01.43.36.36.00). M° Les Gobelins/RER Port-Royal. **Open** by phone 9am-midnight.

Disabled

General information (in French) is available on the Secrétaire d'Etat aux Personnes Handicapées website: www.handicap.gouv.fr.

Electricity

France uses the standard 220-240V, 50-cycle AC system. Visitors with 240V British appliances need an adapter (*adaptateur*). US 110V appliances need an adapter and a transformer (*transformateur*).

Embassies & consulates

Australian Embassy
4 rue Jean-Rey, 15th (01.40.59.33.00/www.france.embassy.gov.au). M° Bir-Hakeim. **Open** *Consular services* 9.15am-noon, 2-4.30pm Mon-Fri. *Visas* 10am-noon Mon-Fri.
British Embassy
35 rue du Fbg-St-Honoré, 8th (01.44.51.31.00/www.amb-grandebretagne.fr). M° Concorde. Consular services 18bis rue d'Anjou, 8th. M° Concorde. **Open** 9.30am-12.30pm, 2.30-4.30pm Mon-Fri. *Visas 16 rue d'Anjou, 8th (01.44.51.31.01).* **Open** 9.30am-noon (by phone), 2.30-4.30pm Mon-Fri.
British citizens wanting consular services (such as new passports) should ignore the queue at 16 rue d'Anjou and walk in at no.18bis.

Canadian Embassy
35 av Montaigne, 8th (01.44.43.29.00/www.amb-canada.fr). M° Franklin D Roosevelt. Consular services (01.44.43.29.02). **Open** 9am-noon Mon-Fri. *Visas 37 av Montaigne (01.44.43.29.16).* **Open** 8.30-11am Mon-Fri.

Irish Embassy
12 av Foch, 16th. Consulate 4 rue Rude, 16th (01.44.17.67.00). M° Charles de Gaulle Etoile. **Open** *Consular/visas* 9.30am-noon Mon-Fri. *By phone* 9.30am-1pm, 2.30-5.30pm Mon-Fri.

New Zealand Embassy
7ter rue Léonard-de-Vinci, 16th (01.45.01.43.43/www.nzembassy.com/france). M° Victor Hugo. **Open** *Sept-June* 9am-1pm, 2-5.30pm Mon-Thur; 9am-1pm, 2-4pm Fri. *July, Aug* 9am-1pm, 2-4.30pm Mon-Thur; 9am-2pm Fri. *Visas* 9am-12.30pm Mon-Fri. Visas for travel to New Zealand can be applied for on the website www.immigration.govt.nz.

South African Embassy
59 quai d'Orsay, 7th (01.53.59.23.23/www.afriquesud.net). M° Invalides. **Open** 8.30am-5.15pm Mon-Fri. *Consulate/visas* 8.30am-noon Mon-Fri.

US Embassy
2 av Gabriel, 8th (01.43.12.22.22/http://france.usembassy.gov). M° Concorde. Consulate and visas 4 av Gabriel, 8th (08.10.26.46.26). M° Concorde. **Open** *Consular services* 9am-12.30pm, 1-3pm Mon-Fri. *Visas 08.92.23.84.72.*

Internet

Milk
31 bd de Sébastopol, 1st (08.20.00.10.00/www.milklub.com). M° Châtelet or Rambuteau/RER Châtelet Les Halles. **Open** 24hrs daily.

Opening hours

Standard opening hours for shops are generally 9am/10am-7pm/8pm Mon-Sat. Some close on Mondays, some for lunch (usually 12.30-2pm) and some in August.

Pharmacies

All *pharmacies* sport a green neon cross. If closed, a pharmacy will have a sign indicating the nearest one open. Staff can provide basic medical services like disinfecting and bandaging wounds (for a small fee) and will indicate the nearest doctor on duty. These are open late:

Matignon
2 rue Jean-Mermoz, 8th (01.43.59.86.55). M° Franklin D Roosevelt. **Open** 8.30am-2am daily.

Pharmacie des Champs-Elysées
84 av des Champs-Elysées, 8th (01.45.62.02.41). M° George V. **Open** 24hrs daily.

Pharmacie Européenne de la Place de Clichy
6 pl de Clichy, 9th (01.48.74.65.18). M° Place de Clichy. **Open** 24hrs daily.

Pharmacie des Halles
10 bd de Sébastopol, 4th (01.42.72.03.23). M° Châtelet. **Open** 9am-midnight Mon-Sat; 9am-10pm Sun.

Police

The French equivalent of 999/911 is **17** (**112** from a mobile), but don't expect a speedy response. If you're assaulted or robbed, report the incident as soon as possible. Make a statement (*procès verbal*) at the *point d'accueil* closest to the crime. To find it, contact the Préfecture Centrale (08.91.01.22.22) or www.prefecture.police.paris.interieur.gouv.fr. You'll need a statement for insurance purposes.

Post

Post offices (*bureaux de poste*) are open 8am-7pm Mon-Fri; 8am-noon Sat, apart from the 24hr one listed below. All are listed in the phone book: under *Administration des PTT* in the *Pages Jaunes*; under *Poste* in the *Pages Blanches*. Most post offices have machines that weigh your letter, print out a stamp and give change, saving you from queuing. You can also buy stamps at a tobacconist.

Main Post Office
52 rue du Louvre, 1st (01.40.28.20.00). M° Les Halles or Louvre Rivoli. **Open** 24hrs daily.

Smoking

Smoking is prohibited in all enclosed public spaces. Hotels can still offer smoking rooms.

Telephones

All French phone numbers have ten digits. Paris and Ile-de-France numbers begin with 01; the rest of France is divided into four zones, 02 to 05. Mobile phone numbers start with 06. Numbers beginning with 08 can only be reached from inside France. The France country code is 33; leave off the first 0 at the start of the ten-digit number. Most public phones use *télécartes* (phonecards). These are sold at post offices and tobacconists, and they cost €7.50 for 50 units or €15 for 120 units.

Time

France is one hour ahead of GMT and uses the 24hr system (for example, 18h means 6pm).

Tipping

A service charge of ten to 15% is legally included in your bill at all restaurants, cafés and bars. However, it's polite to round up the final amount.

Tourist information

Espace du Tourisme d'Ile de France
Carrousel du Louvre, 99 rue de Rivoli, 1st (08.26.16.66.66/www.paris-ile-de-france.com). M° Pyramides. **Open** 8.30am-7pm Mon-Fri.
For Paris and the Ile-de-France.

Maison de la France
20 av de l'Opéra, 1st (01.42.96.70.00/www.franceguide.com). M° Opéra. **Open** 10am-6pm Mon-Fri; 10am-5pm Sat.
The state organisation for tourism.

Office de Tourisme et des Congrès de Paris
Carrousel du Louvre, 99 rue de Rivoli, 1st (08.92.68.30.00/www.parisinfo.com). M° Palais Royal Musée du Louvre. **Open** 9am-7pm daily.
Info on Paris and the suburbs; tickets.
Other locations *Gare de Lyon, 20 bd Diderot, 12th. Gare du Nord, 18 rue de Dunkerque, 10th. Montmartre, 21 pl du Tertre, 18th. Opéra, 11 rue Scribe, 9th. Pyramides, 25 rue des Pyramides, 1st. Tour Eiffel, Champ de Mars, 7th.*

Visas

European Union nationals do not need a visa to enter France, nor do US, Canadian, Australian, New Zealand or South African citizens for stays of up to three months. Nationals of other countries should enquire at the nearest French Consulate before leaving home. If you are travelling to France from one of the countries included in the Schengen agreement (most of the EU, but not Britain or Ireland), the visa from that country should be sufficient.

What's on

Two publications compete for consumers of listings information: *L'Officiel des Spectacles* (€0.35) and *Pariscope* (€0.40).

Vocabulary

General expressions

good morning/hello *bonjour*; **good evening** *bonsoir*; **goodbye** *au revoir*; **hi** *salut*; **OK** *d'accord*; **yes** *oui*; **no** *non*; **how are you?** *comment allez-vous?*; **how's it going?** *comment ça va?/ça va?*; **sir/Mr** *monsieur* (M); **madam/Mrs** *madame* (Mme); **miss** *mademoiselle* (Mlle); **please** *s'il vous plaît*; **thank you** *merci*; **thank you very much** *merci beaucoup*; **sorry** *pardon*; **excuse me** *excusez-moi*; **do you speak English?** *parlez-vous anglais?*; **I don't speak French** *je ne parle pas français*; **I don't understand** *je ne comprends pas*; **speak more slowly, please** *parlez plus lentement, s'il vous plaît*; **good** *bon/bonne*; **bad** *mauvais/mauvaise*; **small** *petit/petite*; **big** *grand/grande*; **beautiful** *beau/belle*; **well** *bien*; **badly** *mal*; **a bit** *un peu*; **a lot** *beaucoup*; **very** *très*; **with** *avec*; **without** *sans*; **and** *et*; **or** *ou*; **because** *parce que*; **who?** *qui?*; **when?** *quand?*; **what?** *quoi?*; **which?** *quel?*; **where?** *où?*; **why?** *pourquoi?*; **how?** *comment?*; **at what time?** *à quelle heure?*; **forbidden** *interdit/défendu*; **out of order** *hors service* (HS)/*en panne*; **daily** *tous les jours* (tlj)

Getting around

where is the (nearest) métro? *où est le métro (le plus proche)?*; **when is the next train for... ?** *c'est quand le prochain train pour...?*; **ticket** *un billet*; **station** *la gare*; **platform** *le quai*; **entrance** *entrée*; **exit** *sortie*; **left** *gauche*; **right** *droite*; **straight on** *tout droit*; **far** *loin*; **near** *pas loin/près d'ici*; **street map** *le plan*; **bank** *la banque*; **is there a bank near here?** *est-ce qu'il y a une banque près d'ici?*

Accommodation

do you have a room (for this evening/for two people)? *avez-vous une chambre (pour ce soir/pour deux personnes)?*; **full** *complet*; **room** *une chambre*; **bed** *un lit*; **double bed** *un grand lit*; **(a room with) twin beds** (*une chambre à*) *deux lits*; **with bath(room)/shower** *avec* (*salle de*) *bain/douche*; **breakfast** *le petit déjeuner*; **included** *compris*

At the restaurant

I'd like to book a table (for three/at 8pm) *je voudrais réserver une table (pour trois personnes/à vingt heures)*; **lunch** *le déjeuner*; **dinner** *le dîner*; **coffee** (espresso) *un café*; **white coffee** *un café au lait/café crème*; **tea** *du thé*; **wine** *du vin*; **beer** *la bière*; **mineral water** *eau minérale*; **fizzy** *gazeuse*; **still** *plate*; **tap water** *eau du robinet/une carafe d'eau*; **the bill, please** *l'addition, s'il vous plaît*

Numbers

0 *zéro*; **1** *un, une*; **2** *deux*; **3** *trois*; **4** *quatre*; **5** *cinq*; **6** *six*; **7** *sept*; **8** *huit*; **9** *neuf*; **10** *dix*; **11** *onze*; **12** *douze*; **13** *treize*; **14** *quatorze*; **15** *quinze*; **16** *seize*; **17** *dix-sept*; **18** *dix-huit*; **19** *dix-neuf*; **20** *vingt*; **21** *vingt-et-un*; **22** *vingt-deux*; **30** *trente*; **40** *quarante*; **50** *cinquante*; **60** *soixante*; **70** *soixante-dix*; **80** *quatre-vingts*; **90** *quatre-vingt-dix*; **100** *cent*; **1000** *mille*; **1,000,000** *un million*

Index

Sights & Areas